Graphic Justice

The intersections of law and contemporary culture are vital for comprehending the meaning and significance of law in today's world. Far from being unsophisticated mass entertainment, comics and graphic fiction both imbue our contemporary culture, and are themselves imbued, with the concerns of law and justice. Accordingly, and spanning a wide variety of approaches and topics from an international array of contributors, *Graphic Justice* draws comics and graphic fiction into the range of critical resources available to the academic study of law. The first book to do this, *Graphic Justice* broadens our understanding of law and justice as part of our human world—a world that is inhabited not simply by legal concepts and institutions alone, but also by narratives, stories, fantasies, images, and other cultural articulations of human meaning. Engaging with key legal issues (including copyright, education, legal ethics, biomedical regulation, and legal personhood) and exploring critical issues in criminal justice and perspectives on international rights, law and justice—all through engagement with comics and graphic fiction—the collection showcases the vast breadth of potential that the medium holds. *Graphic Justice* will be of interest to academics and postgraduate students in: cultural legal studies; law and the image; law, narrative and literature; law and popular culture; cultural criminology; as well as cultural and comics studies more generally.

Thomas Giddens (St Mary's University) is a Lecturer in Law and Co-Director of St Mary's Centre for Law and Culture. Alongside jurisprudence and popular culture, he is interested in the use of comics in law and legal studies, and is founder of the Graphic Justice Research Alliance (graphicjustice.blogspot.com).

Graphic Justice

Intersections of Comics and Law

Edited by Thomas Giddens

Routledge
Taylor & Francis Group
a GlassHouse Book

First published 2015
by Routledge
2 Park Square, Milton Park, Abingdon, Oxfordshire OX14 4RN

and by Routledge
711 Third Avenue, New York, NY 10017

First issued in paperback 2016

Routledge is an imprint of the Taylor & Francis Group, an informa business

British Library Cataloguing in Publication Data

A catalogue record for this book is available from the British Library

Library of Congress Cataloging-in-Publication Data

Graphic justice : intersections of comics and law / edited by Thomas Giddens.
pages cm
Includes index.
ISBN 978-1-138-78799-5 (hardback) — ISBN 978-1-315-76575-4 (ebk)
1. Comic books, strips, etc.—United States—History and criticism.
2. Graphic novels—History and criticism. 3. Law and literature.
4. Justice in literature. I. Giddens, Thomas, editor.
PN6714.G739 2015
741.5'973—dc23 2014037613

ISBN 13: 978-1-138-24166-4 (pbk)
ISBN 13: 978-1-138-78799-5 (hbk)

Typeset in Galliard
by Apex CoVantage, LLC

For Helen, indubitably

Contents

Acknowledgements

Special thanks to the members of the ad hoc peer review board, assembled specifically to review the papers for this collection. They volunteered their time and expertise to provide insight and critical feedback on the various contributions during the volume's development: Jac Armstrong, Benjamin Authers, Neal Curtis, Finola Farrant, Michael Fiddler, Desmond Manderson, Jill Marshall, Kieran McCartan, Amanda Perry-Kessaris, Timothy Peters, Edward Phillips, Luis Gómez Romero, Richard Sherwin, Kieran Tranter, Gary Watt, Kent Worcester and Majid Yar.

Thanks also to the UK Socio-Legal Studies Association, which helped fund the Graphic Justice One-Day Symposium on 11 September 2013 at St Mary's University (then University College), Twickenham, London. It was this event that brought together most of the papers that have been developed into the works now bound within this collection.

Contributors

Kim Barker (University of Wolverhampton) is a Lecturer in Law, and has previously taught at the University of Birmingham and Aberystwyth University. Kim's research interests span intellectual property but also digital properties, intersections of intellectual property and culture, comics and games.

Chris Boge (University of Cologne) is Assistant Professor of English and American Studies. He is an Honorary Research Fellow at the School of Law at Birkbeck where he teaches in the crime fiction and the law module, and a recipient of the Birkbeck Institute for the Humanities Visiting Fellowship.

Chris Comerford (University of Technology, Sydney) is a PhD candidate, whose fascination with Christopher Nolan's *The Dark Knight* in 2008 led him to study Batman and superhero comics at large. As well as pursuing work in academia, he also writes comic book reviews and digressions at http://thewritersmultiverse.wordpress.com.

Graham Ferris (Nottingham Trent University) is a Reader in Law at Nottingham Law School. He has written on legal education, legal history and property law. He is a qualified solicitor and has been teaching law for over two decades. He has been reading comics for over four decades.

Thomas Giddens (St Mary's University) is a Lecturer in Law and Co-Director of St Mary's Centre for Law and Culture. Alongside jurisprudence and popular culture, he is interested in the use of comics in law and legal studies, and is founder of the Graphic Justice Research Alliance (graphicjustice.blogspot.com).

Jérémie Gilbert (University of East London) is a Reader in Law. Among a range of publications, his latest book, *Nomadic Peoples and Human Rights*, was published by Routledge in 2014. He is a consultant for a number of non-governmental organisations on indigenous peoples' and nomadic peoples' rights.

Richard Glancey (Northumbria University) qualified as a solicitor in 2008. He subsequently moved into academia and is now a Senior Lecturer in Law at Northumbria University, where he runs the LLB (Hons) programme. He lectures in public law and civil liberties and his research interests are in those fields and legal education.

Nic Groombridge (St Mary's University) is a former Home Office civil servant turned criminologist. His diverse interests include gender, sexuality, surveillance, green perspectives, sport, media and culture. As a public criminologist he tweets as @criminology4u. He would rather climb trees than buildings.

Shawn HE Harmon (University of Edinburgh) specialises in medical law, ethics, technology convergence and life sciences regulation. He is Deputy Director of the J Kenyon Mason Institute for Medicine, Life Sciences and the Law, Joint Editor of *Medical Law International*, and Programme Director for Edinburgh's LLM Medical Law and Ethics.

David Keane (Middlesex University) is a Senior Lecturer in Law. He has authored a number of books and journal articles on human rights law, including *Caste-Based Discrimination in International Human Rights Law* (Ashgate, 2007), and was awarded the Hart Book Prize for early career scholars.

Chris Lloyd (Oxford Brookes University) is a Lecturer in Law. He holds an LLB (Hons) from Kent Law School and is finalising his PhD at the School of Law, Birkbeck College, University of London. Chris has articles in *The Australian Feminist Law Journal* and *Law Text Culture*, and reviews in *Law, Culture and the Humanities* and *Derrida Today*.

Cleo Lunt is a teacher of maths and science at a special educational needs secondary school. She has written on law and genetic science. She is a science graduate holding a BSc in medical genetics. She has been reading comics for over two decades.

Angus Nurse (Middlesex University) is a Senior Lecturer in Criminology, researching criminology, law, and crime and popular culture. He has published widely on crime cinema, television and literature, and environmental crime. His book, *Animal Harm: Perspectives on why People Harm and Kill Animals*, was published by Ashgate in 2013.

James Petty (University of Melbourne) is a PhD candidate in Criminology. His interests include disadvantage and marginalisation, consumerism, poverty and homelessness, drug policy and reform, cultural criminology, queer theory and representation, comics and film. His thesis is focusing on social marginalisation and perceptions of crisis.

Nickie D Phillips (St Francis College, Brooklyn) is an Associate Professor in Criminal Justice, and director of St Francis's Center for Crime and Popular Culture. She is co-author (with Staci Strobl) of *Comic Book Crime* (New York University Press, 2013). She has also worked on crime reporting and hate crime prosecution, and is currently examining media and entertainment involving 'rape culture'.

Staci Strobl (John Jay College of Criminal Justice) is an Associate Professor in Criminal Justice. She is co-author (with Nickie D Phillips) of *Comic Book Crime* (New York University Press, 2013). She was awarded the 2008 Radzinowicz Memorial Prize for her article on the criminalisation of domestic workers in Bahrain, and currently has projects on Omani children's comics and news reporting on policewomen in Kuwait.

Introduction

Thomas Giddens

We are surrounded by emanations of graphic storytelling: comics-inspired films fill our cinemas; prose narratives become adapted and transported into graphic novels; graphic novels become computer games and television series; superhero merchandise fills the shelves of supermarkets and clothing stores. Feeding from this wide cultural significance, this collection of essays examines the multi-faceted intersections of comics and law. Although there has been increased engagement with literature, film, popular culture, and even 'the visual' in general[1] within legal studies, despite the medium's recent surge in cultural capital, the significance of graphic fiction to law remains conspicuously under researched.[2] At its most basic level, the significance of comics to law can be couched in these terms: comics are an overt and widespread part of contemporary society and culture, and law is in part an attempt to regulate that society and culture and in part a reflection of its values; therefore, an understanding of the intersections of comics with law is important in making sense of law and its place in today's world. But this very general observation is just the beginning.

1 Examples are numerous, but here is a brief indicative selection: C Douzinas and L Nead (eds), *Law and the Image: The Authority of Art and the Aesthetics of Law* (University of Chicago Press 1999); S Greenfield, G Osborn and P Robson, *Film and the Law: The Cinema of Justice* (2nd edn, Hart 2010); WP MacNeil, *Lex Populi: The Jurisprudence of Popular Culture* (Stanford University Press 2007); M Williams, *Empty Justice: One Hundred Years of Law, Literature and Philosophy* (Cavendish 2002).

2 Notwithstanding a few disparate forays, notably the 2012 special issue on 'Justice Framed: Law in Comics and Graphic Novels' in volume 16 of *Law Text Culture*. See the issue's introduction: L Gómez Romero and I Dahlman, 'Introduction – Justice Framed: Law in Comics and Graphic Novels' (2012) 16 *Law Text Culture* 3. Other, more sporadic examples include J Bainbridge, '"This is *the Authority*. This Planet is Under Our Protection" – An Exegesis of Superheroes' Interrogations of Law' (2007) 3 *Law, Culture and the Humanities* 455; T Giddens, 'Comics, Law, and Aesthetics: Towards the Use of Graphic Fiction in Legal Studies' (2012) 6 *Law and Humanities* 85.

Even glancing at the mainstream surface of comics, diverse issues of justice and social order are instantly apparent. *Batman*, *Daredevil*, *Spider-Man* and *The Justice League of America* – all these narrative worlds navigate issues of right and wrong, of morality, of retribution and vengeance, of methodologies of control. Theirs are worlds populated with good and evil, with power and responsibility, with duty and moral choice. But this, too, is only a start. Even lightly scratching at this mainstream surface, one finds a raft of non-superhero narratives. Some of these, like stories in other media, are stories directly about law and justice (crime narratives, legal dramas); others are about making difficult moral choices. Others tap into deep metaphysical questions about the nature of self and what it means to be human in the first place. Like other narrative forms – literature, film, theatre – comics and graphic fiction try to explore and express the multiple and complex dimensions of human life.[3]

Are we there yet? No, far from it. The content and themes of graphic fiction may be richly vast and diverse, but there is more to comics than their content. Narratives can be told in many different ways, using many different tools and devices. A simple oral tale has a certain quality, and related limitations. A huge cinematic production similarly has its own set of capacities. This is not to suggest that these forms are static and unchanging – innovative creators can challenge the way a form is used, or expose previously untapped dimensions. But the form of a narrative shapes its meanings; the way a story is told is *part of* that story. Meaning derives from form as well as content.[4] Graphic fiction is a particular form of narration, and one that (like many things in this world) is not easy to define.[5] But the complexities inherent in the comics' form itself can provide avenues for conceptualising and engaging with issues in legal theory, notably around the relationships between words and images, and the limits of textual representation. Indeed, as the opening chapter, 'Lex comica: on comics and legal theory', demonstrates, comics can even be used as a direct vehicle for legal theory.[6]

From what has been said so far, it is apparent that the significance of comics to law is not simple or unitary, but is complex and multi-faceted. Accordingly, the aim of this collection is to demonstrate (albeit in a necessarily preliminary way) some key examples of the ways in which law and

3 For a more detailed overview of the variety of comics publishing, see Giddens (n 2) 85–87.

4 See RK Sherwin, *When Law Goes Pop: The Vanishing Line between Law and Popular Culture* (University of Chicago Press 2000) 27.

5 For an overview of the definition debate, see R Varnum and CT Gibbons, 'Introduction' in R Varnum and CT Gibbons (eds), *The Language of Comics: Word and Image* (University Press of Mississippi 2001). See also Giddens (n 2) 89–95.

6 See Chapter 1. See also Giddens (n 2).

comics interact. On, through, between, and within the pages of this collection a picture will emerge of the vast and varied potential of comics and graphic fiction for critical reflection on the concerns of law and justice.

Part I gives a brief collection of examples of how comics can contribute to legal debate in a number of areas, from doctrinal copyright law, to legal ethics, education, public discourse, and legal philosophy. Beyond form and content, even beyond broad cultural significance, Kim Barker examines the comics form from a very legal perspective. Unpicking the complex intellectual property rights in a work of comics is not simple, and through her analysis of this complexity Barker demonstrates that understandings of comics in copyright law, particularly around online user-generated content and the copyright that can rest in specific characters (including, absurdly, the Batmobile) can lead to a blurring of fundamental copyright principles such as the distinction between ideas and expressions that have shaped intellectual property law for over a century.[7]

Continuing the focus on the traditionally legal sphere, Graham Ferris and Cleo Lunt look at issues of legal representation in comics. Representation, for Ferris and Lunt, is a dual problem: it is about both the way graphic fiction portrays lawyers and their work to the public (and, importantly, to potential future lawyers), and the ethics of advocating for (that is, 'representing') guilty clients. As they argue, the fictional world of heroic comics may have important significance in their portrayal of the world of the legal profession, but works such as *Daredevil* need to develop a more sophisticated depiction of the ethical difficulties involved in representing the guilty.[8]

Another mainstream legal issue is taken up by Richard Glancey. He is concerned with the education of the students on his undergraduate Constitutional Law module, specifically with the difficulty that is often present when it comes to comprehending the theoretical complexities of core concepts. But comics may also have unique benefits to legal education - in steps *Judge Dredd*, adding a significant experiential dimension, bringing to life ideas such as the rule of law and the separation of powers that can springboard students into deeper understandings of these important concepts.[9]

Continuing the theme of using comics to communicate legal issues and ideas, Shawn HE Harmon shows how futuristic science fiction can be specifically developed and deployed to increase both public understanding and engagement with bioethical issues. Telling the story of his own involvement in a project to do just that, his chapter demonstrates

7 See Chapter 2.
8 See Chapter 3.
9 See Chapter 4.

the potential for graphic fiction to both articulate and participate in legal discourse.[10]

Futuristic science fiction has additional critical importance, as Thomas Giddens shows through his philosophical reflection on the uncertain boundary between human and machine in Shirow Masamune's *The Ghost in the Shell*. This issue is important for law, because law is both created and applied by humans as well as being reliant upon knowing what a human is for the construction of key legal doctrines (such as murder, or the difference between person and property). But, as Giddens argues, the human is fluid and not easily pinned down.[11]

Part II moves to specifically consider one of the most prominent themes apparent in graphic fiction: crime and criminal justice. Looking to the cultural dimensions of crime and how it is mediated through fiction, specifically the communal and social experience of being part of mainstream US comics' readership, Nickie D Phillips and Staci Strobl examine the concept of deathworthiness through the retributive lens of *Cry for Justice* and *Red Team*. Drawing rich links between the notions of justice and desert that these two series articulate and the popular discourse around the real-world killing spree of Christopher Dorner, Phillips and Strobl ultimately show how the narratives of comics are a deeply significant way in which many people process and make sense of complex questions of morality.[12]

Angus Nurse blurs the seemingly clear division between retributive and restorative justice through his analysis of *100 Bullets*. In a world of inequality, where the powerful and those who 'have' make the rules in their own interests, and justice remains elusive for those who 'have not', taking the quintessentially restorative move of giving the victim the ability seek his or her own personal justice becomes a meaningful alternative to official pathways. Through Nurse's analysis, he builds up a picture of an extreme restorative justice, which often spills over into retributive violence and unsettles the boundary between the two.[13]

Turning away from the notion of retribution, James Petty examines a classic of the comics' form: Alan Moore's and Dave Gibbons's *Watchmen*. In his rich conceptual analysis of this work, inspired by cultural and visual criminology, Petty demonstrates how the superhero genre, when deployed with the skill of auteurs such as Moore, can effect a radical critique of western ideologies of justice and violence, and deeply question whether the existence of these spandex-clad guardians of justice would actually make the world a better place.[14]

10 See Chapter 5.
11 See Chapter 6.
12 See Chapter 7.
13 See Chapter 8.
14 See Chapter 9.

Perhaps worryingly following *Watchmen*'s unsettling warning, Nic Groombridge gives a provocative discussion of people actually trying and take up the mantle of the costumed vigilante – but rather than bringing justice to the world (whatever *that* might mean, as Boge highlights in Chapter 13) there seems to be something ineffectual about the would-be heroes Groombridge considers. Regardless, focusing on the use of the superhero in UK fathers' rights protests, Groombridge ultimately communicates the cultural resonance of the superhero in individuals' approach to understanding how to achieve justice outside the official system and the need to deepen our understanding of such phenomena.[15]

Part III takes on a distinctly international flavour, focusing on questions of international law, global justice, and human rights atrocities. Chris Comerford kicks us off by pointing out the connections between Barak Obama and Batman, specifically in terms of their deployment of Agamben's state of exception. Focusing on Obama's executive assassination of Osama bin Laden and the development of *Batman Incorporated*, both of which rely upon the necessity of exceptional action to justify their extreme measures, Comerford suggests that such exceptional actions (to paraphrase the Dark Knight himself) might be what we need, but not what we deserve.[16]

And still levelling critique in Obama's direction, Chris Lloyd examines the US President's controversial drone programme and his killing of US citizens without charge or trial – an examination articulated through the critical and deeply satirical art of *2000AD*'s authoritarian lawgiver, Judge Dredd. Taking his journey with Rancière, Benjamin and Derrida, Lloyd draws out the problematics surrounding Obama's becoming (like Dredd) a terrible conflation of judge, jury and executioner, an authoritarian vision warned against in political philosophy and the critical art of Dredd.[17]

Turning from Obama to a more general analysis of international justice, Chris Boge capitalises on the potential for superhero narratives to help us explore the complex problems of that elusive legal concept, 'justice'. Focusing on two *Justice League* series, and deploying insights from post-colonialism, international law, practical ethics and human rights discourse, he highlights the vast complexity exposed even by seemingly 'straight-forward' or 'non-reflexive' visions of superhero justice, pondering on the difficulty in understanding what global justice might look like.[18]

Lastly, stepping back from analysis of graphic *fiction*, Jérémie Gilbert and David Keane consider how graphic *fact* (specifically, comics aimed at reporting on real-world human rights atrocities) might be a real force

15 See Chapter 10.
16 See Chapter 11.
17 See Chapter 12.
18 See Chapter 13.

for international justice. Examining issues in human rights reporting and the seminal graphic reportage of Joe Sacco, amongst others, Gilbert and Keane clearly identify both a growing body of journalistic comics and the human enrichment that the medium can bring – particularly to the reporting of events such as the deep trauma of mass rights violations.[19]

So ends the collection of chapters in this book. As can be seen, we have come a long way: from the doctrinal view of comics as regulatory objects within intellectual property law, through concerns of representation, education, communication and philosophy, across the complex role of comics in understanding crime and criminal justice and the tensions between reality and fiction, to the value of comics in understanding issues of a truly global significance: exceptional executive violence and international concepts of justice, and ultimately to the use of comics not simply as a tool or object of analysis, but as a meaningful and important participant in the protection of humans against mass harm. The aim of this volume, if it is not already clear, is to demonstrate and showcase the diverse potential for comics and graphic fiction to enrich the various discourses of law, justice and legal studies. But rather than examining the legal potential of comics in the abstract, for the most part the chapters in this book 'argue by doing'. As can be seen: on, through, between, and within its pages you will find rich seams of analysis engaging many themes important to law and justice – and importantly, these are undertaken with comics and graphic fiction as a not-so-silent analytical companion.

It is hoped that following these analyses, when observing a collection of superheroes or their proliferating merchandise, no longer will it simply be a hoard of dazzling superficiality or childish nostalgia that is seen – but a complex array of conceptual models and critical engagements relating to legal theory and the meaning of justice; no more will the comics' aesthetic be pushed from your critical radar as a distraction or mere entertainment – but will be sought out as a source of critical inspiration, example, and insight; never again will the combination of words and images simply mean crude, childish escapism – but will signal the complex limits of law's language and of legitimate knowledge; no more shall legal discourse be constructed only through text – but will be populated by and articulated through engagement with the richly constructed panels and pages of graphic fiction. In short, the combination of diverse texts in this book seeks a unitary aim: that legal studies embrace the medium of comics as a real and significant critical resource and object.

19 See Chapter 14.

Bibliography

Bainbridge J, '"This is *the Authority*. This Planet is Under Our Protection" - An Exegesis of Superheroes' Interrogations of Law' (2007) 3 *Law, Culture and the Humanities* 455.

Douzinas C and Nead L (eds), *Law and the Image: The Authority of Art and the Aesthetics of Law* (University of Chicago Press 1999).

Giddens T, 'Comics, Law, and Aesthetics: Towards the Use of Graphic Fiction in Legal Studies' (2012) 6 *Law and Humanities* 85.

Gómez Romero L and Dahlman I, 'Introduction - Justice Framed: Law in Comics and Graphic Novels' (2012) 16 *Law Text Culture* 3.

Greenfield S, Osborn G and Robson P, *Film and the Law: The Cinema of Justice* (2nd edn, Hart 2010).

MacNeil WP, *Lex Populi: The Jurisprudence of Popular Culture* (Stanford University Press 2007).

Sherwin RK, *When Law Goes Pop: The Vanishing Line between Law and Popular Culture* (University of Chicago Press 2000).

Varnum R and Gibbons CT, 'Introduction' in Varnum R and Gibbons CT (eds), *The Language of Comics: Word and Image* (University Press of Mississippi 2001).

Williams M, *Empty Justice: One Hundred Years of Law, Literature and Philosophy* (Cavendish 2002).

Chapter 1

Lex comica: on comics and legal theory

Thomas Giddens

So, here's another example
I think
... therefore ...
I AM!
LOGICAL LINKS
Assuming I exist to be able to think
2
Also
This is not a person
I think I am ink on a page arranged such that I can be **representationally linked** with the **idea** of a person
3
Thus
... layered with rational connections beyond the (simple) logic of narrative progression...
In other words...
rational grid
LOGIC
REASON
foundations
... which look a lot like the foundations of law...
This is why judges use comics all the time to communicate their highly rational legal decisions

I sentence you to **graphic justice!**
Hold on! This is an **inaccurate** depiction of the legal process!
BANG!
ERGO...
Hmm... but if they're so rational, why **aren't** comics used by judges (or legal theorists, for that matter)? Perhaps there are still other elements at work that are **in tension** with comics' rational dimensions and capacities...

5
THIS IS AN IMAGE
And images, it can be said, work like this:
THIS IS AN IMAGE
sensory perception
So, while **this** may be true:
REASON
So is this:
Oh wow! My senses are perceiving the complex interplay of rational elements represented on this page!
...not to mention this...
emotional response
very sad comic
Reading this very sad comic can be said to be producing * sob * an **emotional response** in me
In other words...
emotions
drama
affect
senses
narrative
experience
LOGIC

This is why graphic novelists actually **do** use comics all the time to communicate their **affective** and **compelling narratives**
6
THE VISUAL PRESENTATION OF TEXT CAN ALSO BE LOADED WITH MEANING HIGHLIGHTING THE NATURE OF TEXT AS AN ABSTRACT IMAGE
And the **rational** grid can be manipulated to profoundly **aesthetic** and **affective** ends…
7
Hey! you!
AARGH!
Hmm… My mind is guilty
Please
No…
BANG!

Textual representation has its limits...
THE PHENOMENAL LIFE OF A. LEGAL SUBJECT
by A. Judge and A. Lawyer
A living human
Hmm... so does rationality
Life
Legal Journal #871
LAW REPORTS
Statutes
Which is a problem for a discipline based on rational language

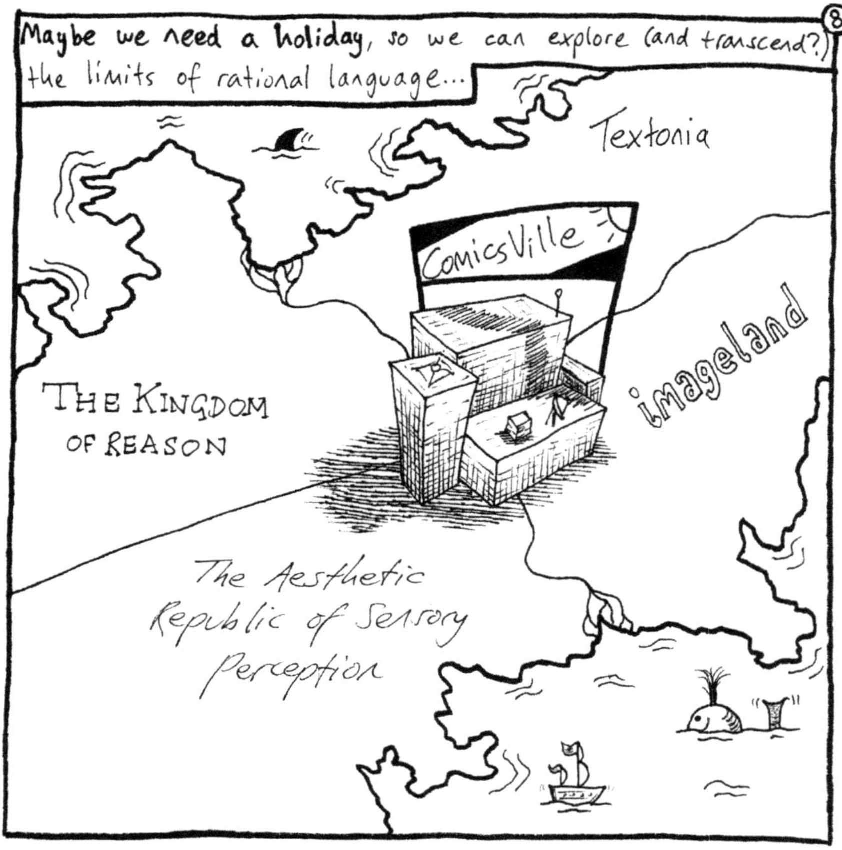
8
Maybe we need a holiday, so we can explore (and transcend?) the limits of rational language...
Textonia
ComicsVille
imageland
THE KINGDOM OF REASON
The Aesthetic Republic of Sensory Perception

Later, at the airport...
NOW BOARDING FOR COMICSVILLE

References:

(1) On the role of the gutter in reading comics, see S McLoud, *Understanding Comics: The Invisible Art* (HarperCollins 1993) 60–92.

(2) See ibid 24–25. On deriving meaning from mere 'ink on the page', see generally S Fish, *Doing What Comes Naturally: Change, Rhetoric, and Practice of Theory in Literary and Legal Studies* (Duke UP 1989) 4, and in comics D Carrier, *The Aesthetics of Comics* (Pennsylvania State UP 2000) 80. On the representational links present in comics, see A Miller, *Reading Bande Dessinée: Critical Approaches to French Language Comic Strip* (Intellect 2007) 77.

(3) On the complex tensions present in comics, see C Hatfield, *Alternative Comics: An Emerging Literature* (UP of Mississippi 2005) 32–67. See also T Giddens, 'Comics, Law, and Aesthetics: Towards the Use of Graphic Fiction in Legal Studies' (2012) 6 *Law and Humanities* 85.

(4) On the separation of law from art, note for example the introduction to C Douzinas and L Nead (eds), *Law and the Image: The Authority of Art and the Aesthetics of Law* (University of Chicago Press 1999) 3. Note, however, that whilst judges may not use them, comics are sometimes used by governments to communicate key legal issues: see, for example, O Laughland, 'Australian Government Targets Asylum Seekers with Graphic Campaign' (*The Guardian*, 11 February 2014) <www.theguardian.com/world/2014/feb/11/government-launches-new-graphic-campaign-to-deter-asylum-seekers> accessed 22 July 2014.

(5) See McCloud (n 1) 24–59 on how comics represent 'reality' through iconic images. And, on how we experience 'reality' through our senses – viz **aesthetically** – see D Manderson, *Songs without Music: Aesthetic Dimensions of Law and Justice* (University of California Press 2000) 3–24.

(6) Hatfield (n 3) 36–37.

(7) See Giddens (n 3) 97–101.

(8) To see more details of this argument **written down**, see ibid.

Acknowledgements: I would like to thank Benjamin Authers, Luis Gomez Romero, Timothy Peters, Stephen Skinner, and Melanie Williams for their helpful thoughts on an earlier version of this chapter.

Part I

Introducing comics and law

Chapter 2

Holy blurring of core copyright principles, Batmobile!

Kim Barker

Introduction

Comics are based around the adventures - and misadventures - of the characters that appear within them.[1] Two successful comic series are those produced by DC Comics - *Batman*[2] - and the Marvel series - *The Avengers*.[3] These comics rely almost exclusively on their characters for their success. These characters are incredibly important - but also distinctive and valuable. As creative products, comics are protected by intellectual property; however, it is now possible that the characters appearing in these comics are also capable of protection in their own right.[4] This chapter considers the protection granted to comics, and to their characters, under the law of copyright, and considers the challenges posed by such decisions, especially in light of the rapid expansion of fan fiction[5] and fan fiction publishing outlets. This work discusses these issues in light of a recent decision protecting the Batmobile as a character in its own right,[6] before evaluating the extent to which 'character' receives copyright protection.

1 *DC Comics v Towle* 2013 WL 541430 (CD Cal Feb 7 2013).

2 See 'The Dark Knight - Batman' (*DC Comics*) <www.dccomics.com/characters/batman> accessed 4 February 2014.

3 See 'Marvel Avengers: Alliance' (*Marvel Database*) <http://marvel.wikia.com/Marvel:_Avengers_Alliance> accessed 4 February 2014.

4 *DC Comics v Towle* (n 1).

5 Fan fiction is generally referred to as stories about characters or settings written by fans of the original works.

6 *DC Comics v Towle* (n 1). Indeed, this chapter argues that granting copyright protection to the Batmobile as a character is absurd - an absurdity that can be seen in the fact that using 'Batmobile' as one would any other character's name does not sit happily in a sentence, see the title of this chapter for an example.

Characters and ComiX

The recent decision in the US case of *DC Comics v Towle*[7] has determined that the 'Batmobile' is to be regarded as a character - one distinct from 'Batman' - and which benefits from individual copyright protection. This decision raises questions surrounding the extent to which characters are protected aside from other characters and other attributes in comics and other fictional works. It also represents a significant change in the legal landscape surrounding characters in literary works.[8] There are now also a number of questions relating to the protection and intellectual property contained within works of fan fiction, which are heavily based upon characters from leading comics. The Batmobile decision is of further significance when it is placed in the context of this fan fiction, and moreover announcements by the ComiXology[9] platform in 2012: this platform now allows self-publishing of entire comics,[10] allowing fans to write comics based on official comics or using the characters from leading comics. This could conceivably now include Batmobile comics; although, in light of the decision in *DC Comics v Towle*, there is potential for user-generated content (UGC), including fan fiction comics, to fall foul of copyright protection.

The ComiXology platform seems to encourage the sharing of works which may be based on characters from other comics. These could potentially be infringing the copyright in characters.[11] Seemingly, the actions of ComiXology conflict with the decision in *DC Comics v Towle* and pose problems for UGC production.

The protective rights-based regime

In England and Wales, the Copyright, Designs and Patents Act 1988 (CDPA 1988) provides protection to a wide range of works[12] from sound

7 *DC Comics v Towle* (n 1).

8 Compare the decision of *DC Comics v Towle* (n 1) to the predated decision in *Warner Bros Pictures Inc v Columbia Broadcasting System, Inc* 216 F 2d 945 (9th Cir 1954), where the court was categorical in stating that a character was not to be afforded distinct copyright protection.

9 A cloud-based comics platform, see <www.comixology.com/about>.

10 'Self-Publishing Comic Books: ComiXology Launches "Submit"' (*Huffington Post*, 3 July 2013) <www.huffingtonpost.com/2013/03/07/self-publishing-comic-books-comixology_n_2829005.html> accessed 30 July 2013.

11 *DC Comics v Towle* (n 1).

12 W Cornish, D Llewelyn and T Aplin, *Intellectual Property: Patents, Copyright, Trademarks and Allied Rights* (8th edn, Sweet and Maxwell 2013) 430–34.

recordings[13] and broadcasts[14] to works such as films[15] and newspapers.[16] These works are all expressions of ideas.[17] Another significant element relates to the fixation or capture in a permanent format of the work itself. The fixation requirement is particularly significant for literary, dramatic, musical or artistic works because there is a need for these works to be recorded or captured in some way in order to benefit from copyright protection.[18] Without there being some form of capturing of the work, copyright subsistence cannot arise[19] and the potential work will not benefit from copyright protection.

A literary work is defined within the CDPA 1988 as a work that is written.[20] Protection is available for literary works, which encompasses protection for books – and works such as comics given their 'written' format, ie the use of images and text.[21] It is possible that comics in particular benefit from additional artistic copyright due to the images and graphics that are merged with the text-based elements. Artistic works, for the purposes of copyright, include things such as graphic works.[22] It is therefore possible that there will be more than one copyright subsisting in the comic as a work – literary copyright and artistic copyright. There is no legislative restriction as to the number of copyrights that can arise in a particular work. For example, it is usual for there to be more than one copyright in books – both the literary work, under section 3 of the CDPA 1988, as well as the typographical arrangement, under section 8. The question of multiple copyrights has arisen in copyright disputes, most notably in *Critchley Components*.[23] Laddie J highlighted that there is no reason why one work cannot be protected by numerous copyrights.[24] In relation to comics, there

13 Section 5B of the CDPA 1988.
14 Section 6 of the CDPA 1988.
15 Section 5A of the CDPA 1988.
16 As, eg, literary works under section 3 of the CDPA 1988, but also as published arrangements under section 8. See also, *Newspaper Licensing Agency Ltd v Marks & Spencer plc* [2000] EWCA Civ 179, [2001] Ch 257.
17 Copyright is concerned with the protection of expressions rather than ideas. See below regarding the idea/expression dichotomy.
18 Section 3(2) of the CDPA 1988.
19 L Bently and B Sherman, *Intellectual Property Law* (3rd edn, Oxford University Press 2009) 58.
20 Section 3(1) of the CDPA 1988.
21 P Torremans, *Holyoak and Torremans Intellectual Property Law* (7th edn, Oxford University Press 2013) 199. See also, C Waelde and others, *Contemporary Intellectual Property Law and Policy* (3rd edn, Oxford University Press 2013) 56–82.
22 Section 4(1) of the CDPA 1988.
23 *Electronic Techniques (Anglia) Ltd v Critchley Components* [1997] FSR 401.
24 Ibid 412–13 (Laddie J).

is likely to be more than one creative effort involved, and on that basis it is unlikely that there will be difficulty in finding multiple copyrights in the same comics work. Two separate and distinct copyrights, potentially for different authors - literary copyright for the person(s) writing the words and artistic copyright for the graphical elements to the comic - are likely to subsist.

However, it is not always straightforward to identify what will be capable of being a 'work'. Deazley and Mathis consider the difficulty of identifying the 'work' forming the subject of copyright protection,[25] indicating that there is already a 'problematic legal landscape'[26] in the sphere of copyright, especially in terms of identifying what will form a work for the purposes of copyright. For example, the scope of copyright protection is difficult to identify if an artistic or literary work is not present. The challenge of identifying the category of works for comics to be protected under is compounded by their very nature.[27] This is especially challenging when considering the differences between comics publishing compared to other forms of publishing. Many comics tend to be published in a series or a number of issues rather than a complete story. As such, it is possible for debate to arise as to whether each of the comic issues benefits from copyright protection, or whether the collected story benefits from the protection, although there are decisions that indicate the courts protect works as a whole rather than in parts (albeit these are not comic-specific cases).

Deazley and Mathis indicate that, depending upon the ways in which a comic is written, it may be possible to protect each page or each panel of a particular comic,[28] perhaps even as individual works of art. The issue of protecting parts of a work or a whole work is one that has caused some difficulty in identifying the work benefiting from copyright protection. For example, in the case of *Hyperion Records*,[29] the court indicated that it was possible for individual notes in a classical composition to benefit from protection individually, although that was not the approach taken in the case. This was also an approach that was considered possible in the earlier case of *Sweeney*,[30] where the court said that individual chapters of a book could be protected separately. This has, however, been a controversial issue

25 R Deazley and J Mathis, 'Writing About Comics and Copyright' (2013) CREATe Working Paper No9<www.create.ac.uk/publications/writing-about-comics-and-copyright/> accessed 31 January 2014.

26 Ibid 9.

27 S McCloud, *Understanding Comics: The Invisible Art* (HarperPerennial 1994) 1–23.

28 Deazley and Mathis (n 25) 8.

29 *Hyperion Records Ltd v Sawkins* [2005] EWCA Civ 565.

30 *Sweeney and another v Macmillan Publishers Ltd and another* [2001] EWHC 460 (Ch), [2001] All ER (D) 332 (Nov).

that was seemingly resolved in *Ladbroke v William Hill*,[31] where the House of Lords indicated that the correct approach to identifying the 'work' was to consider the work in its entirety. As such, it seems that whilst it is possible to protect individual elements of a work, one possible approach that has been adopted by the courts is to protect the work as a whole work, although this is an unresolved area of complexity, compounded if multiple authors are involved in creating a work.

The protection that is afforded to works such as comics ensures that their expressions are protected rather than the ideas embodied within them. This is a fundamental principle that underpins the law of copyright in England and Wales, and is better referred to as the idea/expression dichotomy. This principle originated in the late 1800s[32] and is still regarded as the defining principle of copyright in the absence of a statutory definition, and has been recently reiterated by the Court of Appeal in *Designers Guild*.[33] Morritt LJ stated, 'copyright subsists not in ideas, but in the form in which the ideas are expressed'.[34] This statement reiterated the principle identified at the turn of the 20th century. There are doubts - including the extent to which copyright protects ideas - surrounding whether or not the idea/expression dichotomy offers a useful approach in copyright scenarios, and it is submitted that there is no clear boundary between ideas and expressions. Judge Learned Hand suggests that the dichotomy can at best only offer generic guidance.[35] This debate has been a lengthy one, with Peterson J in 1916 attempting to clarify this, indicating that if something is worth copying then it is worth protecting.[36] If something like a comic (as a literary work), for example, falls within the definitions offered in the CDPA 1988 of 'works'[37] then it will benefit from copyright protection. It therefore seems that elements of comics fit within this uncertainty over idea and expression, and in light of decisions such as that of *DC Comics v Towle* the dichotomy has been weakened further.

Copyright protects literary works and within this category, protection is afforded to comics. What does not benefit from protection are the ideas embodied within the comics themselves. The fundamental basis for copyright rests on the expression of an idea, rather than an idea in itself, although as discussed below, this is now a point of debate.

31 *Ladbroke Football Ltd v William Hill Football Ltd* [1964] 1 WLR 273.
32 *Hollinrake v Truswell* [1894] 3 Ch 420; the idea/expression dichotomy was first identified in the US case of *Baker v Selden* 101 US 99 (1879).
33 *Designers Guild Ltd v Russell Williams (Textiles) Ltd* [2000] All ER (D) 1950.
34 Ibid 128.
35 *Nichols v Universal Pictures* 45 F 2d 119 (2d Cir 1930).
36 *University of London Press v University Tutorial Press* [1916] 2 Ch 601, 618 (Peterson J).
37 Sections 1-8 of the CDPA 1988.

User-generated content, fan fiction and copyright?

UGC is easily recognisable but difficult to define. The phrase refers to content which is produced by consumers and users, for example Amazon customer reviews, blogs, social media sites and uploaded photos.[38] The Organisation for Economic Co-operation and Development (OECD) has identified UGC as being connected to the ability of internet users to express themselves online because the internet has developed to be something that now encourages participation - this is known as the 'participative web'[39] or Web 2.0. The OECD defines UGC as involving three elements: publication, creative effort and creation outside professional creative industries.[40] Combining these factors with the idea that UGC is participative, the three elements suggest that there is some form of creative endeavour produced in a non-traditional industry or format published on the internet. Under this definition, creative endeavours such as fan fiction - and potentially comics - fall within the realm of UGC.

UGC can arise in a number of contexts. Perhaps some of the most notable examples have arisen with the rise in social media sites. Instagram is one - controversial[41] - example of a UGC platform: users share their images online, directly producing the content, which Instagram as a service relies upon and is consisted of.[42] UGC also arises in specific comics contexts, and (as just seen) it is also possible to view online fan fiction as examples of UGC. Fan fiction, as defined by Schwabach, refers to 'Works derived from other works currently protected as intellectual property but not explicitly authorized and not commercially published'.[43]

This differs from the approach adopted by the OECD in its consideration of the participative web, which provides the following definition:

38 *Financial Times*, 'Definition of User Generated Content' (*Financial Times Lexicon*, 2014) <http://lexicon.ft.com/Term?term=user_generated-content-(UGC)> accessed 31 January 2014.

39 OECD Working Party on the Information Economy, 'Participative Web: User Created Content Report' (OECD 2007) <http://www.oecd.org/internet/ieconomy/38393115.pdf> accessed 31 January 2014, 8.

40 Ibid 8.

41 Instagram sparked controversy in late 2012 by changing its terms and conditions to claim ownership over all the images its users had posted through the Instagram service. See for details, M Warman, 'Facebook's Instagram Claims "Perpetual" Rights to Users' Photos' (*The Telegraph*, 18 December 2012) <www.telegraph.co.uk/technology/social-media/9752288/Facebooks-Instagram-claims-perpetual-rights-to-users-photos.html> accessed 31 January 2014.

42 See eg, R Ouzeau, 'Unlock the Power of User Generated Content on Instagram' (*Statigram Blog*, 14 January 2014) <http://blog.statigr.am/unlock-power-user-generated-content-instagram/> accessed 15 January 2014.

43 A Schwabach, *Fan Fiction and Copyright: Outsider Works and Intellectual Property Protection* (Ashgate 2011) 8.

> Fan fiction is a term that describes creative writing (often short stories) that uses pre-existing characters from television, movies or other fiction. Fanfiction.net is such a fan site with thousands of stories, for instance, expanding on the tales of JK Rowling's characters in Harry Potter books.[44]

It is clear from the approaches adopted by Schwabach and by the OECD that fan fiction is the creation of works that are based on pre-existing works. Fan fiction is nothing new *per se*, and has existed since fictional worlds attracted their own distinct followings,[45] but has become more visible since online publishing and self-publishing platforms rose to prominence.[46] Schwabach credits the 'respectability' of fan fiction to the movement in the 1970s of fandom in light of the 1976 *Star Trek: The New Voyages* short stories collection, which combined fictional works written by fans with introductions written by the actors from the *Star Trek* TV show.[47] This in some respects legitimised fan fiction movements where they had previously been deemed to be niche areas. The impact of the internet upon fan fiction generated a plethora of problems from a copyright perspective, including the publishing potential,[48] not to mention potential infringements of established characters - for example Harry Potter[49] - when used in derived works. The example of JK Rowling and the *Harry Potter* series forming a basis for fan fiction has arisen in the UK through the 'Barry Trotter'[50] works. This is in addition to JK Rowling suing for alleged copyright infringement in the 'Tanya Grotter' works in Russia. Both the Tanya Grotter work and the Barry Trotter work are fan fiction works, and both derivative works have been published.

The suggestion that fan fiction is nothing other than UGC, and as such online publishing should not prove problematic, was the argument used as a defence in relation to the wildly popular *Fifty Shades of Grey* series[51] when

44 OECD (n 39) 16.
45 Schwabach (n 43) 9.
46 Schwabach (n 43) 14.
47 Schwabach (n 43) 9.
48 L Stendell, 'Fanfic and Fanfact: How Current Copyright Law Ignores the Reality of Copyright Owner and Consumer Interests in Fan Fiction' (2005) 58 *Southern Methodist University Law Review* 1551.
49 T Wu, 'Harry Potter and the International Order of Copyright' (*Slate*, 27 June 2003) <www.slate.com/articles/news_and_politics/jurisprudence/2003/06/harry_potter_and_the_international_order_of_copyright.single.html> accessed 31 January 2014.
50 P England and D Meale, 'Barry Trotter and the Infringement of Copyright - Parody Rules in the UK' (2008) 178 *Managing Intellectual Property* 34.
51 *Fifty Shades Limited and Universal Studios LLC v Smash Pictures Inc* No CV12-10111 (CD Cal 27 Nov 2012).

copyright infringement claims were lodged against a pornographic production of the work.[52] The defence claimed that the original works could not benefit from copyright protection because they were already in the public domain and had been produced in high percentages on a variety of websites. An additional and more unusual claim arose that there could be no copyright in the *Fifty Shades of Grey* works because they were originally fan fiction based on the *Twilight* series. This is a compelling argument, and one which Sunshine and Cloak highlight needs attention in any creation of fan fiction, 'the fan fiction author needs to be mindful to avoid infringing the underlying work or risk losing copyright protection'.[53] Fischer highlights that a claim such as that made in this case places a substantial emphasis on the contractual licensing of any fan fiction site.[54] This seems to emphasise the importance of reading End User License Agreements,[55] especially when dealing with potentially valuable properties online.[56]

However, UGC differs from fan fiction in one significant way. UGC can be original, whereas fan fiction is derivative; it is based on a previous work (and therefore is based on a work which will benefit from copyright protection). This poses problems for the copyright subsistence in fan fiction, largely because of the idea/expression dichotomy, and the basing of fan fiction on the original works. It also poses potential difficulties when determining whether there has been copyright infringement by someone producing fan fiction.

This is a particular problem when fan fiction is widely published and shared on fan fiction sites. A brief survey of one leading site[57] reveals that there are over 10,000 fan fiction stories relating to Batman alone.[58] It is potentially a problem following the announcement by ComiXology that there is a move towards commercial self-publication of fan fiction comics. The ComiXology platform is one that publishes online comics, and which

52 E Gardner, 'Universal Sues over "Fifty Shades of Grey" Porn Adaptation' (*The Hollywood Reporter*, 29 November 2012) <www.hollywoodreporter.com/thr-esq/fifty-shades-grey-porn-adaptation-395478> accessed 2 February 2014.

53 DB Sunshine and JT Cloak, 'Fifty Shades of Copyright' *Intellectual Property Magazine* (London, May 2013) 47.

54 MA Fischer, 'Fifty Shades of Grey and Fan Fiction: Do You Own Your User Generated Content?' (*Lexology*, 12 March 2013) <www.lexology.com/library/detail.aspx?g=5cd41c40-3d90-486d-8510-4a9f86dd7bfa> accessed 6 February 2014.

55 Contractual agreements governing the relationship between the providers and users of software and websites, including fan fiction sites.

56 K Barker, 'MMORPGing – The Legalities of Game Play' (2012) 3 *European Journal for Law and Technology* 1.

57 'Batman FanFiction Archives' (*FanFiction.Net*) <www.fanfiction.net/comic/Batman/> accessed 30 August 2013.

58 'Self-Publishing Comic Books' (n 10).

in July 2013 announced that self-publishing of comics would be supported for the first time. This service allows fan fiction authors, and authors of their own comics, to submit them to the ComiXology platform and see them published. Whilst this was not the only platform to launch such a submission system - with Amazon also launching a similar service[59] - it is one which focuses especially on comics and graphic works, and in light of problems surrounding not only copyright subsistence in comics, but also comic character copyright, it is a significant development. Given that comics are protected by copyright, and that UGC can include works of fan fiction, such developments provide broad challenges for copyright. These challenges are exacerbated in light of decisions indicating that comics characters are protectable by copyright in themselves.

The Batmobile 'character' problem

As discussed, copyright protection extends to the expressions of ideas rather than to the ideas themselves. In July 2013, Judge Lew, in a Californian court, decided that the Batmobile was a character and therefore capable of distinct copyright protection, paying scant regard to the question of design rights. In *DC Comics v Towle*,[60] Mr Towle had been operating 'Gotham Garages',[61] where customers could order replica vehicles based on the Batmobile from the 1989 *Batman* film, and the 1966 TV series. DC Comics, as the publisher of comic books featuring both the Batmobile and the Batman character, sued Towle for copyright infringement on the basis that Towle had been producing replica vehicles modelled on those that had appeared in the TV series, films and comics. The decision came before Judge Lew, who, in considering his judgment, identified the significance of a character in any work of copyright.

If the idea/expression dichotomy is applied to the facts of *DC Comics v Towle*, it seems difficult to reach a conclusion other than the Batmobile replica cars being a different form of expression, and therefore protectable as a different work from the comic books, films and TV series. This would appear to be the correct stance, especially on the basis of what was determined in cases such as *Designers Guild*,[62] where a distinction was held

59 See eg, Kindle Direct Publishing <https://kdp.amazon.com/>.
60 *DC Comics v Towle* (n 1).
61 Gotham Garages <www.gothamgarage.net/cars.html>, although the website now indicates that Gotham Garages does not own the trademarks in vehicles such as 'Herbie the Lovebug' or the 'Munsters Koach'.
62 *Designers Guild* (n 33). It may be observed that this is a UK authority, and the Batmobile decision is not; nevertheless, both the United States and the UK have adopted the idea/expression dichotomy as the fundamental basis for their respective copyright systems. In the United States, this was identified in the fundamental case of *Baker v Selden* 101 US 99 (1879).

between ideas and expressions. Surely, the expressions of the Batmobile in the comics and film were different from the expression in the form of a replica car by Mr Towle?

Nevertheless, the approach Judge Lew in *DC Comics v Towle* followed was different. He stipulated that the Batmobile (in the comics, TV series and book) was a character which was particular and distinctive; therefore entitled to separate copyright protection. In making such a judgment, Judge Lew held that Mr Towle had been infringing the copyright of DC Comics. This was the decision reached, regardless of the fact that the Judge was aware that the Batmobile appeared differently each time it appeared:

> The Batmobile is known by one consistent name that identifies it as Batman's personal vehicle. It also displays consistent physical traits . . . Even though the Batmobile is not identical in every comic book, film or television show, it is still widely recognizable because it often contains bat-like motifs, such as bat-faced grill, or bat-shaped tailfins in the rear of the car, and it is almost always jet black.[63]

It is clear from the judgment that Judge Lew was aware of the differences between the various representations the Batmobile has taken on in different media. Nevertheless, he highlighted a variety of common features, which he indicated were distinctive enough to allow a finding of character in the Batmobile. The Judge also indicated that because the Batmobile had a distinctive character, and was protected by copyright, Mr Towle was infringing that copyright, even by transferring the expression of the Batmobile from a two-dimensional representation into a three-dimensional representation.[64] This has proved to be a controversial decision, and is far from problem-free, because the scope of the judgment essentially means that even where there is a functional element to the expression, a copyright finding of character will be sufficient for infringement to arise.[65] The difficulty with this decision stems directly from the idea/expression dichotomy: the expression of the Batmobile in Mr Towle's car was a different expression from that in the comic books, film and TV series. If core copyright principles are applied, such a decision should not have arisen - it is within the scope of the law to provide protection for both expressions.

A similar issue arose in the *Lucasfilm*[66] litigation in the UK in relation to whether or not copyright protection extended to replica Stormtrooper

63 *DC Comics v Towle* (n 1) 37–38 (Judge Lew).

64 *DC Comics v Towle* (n 1) 39 (Judge Lew).

65 KA Henry, 'Holy Copyrightability! The Batmobile is a Superhero. . .' (*Media Law Monitor*, 9 April 2013) <www.medialawmonitor.com/2013/04/holy-copyrightability-batman-the-batmobile-is-a-superhero/> accessed 30 August 2013.

66 *Lucasfilm Ltd v Ainsworth* [2011] UKSC 39.

Helmets that had originally been made for the 1970s film, *Star Wars Episode IV: A New Hope*. The Supreme Court was required to adjudicate on a copyright infringement claim arising in the helmets being produced by Ainsworth without permission of Lucasfilm. The court considered that the helmets could potentially be capable of copyright protection, albeit not in this instance. This decision turned on the consideration given by the court to the 'purpose' of the helmets, stipulating that there could be no copyright in the helmet because it was not the helmet forming the work of art, 'It was the Star Wars film that was the work of art . . . The helmet was utilitarian in the sense that is was an element in the process of production of the film'.[67]

This reasoning, if applied to decisions like *DC Comics v Towle*, indicates that the decision made by Judge Lew could be correct, if the rationale was that the 'work of art' in question was something more than merely the Batmobile. As such, it is possible that the reasoning of Judge Lew was that protection had to be granted to the Batmobile as a character because it was an extension of Batman as a work of art. Whether this rationale would be applied in the UK is an interesting question. Irrespective of this, the decision reached in another UK case, *Temple Islands v New English Teas*,[68] also concerned the scope of copyright protection. This case was not concerned with character protection, but with the protection afforded to photographs that have been edited. The issue arose over a question of copyright infringement in images of the Houses of Parliament, taken with a London bus in the foreground, later edited so that there was a monochrome background with a red bus in the foreground.[69] The two images, taken by different people, were similar but were taken from slightly different positions on the banks of the River Thames in London. Judge Birss in the Patents County Court was required to consider whether there had been copyright infringement, and held that there was infringement of the first image, although there are concerns as to whether or not this case establishes good law.

The implications of the *Temple Islands* decision are potentially significant, and evidence the emanation of the underlying confusion prevalent in the idea/expression dichotomy.[70] The dichotomy does not protect ideas,[71]

67 Ibid 44.

68 *Temple Island Collections Ltd v New English Teas Ltd and Anor* [2012] EWPCC 1.

69 See eg, C Lee, 'The Wheels on the Birss' (*The IPKat*, 25 January 2012) <http://ipkitten.blogspot.co.uk/2012/01/wheels-on-birss.html> accessed 26 January 2014.

70 S Innes, 'Snaps: Temple Island Collections v New English Teas Ltd [2012] EWPCC 1' (*Lexology*, 3 April 2012) <www.lexology.com/library/detail.aspx?g=4a5a2656-512e-4036-96fb-2e7d63cd263c> accessed 14 January 2014.

71 S Ang, 'The Idea-Expression Dichotomy and Merger Doctrine in the Copyright Law of the US and the UK' (1994) 2 *International Journal of Law and Information Technology* 111; *Hollinrake v Truswell* [1894] 3 Ch 420; *Designers Guild* (n 33).

yet the decision in *Temple Islands* has had the effect of giving protection to the underlying idea of editing the photograph rather than protecting two expressions of the same, or a very similar, idea. Rahmatian indicates that the court reached the correct decision, but that the law is to blame for producing the wrong result;[72] however, it is submitted that this is an unjustifiable legal position. Nevertheless, the court did not consider in its judgment in *Temple Islands* the idea/expression dichotomy. Consequently, it seems that the effect of the *Temple Islands*, *Lucasfilm* and *DC Comics v Towle* cases have all weakened and blurred the dichotomy. In addition to that, it is also apparent that from the *Temple Islands* and *DC Comics v Towle* judgments that copyright protection is extending to include protection of underlying ideas. This is likely to be particularly problematic, given the ease with which fan fiction comics can be produced and published through platforms such as ComiXology.

DC Comics v Towle is not the only case concerning intellectual property rights in characters. Nor is it the only case discussing characters in cars. A related case dealing with rights in car characters is *Halicki Films*.[73] This case was concerned with the copyright in the name of the car 'Eleanor' which had appeared in the original *Gone in 60 Seconds*. The dispute arose because of the Disney remake of the film in 2000, and the use of the rights to sell merchandise. The court was required to adjudicate on a number of issues relating to the character of the car, and, whilst not ruling that the car appearing in the original could be entitled to 'comic book-like copyright',[74] indicated that there were distinctive elements, which may allow such protection to arise. Brehm and May have suggested that the leading reason why such a finding could be possible is because of the particularly distinctive features the characters have.[75] The Batmobile had its features discussed at length, with the Judge concluding that the features themselves were distinctive.[76] Similarly, in *Halicki*, 'Eleanor' was a bright yellow 1970s car – again, distinctive enough to be memorable.

There have been other US cases dealing with the protection afforded to characters under the law of copyright, although these have not – in contrast to the Batmobile and 'Eleanor' decisions – been concerned *per se* with physical embodiments of those characters. Schwabach indicates that the US courts have changed their scope of protection in relation to characters,

72 A Rahmatian, '*Temple Islands Collections v New English Teas*: An Incorrect Decision Based on the Right Law?' [2012] *European Intellectual Property Review* 796.

73 *Halicki Films LLC v Sanderson Sales and Marketing* 547 F 3d 1213 (9th Cir 2008).

74 Ibid.

75 AS Brehm and EW May, 'Copyright Protection for Fictional Characters' (2012) 84 *Bloomberg BNA's Patent, Trademark and Copyright Journal* 285.

76 *DC Comics v Towle* (n 1) 37–38 (Judge Lew).

using different tests.[77] This change in approach from the US courts has meant that they adopted a strict stance in that characters were deemed to be un-protectable in the 1950s, yet that approach changed post-2012. The first test, indicating that characters are not protectable, arose in relation to the character of Sam Spade in *The Maltese Falcon* in 1954.[78] The court in this case indicated that irrespective of the assignability or otherwise of copyright in *The Maltese Falcon*, there was no copyright in the character Sam Spade, 'The character is only the chessman in the game of telling the story, he is not within the protection afforded by copyright'.[79]

This restrictive approach seems consistent with the idea/expression approach to copyright. The Sam Spade character, under this restrictive approach or the so-called 'story-being told'[80] test, did not benefit from copyright protection. This is perhaps because of the claim made by the author Hammett in the 1934 edition, 'Spade has no original. He is a dream man'.[81] This is reiterated by Schwabach, who indicates that there were no particularly distinctive features of Sam Spade.[82] It is perhaps this that distinguishes the 1954 decision, from the much later cases of *DC Comics v Towle* and *Halicki*.

The second test, known as the 'sufficiently delineated' test, was adopted initially in *Air Pirates*,[83] where the court indicated the shortcomings of the 'story being told test' when applied to characters accompanied by graphical representations. It is therefore apparent that under the 'story being told' test it is unlikely that the Batmobile of Mr Towle would have been found to be infringing copyright on the basis that there is no copyright in characters. However, under the less restrictive 'sufficiently delineated' test, which focuses on the character being drawn so sufficiently that the representation of the character moves from an idea to being an expression, it is:

> plausible to interpret *Air Pirates* as applying a less stringent test for protectability of graphic characters ... As a practical matter, a graphically depicted character is much more likely than a literary character to be fleshed out in sufficient detail so as to warrant copyright protection.[84]

77 Schwabach (n 43) 28.

78 *Warner Bros Pictures Inc v Columbia Broadcasting System Inc* 216 F 2d 945 (9th Cir 1954).

79 *Halicki Films LLC* (n 73) 1224.

80 Schwabach (n 43) 24.

81 D Hammett, 'Dashiell Hammet's Introduction to *The Maltese Falcon* (1934 edition)' (*The Thrilling Detective Web Site*) <www.thrillingdetective.com/trivia/triv244.html> accessed 31 January 2014.

82 Schwabach (n 43) 29.

83 *Walt Disney Productions v Air Pirates* 581 F 2d 751 (9th Cir 1978).

84 *Anderson v Stallone* 1989 WL 206431 (CD Cal 1989).

Under this interpretation, adopted in 1989,[85] it is clear that the courts have adopted a lower threshold which identifies that there will be more detail required in order to protect a character under copyright. Nevertheless, this is not without its problems. And it is within such vagueness as 'sufficient detail' that decisions like *DC Comics v Towle* are made. This again blurs the lines between idea and expression, and is likely to prove problematic in subsequent cases.

The blurring of ideas – a comic tragedy?

The decision relating to the Batmobile is concerning for fans of the Batman series, be it films, comic books or a television series. Fan fiction has to begin somewhere, and that is very often with the original work, and the original expression of a character. If, as indicated in the US cases, characters are protected by copyright, it is highly likely that fans who continue to produce fan fiction based on the leading characters - such as Batman and the Batmobile - will fall foul of copyright laws. This is even more likely given the volume of fan fiction, which is published through online platforms such as ComiXology.

Digital platforms such as ComiXology encourage creativity, and reflect the underpinnings of the intellectual property system. However, whilst encouraging creativity, they are also simultaneously encouraging users and fans to engage in activities which may lead to copyright infringement. This is particularly problematic in light of the *DC Comics v Towle* decision that subordinate characters in established comics can benefit from protection. The court, in making such a determination, may have reached the correct decision based on the facts. The court in *DC Comics v Towle* equally may have made the incorrect decision, especially after the decision in *Lucasfilm*, where the focus rested on the utilitarian function and purpose of the items created. In focusing on the purpose here, the Batmobile was part of the film and was not part of the original expression, so does not fall within the copyright of the Batmobile. By protecting a character, the court has stretched the boundaries of copyright, and has twisted - perhaps irreparably - the distinction between ideas and expressions. It seems from the decision that underlying ideas - such as the Batmobile - are now protected by copyright, rather than the expression of them.

If the court had protected the expression of Mr Towle's Batmobile, rather than the Batmobile *per se*, the scope of copyright would not have been damaged. The court could have made such a decision on the basis of UGC justifications - Mr Towle's Batmobile is his expression of the idea behind the Batmobile. The decision in the United States seems to do something

85 Ibid.

very similar to that which was done in the UK case of *Temple Islands* – the law has been interpreted and applied by both courts in two different jurisdictions, and in their application they have given protection to the ideas underlying expressions rather than the expressions themselves. In addition to this, they have significantly altered the potential for fiction, and that detracts not only from the characters themselves, but also from the enjoyment of those characters. UGC and fan fiction enterprises have had their creative freedom curtailed by two problematic decisions which have changed the scope of copyright protection.

Cases

Anderson v Stallone 1989 WL 206431 (CD Cal 1989)
Baker v Selden 101 US 99 (1879)
DC Comics v Towle 2013 WL 541430 (CD Cal Feb 7 2013)
Designers Guild Ltd v Russell Williams (Textiles) Ltd [2000] All ER (D) 1950
Electronic Techniques (Anglia) Ltd v Critchley Components [1997] FSR 401
Fifty Shades Limited and Universal Studios LLC v Smash Pictures Inc No CV12-10111 (CD Cal 27 Nov 2012)
Halicki Films LLC v Sanderson Sales and Marketing 547 F 3d 1213 (9th Cir 2008)
Hollinrake v Truswell [1894] 3 Ch 420
Hyperion Records Ltd v Sawkins [2005] EWCA Civ 565
Ladbroke Football Ltd v William Hill Football Ltd [1964] 1 WLR 273
Lucasfilm Ltd v Ainsworth [2011] UKSC 39
Newspaper Licensing Agency Ltd v Marks & Spencer plc [2000] EWCA Civ 179, [2001] Ch 257
Nichols v Universal Pictures 45 F 2d 119 (2d Cir 1930)
Sweeney and another v Macmillan Publishers Ltd and another [2001] EWHC 460 (Ch), [2001] All ER (D) 332 (Nov)
Temple Island Collections Ltd v New English Teas Ltd and Anor [2012] EWPCC 1
University of London Press v University Tutorial Press [1916] 2 Ch 601
Walt Disney Productions v Air Pirates 581 F 2d 751 (9th Cir 1978)
Warner Bros Pictures Inc v Columbia Broadcasting System Inc 216 F 2d 945 (9th Cir 1954)

Bibliography

Ang S, 'The Idea-Expression Dichotomy and Merger Doctrine in the Copyright Law of the US and the UK' (1994) 2 *International Journal of Law and Information Technology* 111.
Barker K, 'MMORPGing – The Legalities of Game Play' (2012) 3 *European Journal for Law and Technology* 1.
'Batman FanFiction Archive' (*FanFiction.Net*) <www.fanfiction.net/comic/Batman/> accessed 30 August 2013.
Bently L and Sherman B, *Intellectual Property Law* (3rd edn, Oxford University Press 2009).

Brehm AS and May EW, 'Copyright Protection for Fictional Characters' (2012) 84 *Bloomberg BNA's Patent, Trademark and Copyright Journal* 285.

Cornish W, Llewellyn D and Aplin T, *Intellectual Property: Patents, Copyright, Trade marks and Allied Rights* (8th edn, Sweet and Maxwell 2013).

Deazley R and Mathis J, 'Writing about Comics and Copyright' (2013) CREATe Working Paper No 9 <www.create.ac.uk/publications/writing-about-comics-and-copyright/> accessed 31 January 2014.

England P and Meale D, 'Barry Trotter and the Infringement of Copyright – Parody Rules in the UK' (2008) 178 *Managing Intellectual Property* 34.

Financial Times, 'Definition of User Generated Content' (*Financial Times Lexicon*, 2014) <http://lexicon.ft.com/Term?term=user_generated-content-(UGC)> accessed 31 January 2014.

Fischer MA, 'Fifty Shades of Grey and Fan Fiction: Do You Own Your User Generated Content?' (*Lexology*, 12 March 2013) <www.lexology.com/library/detail.aspx?g=5cd41c40-3d90-486d-8510-4a9f86dd7bfa> accessed 6 February 2014.

'Gotham Garages' <www.gothamgarage.net/cars.html> accessed 6 February 2014.

Gardner E, 'Universal Sues over "Fifty Shades of Grey" Porn Adaptation' (*The Hollywood Reporter*, 29 November 2012) <www.hollywoodreporter.com/thr-esq/fifty-shades-grey-porn-adaptation-395478> accessed 2 February 2014.

Hammett D, 'Dashiell Hammet's Introduction to *The Maltese Falcon* (1934 edition)' (*The Thrilling Detective Web Site*) <www.thrillingdetective.com/trivia/triv244.html> accessed 31 January 2014.

Henry KA, 'Holy Copyrightability! The Batmobile is a Superhero . . .' (*Media Law Monitor* 9 April 2013) <www.medialawmonitor.com/2013/04/holy-copyrightability-batman-the-batmobile-is-a-superhero/> accessed 30 August 2013.

Innes S, 'Snaps: *Temple Island Collections v New English Teas Ltd* [2012] EWPCC 1' (*Lexology*, 3 April 2012) <www.lexology.com/library/detail.aspx?g=4a5a2656-512e-4036-96fb-2e7d63cd263c> accessed 14 January 2014.

Lee C, 'The Wheels on the Birss' (*The IPKat*, 25 January 2012) <http://ipkitten.blogspot.co.uk/2012/01/wheels-on-birss.html> accessed 26 January 2014.

'Marvel Avengers: Alliance' (*Marvel Database*) <http://marvel.wikia.com/Marvel:_Avengers_Alliance> accessed 4 February 2014.

McCloud S, *Understanding Comics: The Invisible Art* (HarperPerennial 1994).

OECD Working Party on the Information Economy, 'Participative Web: User Created Content Report' (OECD 2007) <www.oecd.org/internet/ieconomy/38393115.pdf> accessed 31 January 2014.

Ouzeau R, 'Unlock the Power of User Generated Content on Instagram' (*Statigram Blog*, 14 January 2014) <http://blog.statigr.am/unlock-power-user-generated-content-instagram/> accessed 15 January 2014.

Rahmatian A, '*Temple Islands Collections v New English Teas*: An Incorrect Decision Based on the Right Law?' [2012] *European Intellectual Property Review* 796.

Schwabach A, *Fan fiction and Copyright: Outsider Works and Intellectual Property Protection*' (Ashgate 2011).

'Self-Publishing Comic Books: ComiXology Launches "Submit"' (*Huffington Post UK*, 3 July 2013) <www.huffingtonpost.com/2013/03/07/self-publishing-comic-books-comixology_n_2829005.html?utm_hp_ref=tw> accessed 30 July 2013.

Stendell L, 'Fanfic and Fanfact: How Current Copyright Law Ignores the Reality of Copyright Owner and Consumer Interests in Fan fiction' (2005) 58 *Southern Methodist University Law Review* 1551.

Sunshine DB and Cloak JT, 'Fifty Shades of Copyright' *Intellectual Property Magazine* (London, May 2013) 47.

'The Dark Knight - Batman' (*DC Comics*) <www.dccomics.com/characters/batman> accessed 4 February 2014.

Torremans P, *Holyoak and Torremans Intellectual Property Law* (7th edn, Oxford University Press 2013).

Waelde C and others, *Contemporary Intellectual Property Law and Policy* (3rd edn, Oxford University Press 2013).

Warman M, 'Facebook's Instagram Claims "Perpetual" Rights to Users' Photos' (*The Telegraph*, 18 December 2012) <www.telegraph.co.uk/technology/social-media/9752288/Facebooks-Instagram-claims-perpetual-rights-to-users-photos.html> accessed 31 January 2014.

Wu T, 'Harry Potter and the International Order of Copyright' (*Slate*, 27 June 2003) <www.slate.com/articles/news_and_politics/jurisprudence/2003/06/harry_potter_and_the_international_order_of_copyright.single.html> accessed 31 January 2014.

Chapter 3

Devil's advocate: representation in heroic fiction, *Daredevil* and the law

Graham Ferris and Cleo Lunt

Two worlds

Graphic fiction tells stories using words and pictures.[1] Within this narrative form we are concerned only with stories of heroes. That is our first world. The law is a set of practices and of ideas and of techniques: each of which requires some fidelity or loyalty.[2] Law has a pervasive and demanding influence on the practitioner: framing professional work and even affecting one's sense of identity.[3] Within legal practice we are concerned only with lawyers engaged in criminal defence. That is our second world.

The relationship between the worlds of law and narrative is approaching sub-discipline status. Legal education has sought support from disciplines concerned with how and why people tell stories. In *Minding the Law* the authors assert:

> To be sure, law has special functions, institutional and cognitive. The law, we are told, saves us from forgetfulness of our most basic obligations to each other and the state, from endless cycles of revenge, from the tyrannies of public powers and the blindness of private passions, from fecklessness and faction. Yet if the law does any of these things at all well, it must do them by establishing continuities with the ways in which the people of a society conceive of it and of themselves, the

1 W Eisner, *A Contract with God* (WW Norton 2006). See Virginia Commonwealth University, 'PS Magazine, the Preventive Maintenance Monthly' <http://dig.library.vcu.edu/cdm4/index_psm.php?CISOROOT=/psm> accessed 21 August 2013. How graphic fiction does this is contentious, see RC Harvey, 'Describing and Discarding "Comics" as an Impotent Act of Philosophical Rigor' in J McLaughlin (ed), *Comics as Philosophy* (University Press of Mississippi 2005); C Hatfield, *Alternative Comics: An Emerging Literature* (University Press of Mississippi 2005).

2 LL Fuller, *The Morality of Law* (Yale University Press 1969).

3 WM Sullivan and others, *Educating Lawyers: Preparation for the Profession of Law* (Jossey-Bass 2007).

> ways in which they classify and comprehend, envision and dispute and puzzle out who they are and what they need and want, and why.[4]

Minding the Law is about law learning from narrative, a movement from ideals of logic, deduction and linguistic analysis towards rhetoric, story and drama in one US law school. Indeed, this direction is indicated by the book's sub-title, 'How courts rely on storytelling, and how their stories change the ways we understand the law - and ourselves'.

This chapter tries to travel in the other direction. It is an attempt to identify what narrative has to learn from legal practice to be able to inhabit and explore that world. Any lessons will come from legal professional practice and the professional ethics that developed from that practice. Thus, it is the culture of the law, specifically the culture of the defence advocate, that we want to make available to the storyteller. The telling of a modern professional life is the challenge, and if people need stories to cross thresholds as Joseph Campbell argued,[5] then we need stories of the crossing over into the mental world of professional life:

> It has to do with your having entered a community in whose extended intelligence you share. It is that subtle 'sharing' that constitutes distributed intelligence. By entering into such a community, you have entered not only upon a set of conventions of praxis but upon a way of exercising intelligence.[6]

Thus, our two worlds are set out: story-telling in written words and pictures; and the defence of criminal defendants that lies at the heart of the criminal justice system.[7] This chapter identifies problems of communication between the two worlds, explores the world of the practitioner, and considers examples of distortions in the depiction of legal defence work. The ambition is to facilitate depiction of the professional world in heroic graphic fiction in a manner that will enrich graphic narrative, whilst helping those who intend to enter into legal practice and informing those who, as citizens, support or undermine the legal system. In democratic states how ordinary people understand law and justice will eventually impact upon the quality of those legal systems.[8] Thus, we are concerned with the impact of heroic graphic fiction upon the professional identity

4 AG Amsterdam and J Bruner, *Minding the Law* (Harvard University Press 2002).
5 J Campbell, *The Hero With a Thousand Faces* (Fontana Press 1993) 3–46.
6 J Bruner, *The Culture of Education* (Harvard University Press 1996) 154.
7 Although such practice is not typical of professional work, see D Howarth, *Law as Engineering: Thinking about what Lawyers Do* (Edward Elgar 2013) 22–50.
8 TR Tyler, *Why People Obey the Law* (Princeton University Press 2006).

and integrity of those entering the legal services market and ultimately its impact on justice in the modern democratic state.

The arguments are illustrated with materials on legal ethics taken from the United States, England and Wales, and Australia. We illustrate the narrative worlds primarily with reference to stories about the superhero *Daredevil*, whose alter ego is the lawyer Matt Murdock. *Daredevil* is a particularly useful comic to consider because of the centrality of the lawyer role and the opportunities it provides the writers to explore both the role of the lawyer and the tensions that arise between the vigilante and the legal professional.

Defence lawyers are seldom central characters in heroic comics. Sometimes they are peripheral and very negatively portrayed, as in the graphic adaptation of *The Stand* by Stephen King.[9] Sometimes they are peripheral and given sympathetic treatment, as in *Small Gods* where a defence lawyer, Mr Kerr, is portrayed as facing personal uncertainty about his client's story, and police obstruction of his efforts to establish the truth.[10] In Matt Murdock, the role of the lawyer is central to the heroic character. Tellingly, the defence lawyers at each end of this spectrum are portrayed in a way that assumes a moral identity of representative and represented - either a bad man defends the guilty in *The Stand* or a good man defends the innocent in *Daredevil*.

What happens when two worlds collide?

The failure of heroic fiction to enter the mental world of the legal practitioner is explicable by structural differences between the two worlds that are explored below. Before that exploration it is sensible to consider why we might want to bring these two very different worlds into closer contact, or even collision.[11] In short, heroic graphic fiction could be enriched by an exploration of the role of the criminal defence advocate. First, it would enable readers to understand through empathic identification something of that world, and the difficulties and rewards it brings. Second, it would enable the readers to understand a difficult systemic issue: the necessity for good men and women to defend the guilty.[12]

Lastly, it would be an opportunity to explore questions about sincerity and authenticity that are central to modern life. Trilling has argued that sincerity, being and speaking true to one's genuine belief rather than dissembling, has been of interest only since the early modern era. It was the

9 R Aquirro-Sacasa and M Perkins, *The Stand Omnibus* (Marvel 2012).
10 J Rand, J Ferreyra and K Simon, *Small Gods: Killing Grin* (Image Comics 2005).
11 LM Friedman, 'Law, Lawyers, and Popular Culture' (1989) 98 *Yale Law Journal* 1579.
12 CJ Ogletree, 'Beyond Justifications: Seeking Motivations to Sustain Public Defenders' (1993) 106 *Harvard Law Review* 1239, 1244–60.

use of false-seeming words and actions in everyday life that made sincerity noteworthy.[13] The advocate is paid to speak on behalf of another and not on his or her own behalf. This denies the advocate sincerity in professional action and raises a real problem of authenticity: the congruence of action and speech with one's own true self. Lawyers need to develop an ability to align their perspective with that of the client without losing professional 'objectivity' or their own personal moral stance. Not only is sincerity unavailable but the authenticity of the lawyer is threatened, and that can imperil personal identity.

Trilling's argument applied to cultural narratives. Problems of sincerity and authenticity also arise for legal professionals in the work world of the lawyer. The issue has been explicated by Maslach in terms of types of 'empathy':

> A person can overidentify with someone else's plight . . . Emotional closeness may bias perceptions and influence judgments in ways that are more detrimental than helpful . . . most definitions [of empathy] refer to the ability to 'get inside' another person, some describe an intellectual role-taking while others describe an emotional sharing. In the first case, the individual *sees* things from the other person's perspective, while, in the second, he or she *feels* the other person's emotions. In a helping relationship, the ideal may be the intellectual understanding but not the emotional involvement – that is, to understand the person's viewpoints on the problem but not to take on his or her feelings of fear, anger, shame, and so on.[14]

Explorations of these themes could enrich heroic graphic fiction. They ask exactly the types of question about character, loyalty and judgment that heroic fiction is well suited to explore.

Public discourse might benefit from popular exploration of this world of legal practice. The way culture portrays the defence lawyer has a powerful impact upon how people perceive defence lawyers in the real world.[15]

13 L Trilling, *Sincerity and Authenticity* (Harvard University Press 1972) 9.

14 C Maslach, *Burnout: The Cost of Caring* (Malor Books 2003) 951–60. For problematic loss of objectivity, see AM Perlman, 'A Behavioural Theory of Legal Ethics' (Suffolk University Law School Research Paper No 13-31, 2013) <http://papers.ssrn.com/sol3/papers.cfm?abstract_id=2320605> accessed 19 December 2013. On burnout and empathy in criminal defence work: Ogletree (n 12).

15 For cultural portrays of lawyers in the United States, see A Chase, 'Lawyers and Popular Culture: A Review of Mass Media Portrayals of American Attorneys' (1986) 11 *American Bar Foundation Research Journal* 281; A Sarat and S Scheingold, *The Cultural Lives of Cause Lawyers* (Cambridge University Press 2008).

Mindes and Acock identified three 'labels' applied to lawyers by the general public and lawyers themselves: hero, trickster and helper.[16] They found that the hero label was the most resonant with the general public and lawyers, but that the trickster label was also highly salient, and in some aspects quite anti-social, what they termed 'shyster'. A better informed exploration of the modern hero, as someone who has to struggle to maintain authenticity whilst setting professional boundaries on sincerity, might play a powerful role in exploring the tensions between the three overlapping but not congruent popular images of the lawyer.

For those few who practice in the criminal courts, a failure to tell stories of the transition from student to criminal advocate may take a heavier toll; in the words of Babcock:

> [T]he indifference to their clients' guilt takes its psychological toll on members of the defense bar. Although the books and articles are filled with stories of great victories, the lawyers reveal their feelings of isolation. They alone go through life being asked constantly to explain their professional existence.[17]

The lack of a satisfactory transition story for criminal advocates would account for what Babcock describes: hollow victories by heroes that do not perform their symbolic purpose for the person telling the story or future initiates. As noted above, the problem is one of 'modernity', in the words of Campbell:[18]

> There can be no question: the psychological dangers through which in earlier generations were guided by the symbols and spiritual exercises of their mythological and religious inheritance, we today . . . must face alone, or at best, with only tentative, impromptu, and not often very effective guidance. This is our problem as modern, 'enlightened' individuals, for whom all gods and devils have been rationalised out of existence.[19]

We can use the stories of real life defence advocates as moral exemplars in supporting those adopting a professional identity, especially young people who have limited life experiences to help them negotiate the transition:

16 MW Mindes and AC Acock, 'Trickster, Hero, Helper: A Report on the Lawyer Image' (1982) 7 *American Bar Foundation Research Journal* 177.

17 BA Babcock, 'Defending the Guilty' (1983–84) 32 *Cleveland State Law Review* 175, 180–81.

18 Campbell (n 5) 104.

19 Campbell (n 5) 104.

> [W]e do know that for students to incorporate the profession's ethical-social values into their own, they need to encounter appealing representations of professional ideals, connect in a powerful way with engaging models of ethical commitment within the profession, and reflect on their emerging professional identity in relation to those ideals and models.[20]

However, we can succeed only if we understand the nature of the story we are telling, only if we manage to combine our two worlds.

We can highlight the problems for the story teller who wants to tell the story of the defence advocate by analysing two dichotomies between the two worlds: the nature and function of 'representation' and the epistemological conditions.

Different types of representation

A necessary assumption behind work such as Campbell's is that the functional identity of the particular character is accepted across myths and hero stories. The hero may have any number of personally unique motivations, qualities, reactions to events, or difficulties to overcome – the joy of stories lies in part in the immense fertility and diversity of the surface details. However, Gautama Sakyamuni (Buddha) plays the same functional roles and undergoes the same functional trials as Gilgamesh.[21] In heroic fiction, representation is identity. Campbell identified features of the hero type – a type he believed was necessary for people to make life transitions: his hero leaves the ordinary world for an extraordinary one and returns with new insight.[22] The hero in the story undergoes a rite of passage for the vicarious benefit of the hearer or reader. The listener or reader identifies with the hero and is thereby helped to undergo a life changing transition, 'It has always been the prime function of mythology and rite to supply the symbols that carry the human spirit forward, in counteraction to those other constant human fantasies that tend to tie it back'.[23] For Campbell, a failure of myth or rite was possible, but people would then generate their own auto-myth, 'Apparently, there is something in these initiatory images so necessary to the psyche that if they are

20 Sullivan and others (n 3) 135; see also 156–58 for the importance of role models who can inform students' 'internalized images of lawyers or others they admire and wish to be like' 156.

21 Gilgamesh is the hero of the Sumerian epic tale of a warrior King of Uruk in the oldest known heroic or epic poem.

22 Campbell (n 5) 30.

23 Campbell (n 5) 11.

not supplied from without, through myth and ritual, they will have to be announced again, through dream, from within. . .'.[24]

For Campbell the transitions necessary for personal growth depended upon mythical or ritual enactment. If the story was not told the individual could not grow. What Campbell stresses is the importance of the double representation: individual character (eg Sir Galahad) is hero and is also hearer or reader (initiate). Each representation has to be through identity to be effective ('is' not 'similar to'). It has been argued that modern popular culture generally is generating its own mythical hero characters, specifically from the comic book world the character of Batman has been described as a hero in the Christian tradition.[25] Heroic comics, including *Daredevil*, fit well into Campbell's theoretical account of heroic stories, hence the popular designation of such characters as 'super*heroes*'. Campbell insists the stories of heroes are necessary and will be produced by individual psyches if the need is not met by cultural means. Myth cannot be superseded by rational modernity, it merely shifts its form.

Representation in legal proceedings is not identity. This is obvious, and yet a hard truth to keep hold of - both in public discourse and in practice. Lord Erskine explicated legal representation during the trial of Tom Paine for seditious libel following publication of *The Rights of Man*. Lord Erskine was countering an argument by the prosecutor, the Attorney General, who told the jury, allegedly to scotch a rumour, that bringing the prosecution was not only his duty, but right in his personal opinion, and it would be shameful to think otherwise.[26] The Attorney General wanted the rhetorical advantage to be gained by shifting from doing his impersonal duty to a personal identification with the prosecution. He thus adopted the story-telling approach to representation and identified himself with what he said and did. He claimed to be both sincere and authentic in his official actions. The Attorney General's position was problematic for the administration of justice[27] and for Lord Erskine.

First, it was unusual. It was being said to bring home just how bad this defendant was. Paine had supported the American rebels in 1776, and now he supported the revolutionaries of France, and argued for a democratic Republic in Great Britain. The jury was being invited to take sides. The rhetorical

24 Campbell (n 5) 12.

25 TD Peters, 'Unbalancing Justice: Overcoming the Limits of the Law in *Batman Begins*' (2007) 16 *Griffith Law Review* 247.

26 J Gurney, *The Whole Proceedings on the Trial of an Information Exhibited by the King's Attorney-General against Thomas Paine* (1793 London) 107. Tom Paine wrote and published his book - the 'only' issue was whether the book was a seditious libel.

27 The problem is recognised by modern professional codes of ethics, see eg, American Bar Association, *Code of Professional Responsibility* (ABA 1980) DR 7-106 (C)(4).

device forced the jury to ask itself, 'Whose side are you on?'. Second, it left the representative for the defence in an invidious position. Lord Erskine could not attack the good faith of the Attorney General. He did not want to reply in kind by an equivalent claim that would tie himself to a political radical whom he did not agree with. But not responding would have left the impression of weakness, as if the point was good and had hit home.

Yet the point was not good. It was effective purely through prejudice, and was not evidence or legal argument. In an underhand but brilliant manoeuvre, the Attorney General had managed to get the jury to ask itself of Lord Erskine, 'How can he defend the guilty?'.

This is Lord Erskine's reply:

> I will forever, at all hazards, assert the dignity, independence, and integrity of the *English Bar* without which, impartial justice, the most valuable part of the English constitution, can have no existence. For, from the moment that any advocate can be permitted to say, that he will or will not stand between the crown and a subject arraigned in the court where he daily sits to practise, from that moment the liberties of England are at an end. If the advocate refuses to defend, from what he may think of the charge or of the defence, he assumes the character of the judge; nay, he assumes it before the hour of judgment. . .[28]

Lord Erskine asserted a different concept of representation. He asserted not identity, nor even agreement between the represented and the representative; he asserted an idea of deference by the advocate to the trial process. If the law seeks truth through adversarial trial, then this can only be effective if defence advocates withhold their personal judgment and make all proper efforts to defend their clients. To refuse to defend is to prejudge and usurp the role of the court. Lord Erskine represented Paine for the sake of the legal system, he played a necessary role, he was not claiming allegiance to Paine, but to the law.[29]

The duty to the system is manifested in duties to the court. The United States, England and Wales, and Australia each have principles and rules of conduct that embody duties to the court that are capable of overriding duties to the client.[30] Adversarial trial process is a test of the prosecution's

28 Gurney (n 26) 108.

29 Lord Erskine asserts it is not his personal values or allegiances that are in question, but the duties imposed by his 'role' as a barrister. See T Schneyer, 'Reforming Law Practice in the Pursuit of Justice: The Perils of Privileging "Public" over Professional Values' (2002) 70 *Fordham Law Review* 1831.

30 ABA (n 27) EC 7-1 and American Bar Association, *Model Rules of Professional Conduct* (ABA 1983) rule 3.3.

case. If the cases of prosecutors were never tested then they would have no external incentive or sanction to seek out the best evidence or the true culprit.[31]

Different relationships to knowledge

Our second dichotomy is epistemological. Graphic fiction shows the story, and everything necessary to the narrative should be revealed by its end. Graphic fiction can subvert this apparent certainty that arises from the form of the story-telling. In the Daredevil story *Guardian Devil*, Kevin Smith showed the mistaken perceptions of Daredevil and revealed the true state of affairs only after the identity of the antagonist had been uncovered.[32] However, graphic fiction naturally facilitates narrative omniscience, and artists and writers have to consciously resist omniscience if they wish to avoid it for artistic or thematic reasons.

In the criminal justice system, factual, moral and legal truths are far more elusive. Lawyers who work for criminal defendants become cynical because they deal with a lot of guilty clients, and some of them are not honest with their lawyers. Lawyers are also subject to systemic pressures that favour negotiating guilty pleas and avoiding trial.[33] Sometimes what constitutes guilt is a complex question, and if the lawyer substitutes his or her judgment for that of the court, then he or she usurps the court's truth finding function. A famous case from Australia illustrates this point well.

Tuckier v The King[34] led to the setting out of conduct guidance and rules for advocates whose clients reveal their guilt during trial in Australia.[35] The charge was murder, and the defendant ('Tuckier' or Dhakiyarr) was an Aboriginal elder. Dhakiyarr was accused of murder by fatal spearing of a policeman who was holding Aboriginal women prisoner in the Northern Territory. The spearing seems to have been undisputed by Dhakiyarr. On the evidence it is possible Dhakiyarr thought he was justified in his action under Aboriginal custom. In legal terms he may have been acting in self-defence or he may have been provoked.

31 See T Schneyer, 'Some Sympathy for the Hired Gun' (1991) 41 *Journal of Legal Education* 11.

32 K Smith, J Quesada and J Palmiotti, *Guardian Devil* (Marvel Comics 2001). See also, D Lapham, *Stray Bullets: Uber Alles Edition* (Image Comics 2014) 635–64.

33 See DE Curtis and J Resnik, 'Grieving Criminal Defense Lawyers' (2002) 70 *Fordham Law Review* 1615.

34 (1934) 52 CLR 335. See C Parker and A Evans, *Inside Lawyers' Ethics* (Cambridge University Press 2007) 108–9.

35 Law Council of Australia, *Model Rules of Professional Conduct and Practice* (LCA 2002) 15.2.

During the trial proceedings Dhakiyarr gave instructions to his counsel, through an interpreter who worked for the police.[36] The lawyer decided his client was guilty. He declared himself in the 'worst predicament of his legal career' in open court, and requested permission to speak to the judge without the jury.[37] He conducted no further defence of his client, who was convicted, and after the verdict had been delivered he gave a publicly reported account of Dhakiyarr's confession and guilt. The confidence counsel felt in Dhakiyarr's guilt seems to have been informed by his lack of understanding of, or empathy for, his client's perceptions, instructions, and reasoning. It seems very unlikely that the flustered counsel reflected upon possible defences under the law, such as provocation or self-defence.[38] Counsel displayed far more concern for the reputation of the dead policeman than for the reputation, safety or life of his client.[39] What constitutes guilt in law is often complex, and a defence advocate is not always in the best situation to decide the issue.[40]

Lastly, there are incentives to falsely confess guilt as a guilty plea speeds up the process, and earns a reduced sentence; as well as more obvious incentives to falsely claim innocence to avoid punishment.[41] Professionals working within the system as lawyers for the criminal defendant tend to become cautious about asserting where truth or justice is to be found.[42]

Portrayal of the lawyer in *Daredevil*

Matt Murdock is the blind alter ego of the costumed crime-fighter Daredevil. He has preternaturally heightened senses: although he is blind he can sense objects with a unique radar ability, and he has super-sensitive hearing, smell and touch. Murdock is a lawyer who represents criminal defendants. He practices with his long-time friend Foggy Nelson. Murdock is the heroic comic equivalent of Atticus Finch, the lawyer as hero archetype. Finch is both a well-respected and tolerant member of his community and a lawyer willing to face opprobrium and personal damage in the conduct of his professional work as a court-appointed defence

36 The interpretative problems of taking instructions under such conditions were recognised, see *Tuckier* (n 34) 352.

37 *Tuckier* (n 34) 341.

38 *Tuckier* (n 34) 342, 352.

39 *Tuckier* (n 34) 354–55.

40 The case forms the background to A Collins and T Murray (eds), *Dhakiyarr vs The King* (Mayfan 2003).

41 See ME Vogel, *Coercion to Compromise: Plea Bargaining, the Courts and the Making of Political Authority* (Oxford University Press 2007). See also, B Schlink, *The Reader* (Phoenix 2011).

42 See Babcock (n 15) 183–84.

lawyer. Daredevil is both a vigilante crime fighter and a member of the legal profession active in criminal trials.

One important difference is the ability to choose clients. Finch accepts the role the trial judge assigns him,[43] and does not know when he agrees to act whether his client is guilty or innocent. Murdock does not represent the guilty because he can use his powers to identify the innocent and, we presume, he does not want to use his talents in the service of criminals. Murdock's unique access to information lets him exercise a choice unavailable to other people and avoid a tension inherent in the real life role of criminal defence advocate.

Murdock only defends the innocent in court and he identifies them by using his in-built lie detector, paying particular attention to heartbeat. Murdock can be fooled: by people who have electronic devices that keep heartbeat regular (see Figure 3.1);[44] or people who are themselves firmly convinced of an untruth;[45] or by people who have unnaturally extensive powers of self-control;[46] or very occasionally he simply makes a slip and misses something.[47] Occasionally, he is also willing to help a person who is technically guilty when the person is morally innocent.[48]

Although *Daredevil*'s writers have explored Murdock's relationship with the courts, and he has even lied in open court to protect his secret identity, they have not placed him in the position of knowingly defending the guilty. He is continually faced with what has been described as the more difficult task of defending the innocent: more difficult because failure by the defence advocate results in the punishment of an innocent person.[49] An in-built lie detector means that one knows apparently guilty people are at grave risk of suffering a miscarriage of justice. This can place an unwelcome obligation on Murdock to take cases he would rather avoid. In this Murdock shares a trait with Finch: both lawyer-heroes are willing to represent clients they know will cause them

43 H Lee, *To Kill a Mockingbird* (Arrow 1997) 180, 238.

44 F Miller and K Janson, *Daredevil #184* (Marvel Comics 1982).

45 Smith, Quesada and Palmiotti (n 32). The young woman believes she was impregnated by the holy ghost.

46 The Black Widow in BM Bendis and A Maldeev, *The Widow* (Marvel Comics 2004).

47 BM Bendis and A Maldeev, *Out* (Marvel Comics 2002). He did not notice a juror had lied and she was prejudiced against his client the White Tiger.

48 The Gladiator is a recurring character who Murdock has been sympathetic towards and helped, see BM Bendis and A Maldeev, *Golden Age* (Marvel Comics 2005). This willingness resembles the willingness of Atticus Finch to collude in not prosecuting Boo Radley, see T Dare, 'The Secret Courts of Men's Hearts: Legal Ethics and Harper Lee's *To Kill A Mockingbird*' in K Economides (ed), *Ethical Challenges to Legal Education and Conduct* (Hart 1998).

49 A Smith, 'Defending the Innocent' (2000) 32 *Connecticut Law Review* 485. Bendis and Maldeev (n 47) explored this with the White Tiger trial storyline.

Figure 3.1 From F Miller and K Janson, *Daredevil #184* (Marvel Comics 1982). ©2014 MARVEL. Murdock's built-in lie detector from *Daredevil #183*: it transpires Hogman had a pacemaker and Murdock was deceived by his regular heartbeat.

reputational damage.[50] In the White Tiger storyline, Murdock is under suspicion of being Daredevil and wants to avoid being associated with the superhero community or superhero activity, furthermore, superheroes are unpopular with the public due to recent events. The White Tiger is a vigilante or superhero who is accused of the killing of a police officer. The evidence is circumstantial and Murdock interviews the man who is being held in prison awaiting trial. Matt Murdock's reluctance to represent the White Tiger, and his reliance upon his super-senses, are illustrated by the panels reproduced in Figure 3.2.

In this way, the writers have presented Murdock with the task of defending unpopular defendants, and thereby touched upon one of the pressures associated with the representation of criminal defendants. The most unpopular defendants are often politically offensive to the government and public opinion, as was the case with Tom Paine,[51] or are charged

50 Lee (n 43) 180, Bendis and Maldeev (n 47).
51 Gurney (n 26).

Figure 3.2 From BM Bendis and A Maldeev, *Out* (Marvel Comics 2002). © 2014 MARVEL. Murdock and Nelson interview the White Tiger in prison and Murdock feels obliged to defend a man his super senses tell him is innocent.

with offences that cause moral repugnance in the public,[52] and sometimes both.[53]

The in-built lie detector prevents Murdock having to deal with uncertainty over guilt. However, writers of *Daredevil* have wanted to explore the tensions exposed by the need to act under conditions of uncertainty and to risk being aligned with the immoral:

> In law school, there's a second, less academic curriculum - beyond the standard textbook stuff. You're taught to develop what they refer to as a 'judgmental vacuum'. It's the emotional void a lawyer has to find for himself in order to defend a client you feel may not be completely innocent - or just flat-out guilty.[54]

52 In the United States, the legal community in Guam was reluctant to accept campaigners for freer abortion laws in a small and overwhelmingly Catholic community. See *Guam Society of Obstetricians and Gynaecologists v Ada* 100 F 3rd 691 (9th Cir 1996) and discussion in TS Collett, 'The Common Good and the Duty to Represent: Must the Last Lawyer in Town Take Any Case?' (1999) 40 *South Texas Law Review* 137, 143–45.

53 Those implicated with the destruction of the World Trade Towers in the United States were both hated politically and objects of revulsion for the carnage they had helped to cause. See A Smith, 'Defending the Unpopular Down-Under' (2006) 30 *Melbourne University Law Review* 495, 498 n 15.

54 Smith, Quesada and Palmiotti (n 32).

Of course, defending the guilty is unavoidable in criminal defence work if one does not have an in-built lie detector. The professional ethics of the United States differ from Australia and England on the question of client selection. In England and Wales and Australia, the 'cab-rank' principle precludes client selection in principle.[55] In the United States, a professional obligation is only imposed if an attorney is appointed to represent an accused by the court, or it has been argued when no other representation is available.

When Murdock selects only the innocent to defend, he puts pressure on several principles protected by cab-rank rules or by what in the United States has been described as the duty of the 'last lawyer in town'.[56] He decides upon guilt prior to trial. Yet even Murdock with his lie detector can be deceived; and his super-powers do not free him from sources of error that originate in legal ambiguity or cultural ignorance.

There is also the problem of the unpopular and probably guilty defendant who still requires a defence if justice is to be done and to be seen to be done. Murdock is willing to risk his reputation, but only in the defence of the innocent. The possibility of not acting for the guilty as a point of principle risks leaving some defendants without representation because the belief in their guilt is so widespread and by choosing to defend them the lawyer involved will be seen as associating with them. If any lawyer can claim to be a conscientious objector then all lawyers could claim contentious objection with respect to a class of defendants. For Atticus Finch, the client group was Afro-Americans in the Jim Crow south, for American lawyers in the immediate aftermath of the destruction of the World Trade Towers, it was suspected Islamic terrorists,[57] for Daredevil, the guilty. It is the obligation on the profession as a group that has to be met by individual lawyers. As Atticus Finch put it, 'Scout, simply by the nature of the work, every lawyer gets at least one case in his lifetime that affects him personally. This one's mine I guess'.[58] Refusing to represent those who seem guilty, or those who plead guilty, undermines the system of criminal justice.

Daredevil over the years has explored some of the tensions inherent in the role of the legal representative. However, the writers have not been willing to test the key structural differences between heroic and legal representation identified above. This leaves heroic graphic fiction still unable to integrate the heroic and trickster images of the lawyer. We need a lawyer who accepts his or her fallibility but still tries to do his or her

55 ABA (n 27) EC 2-26.
56 Collett (n 52).
57 Smith (n 53) 498 n 15.
58 Lee (n 43) 84.

best under conditions of uncertainty. If heroic fiction is able to enter this realm of compromised sincerity and challenged authenticity, then it can engage with central problems of modernity. Flawed heroes have been popular successes: Batman, Iron Man, and Daredevil himself have all been portrayed as men struggling to control their own demons. What remains to be explored is the situational stresses upon personal integrity that the role of defence lawyer can place upon a legal professional who must act with circumspection in an uncertain world.

Lastly, law needs fiction to help it sustain itself; although criminal defence work is justifiable, it needs motivated lawyers to sustain it:

> However, these theoretical justifications, though logically compelling, are often of limited utility to the public defender. When faced with a conflict between her professional role and her visceral reaction to her clients . . . that lawyer may not zealously represent a criminal defendant absent a sufficiently compelling *motivation* – an impetus to do the work, rather than a theory that merely argues that it is *defensible*, *excusable*, or *laudable* for someone to do that work.[59]

Conclusion – Why graphic fiction?

Heroic graphic fiction is a form of popular fiction consumed, *inter alia*, by many young people. If those considering future entrance into the legal professions need an initiatory 'rite of passage' then this genre is well placed to provide it. However, there are intrinsic or formal reasons to think graphic fiction is a medium capable of overcoming the problem of dissonance between heroic and legal representation. Graphic fiction has great potential for portraying simultaneous disparate viewpoints. It can represent underlying tensions using familiar devices: the reflective textual narrative deployed in oblong boxes against dissonant pictures; the use of simultaneous parallel panels using the page as super panel;[60] the use of discordant drawing styles or colour.[61] The elegance and power of such techniques can be illustrated by the images from *Daredevil* reproduced above.

Figure 3.1 illustrates use of a graphic device derived from the oscilloscope to show the built-in lie detector at work. The images and text show three separate channels of information: the words spoken (Hogman's words represented by text in a speech balloon); the thoughts of Murdock (represented by text in a thought balloon); Murdock's aural perception of

59 Ogletree (n 12) 1242.
60 W Eisner, *Comics and Sequential Art* (WW Norton & Co 2008) 82–89.
61 As in D Mazzucchelli, *Asterios Polyp* (Pantheon Books 2009).

Hogman's heartbeat (the superimposed oscilloscope line). Time passing is captured by panel sequence: the words are spoken, they and the heartbeat are heard, Murdock realises the importance of the two things he is hearing.

Figure 3.2 illustrates another way of portraying multiple channels of information. The first panel is divided into two vertically: so the divide does not suggest the passage of time, normally represented by panel progression horizontally from left to right. The top half of the panel is the head and words of the White Tiger. The bottom half shows his chest, from which his heartbeat will sound. The thoughts of Murdock are represented in oblong boxes, as he is not pictured, and the thought is reflective. In the next panel time passes and the reader is returned to a view of events happening in public space. Murdock, whose own life is being disrupted by his vigilante life as Daredevil asks the White Tiger the question that is tormenting Murdock personally, 'Why risk everything else in life to be a costumed crime fighter?'.

What is said, what is believed and what is valued are the three factors that are at play in situations of sincerity and authenticity; comics can carry all three channels simultaneously. What the defendant says, what the lawyer believes and what the lawyer says and does are the three factors in play in legal representation; again, comics can carry all three channels simultaneously. The medium is rich in multiple channels of communication: text; calligraphy; word balloons; lexicon; colour and text; image as information; style of drawing; panel arrangement; colour and image. One can combine visceral immediacy of film with the opportunity to review and reassess when more information is available, as demonstrated in *Guardian Devil*.

Heroic graphic fiction has already explored some of the tensions inherent in the representation of criminal defendants in the mass-market continuing narrative of *Daredevil*. It is formally capable of handling the complexity of the world of legal defence work. If the medium embraces this challenging complexity, then exploration of such core problems of modernity as sincerity and authenticity may lie just beyond the horizon.

Case

Guam Society of Obstetricians and Gynaecologists v Ada 100 F 3rd 691 (9th Cir 1996)
Tuckier v The King (1934) 52 CLR 335

Bibliography

American Bar Association, *Code of Professional Responsibility* (ABA 1980).
American Bar Association, *Model Rules of Professional Conduct* (ABA 1983).
Amsterdam AG and Bruner J, *Minding the Law* (Harvard University Press 2002).
Aquirro-Sacasa R and Perkins M, *The Stand Omnibus* (Marvel 2012).

Babcock BA, 'Defending the Guilty' (1983–84) 32 *Cleveland State Law Review* 175.
Bendis BM and Maldeev A, *Out* (Marvel Comics 2002).
Bendis BM and Maldeev A, *The Widow* (Marvel Comics 2004).
Bendis BM and Maldeev A, *Golden Age* (Marvel Comics 2005).
Bruner J, *The Culture of Education* (Harvard University Press 1996).
Campbell J, *The Hero With a Thousand Faces* (Fontana Press 1993).
Chase A, 'Lawyers and Popular Culture: A Review of Mass Media Portrayals of American Attorneys' (1986) 11 *American Bar Foundation Research Journal* 281.
Collett TS, 'The Common Good and the Duty to Represent: Must the Last Lawyer in Town Take Any Case?' (1999) 40 *South Texas Law Review* 137.
Collins A and Murray T (eds), *Dhakiyarr vs The King* (Mayfan 2003).
Curtis DE and Resnik J, 'Grieving Criminal Defense Lawyers' (2002) 70 *Fordham Law Review* 1615.
Dare T, 'The Secret Courts of Men's Hearts: Legal Ethics and Harper Lee's *To Kill A Mockingbird*' in Economides K (ed), *Ethical Challenges to Legal Education and Conduct* (Hart 1998).
Eisner W, *A Contract with God* (WW Norton 2006).
Eisner W, *Comics and Sequential Art* (WW Norton 2008).
Friedman LM, 'Law, Lawyers, and Popular Culture' (1989) 98 *Yale Law Journal* 1579.
Fuller LL, *The Morality of Law* (Yale University Press 1969).
Gurney J, *The Whole Proceedings on the Trial of an Information Exhibited by the King's Attorney-General against Thomas Paine* (London 1793).
Harvey RC, 'Describing and Discarding "Comics" as an Impotent Act of Philosophical Rigor' in J McLaughlin (ed), *Comics as Philosophy* (University Press of Mississippi 2005).
Hatfield C, *Alternative Comics: An Emerging Literature* (University Press of Mississippi 2005).
Howarth D, *Law as Engineering: Thinking about what Lawyers Do* (Edward Elgar 2013).
Lapham D, *Stray Bullets: Uber Alles Edition* (Image Comics 2014).
Law Council of Australia, *Model Rules of Professional Conduct and Practice* (LCA 2002).
Lee H, *To Kill a Mocking Bird* (Arrow 1997).
Maslach C, *Burnout: The Cost of Caring* (Malor Books 2003).
Mazzucchelli D, *Asterios Polyp* (Pantheon Books 2009).
Miller F and Janson K, *Daredevil #183–184* (Marvel Comics 1982).
Mindes MW and Acock AC, 'Trickster, Hero, Helper: A Report on the Lawyer Image' (1982) 7 *American Bar Foundation Research Journal* 177.
Ogletree CJ, 'Beyond Justifications: Seeking Motivations to Sustain Public Defenders' (1993) 106 *Harvard Law Review* 1239.
Parker C and Evans A, *Inside Lawyers Ethics* (Cambridge University Press 2007).
Perlman AM, *A Behavioural Theory of Legal Ethics* (Suffolk University Law School Research Paper No 13-31, 2013) <http://papers.ssrn.com/sol3/papers.cfm?abstract_id=2320605> accessed 19 December 2013.
Peters TD, 'Unbalancing Justice: Overcoming the Limits of the Law in *Batman Begins*' (2007) 16 *Griffith Law Review* 247.
Rand J, Ferreyra J and Simon K, *Small Gods: Killing Grin* (Image Comics 2005).

Sarat A and Scheingold S (eds), *The Cultural Lives of Cause Lawyers* (Cambridge University Press 2008).
Schlink B, *The Reader* (Phoenix 2003).
Schneyer T, 'Some Sympathy for the Hired Gun' (1991) 41 *Journal of Legal Education* 11.
Schneyer T, 'Reforming Law Practice in the Pursuit of Justice: The Perils of Privileging "Public" over Professional Values' (2002) 70 *Fordham Law Review* 1831.
Smith A, 'Defending the Innocent' (2000) 32 *Connecticut Law Review* 485.
Smith A, 'Defending the Unpopular Down-Under' (2006) 30 *Melbourne University Law Review* 495.
Smith K, Quesada J and Palmiotti J, *Guardian Devil* (Marvel Comics 2001).
Sullivan WM, Colby A, Wegner JW, Bond L and Shulman LS, *Educating Lawyers: Preparation for the Profession of Law* (Jossey-Bass 2007).
Trilling L, *Sincerity and Authenticity* (Harvard University Press 1972).
Tyler TR, *Why People Obey the Law* (Princeton University Press 2006).
Virginia Commonwealth University, 'PS Magazine, the Preventive Maintenance Monthly' <http://dig.library.vcu.edu/cdm4/index_psm.php?CISOROOT=/psm> accessed 21 August 2013.
Vogel ME, *Coercion to Compromise: Plea Bargaining, the Courts and the Making of Political Authority* (Oxford University Press 2007).

Chapter 4

I am the law teacher! An experiential approach using *Judge Dredd* to teach constitutional law

Richard Glancey

Students of public or constitutional law often struggle to meaningfully engage with the theoretical components of the topic. As the UK has no codified (often referred to as written) constitution, in order to gain a critical understanding of the UK constitution, students need to engage with theoretical concepts such as the separation of powers, the rule of law, and parliamentary sovereignty. In the absence of a codified constitution, these theoretical concepts underpin and help us to understand the constitutional position and relationships of the different organs of the state. Given their significance and importance, the reticence of many students to meaningfully engage with these theories prevents them from developing such a critical understanding of the UK constitution. As a lecturer in public law, this concerns me. My concerns are twofold: the effectiveness of the learning and teaching methodologies utilised in public law; and, the depth of learning achieved by the students. These two concerns are patently connected. I am always striving to do better in both of these areas, and in this chapter I set out and explore my proposal for how they can be improved - namely, that using graphic fiction as an additional learning and teaching methodology for constitutional theory can enhance the depth of learning achieved by students in these areas.

My proposal is that reference to specific graphic fictional characters and worlds when teaching constitutional theory can be used as a pedagogical tool to enhance students' understanding of the theories. The characteristics of certain heroes and their worlds can be equated to characteristics of constitutional theories, thereby providing characterisation of these complex constitutional theories allowing a valuable introduction to their study. Characterisation brings life to an otherwise dead entity - it animates. Animating something makes it real, makes it interactive, increases enjoyment and elicits a response: it therefore makes the learner *active* as opposed to *passive*, and this change of dynamic allows deeper and more meaningful learning to take place. Such references to graphic fiction are proposed as an added ingredient to a constitutional law course and not a replacement for any current content. The suggestion is that the power of graphic fiction can enhance the learning and teaching of constitutional law students, and therefore could be a valuable pedagogical tool that it is worth exploring. I explore these elements in this chapter, focusing on the world of *Judge Dredd*, in two main parts. The first part explores the pedagogical value of using graphic fiction with reference to experiential learning theory. The second part contains two case studies to demonstrate the experiential approach discussed in the first section.

Pedagogical theory and graphic fiction in law

Why will using graphic fiction to teach law work from a pedagogical perspective? Whilst it is not a classical experiential model, as such an approach typically involves learning through work-based tasks, I believe it does have experiential virtues and therefore the benefits of an experiential approach can be felt.

Classical experiential learning can be seen in clinical work, which started in the medical academy, but is becoming more popular in law.[1] Clinical legal work can be seen in law schools around the globe and takes many different forms, from taking on real cases and advising clients under the supervision of practitioners,[2] to getting involved with policy work and helping to shape legal developments.[3] Whist using graphic fictional heroes to teach constitutional theory is a rather different learning application to working in a solicitor's office advising a client, I outline three aspects of pedagogical theory to demonstrate the experiential pedigree and value of using graphic fiction to teach law: what experiential learning is and why using graphic fiction can be classed as experiential; the benefits of using an experiential approach; and, the impact that using graphic fiction has upon critical thought.

What is experiential learning?

John Dewey is often credited with giving credence to the value of learning through experience,[4] with others such as David Kolb adding further

1 For a good variety of academic source material about legal clinical work, see generally *International Journal of Clinical Legal Education* (<www.northumbriajournals.co.uk/index.php/ijcle>).
2 An example of this is the Student Law Office at Northumbria Law School, Northumbria University.
3 This type of clinic, often called a 'policy clinic' is popular in US law schools.
4 J Dewey, *Experience and Education* (Kappa Delta Pi 1938).

to the theoretical foundations.[5] Kolb summarised experiential learning in one passage as follows:

> Experiential learning theory offers a fundamentally different view of the learning process from that of the behavioural theories of learning based on an empirical epistemology or the more implicit theories of learning that underlie traditional educational methods, methods that for the most part are based on rational, idealist epistemology . . . [It] emphasises the central role that experience plays in the learning process. This differentiates experiential learning from rationalist and other cognitive theories of learning that tend to give primary emphasis to acquisition, manipulation, and recall of abstract symbols, and from behavioural learning theories that *deny any role* for consciousness and *subjective experience* in the learning process . . . experiential learning theory [is not] an alternative to behavioural and cognitive learning theories, but rather [it provides] a holistic integrative perspective on learning that combines experience, perception, cognition and behaviour.[6]

Using graphic fiction heroes as case studies could be seen as a form of experiential learning. Students are taking 'factual' scenarios (the worlds of the graphic fiction heroes), akin to a problem scenario used in Problem-Based Learning,[7] which students then use to conduct learning through utilising their subjective experience of assimilating the graphic fiction worlds with the constitutional theories; students can be seen to be learning by doing. One of the key arguments as to why experiential learning is effective is that it creates a 'real' learning environment that invites students to take ownership and responsibility of their learning. The result of this is a deeper and more meaningful learning experience.[8]

There could be, however, a problem with classing this type of learning as 'experiential'. Beard has explored some different definitions of what

5 D Kolb, *Experiential Learning: Experience as the Source of Learning and Development* (Prentice-Hall 1984).

6 Ibid 20, emphasis added.

7 Problem-Based Learning is where students are given a problem scenario at the outset, generally without having been lectured upon the topic, and undertake their own research into the areas they identify under supervision of academic staff. The problem serves as the starting point and basis of the learning as opposed to the traditional approach which uses problem scenarios at the end of a learning cycle to test knowledge. See M Savin-Baden and C Howell Major, *Foundations of Problem-Based Learning* (The Society for Research into Higher Education and Oxford University Press 2004).

8 See P Ramsden, *Learning to Teach in Higher Education* (2nd edn, RoutledgeFalmer 2003) ch 4, which discusses the difference between 'surface' and 'deep' learning.

experiential learning means.[9] One such definition he gives by Keeton and Tate is:

> Learning in which the learner is directly in touch with the realities being studied. It is contrasted with learning in which the learner only reads about, hears about, talks about, or writes about these realities but never comes into contact with them as part of the learning process.[10]

It could be argued that merely reading graphic fiction falls into the category mentioned by Keeton and Tate as that which can be contrasted with experiential learning. I believe it is a more sophisticated process than that, however, as it does put students in touch with the realities being studied. Removing the graphic fictional heroes from the page and exploring their worlds in a practical way elevates the process beyond reading, talking or writing, and is learning by doing, or by 'experience'. This is further evidenced by what Kayes refers to as the *process* versus *content* form of education.[11] Whilst traditional pedagogical approaches, such as lectures, focus upon *content* and are evaluative, experiential pedagogy focuses upon the *process* and is developmental. My assertion is that using graphic fiction to teach law is a *process*-based pedagogy designed to assist the development of students.

The benefits of experiential learning

There are many benefits of using an experiential approach in learning and teaching. Beard refers to the richer experience offered by experiential learning through what he calls the 'giraffe effect'.[12] He gives the analogy that people usually see giraffes either in a zoo or in the wild on safari. In both instances they are observed from a distance, either in a cage or enclosure or roaming free on a plain. He then refers to the practice of some safari parks to allow giraffes to be observed from cars and fed from open car windows. He says this is a far different experience of the animal, as they can be smelt, felt, touched, and it gives a real impression of the size and power of the animals. Beard summarises by saying the richness of the latter experience is more engaging as the *experience* takes centre stage. He concludes the learning has shifted, from taking place at a distance, to

9 C Beard, *The Experiential Learning Toolkit: Blending Practice with Concepts* (Kogan Page 2010).

10 Ibid 17, citing Keeton and Tate.

11 C Kayes, 'Institutional Barriers to Experiential Learning Revisited' in M Reynolds and R Vince (eds), *The Handbook of Experiential Learning and Management Education* (Oxford University Press 2007).

12 Beard (n 9) 15.

being immersed in it – in his words, from transmission to transformation – and this is what experiential learning should be doing. It is going beyond 'outer' experiences and allows 'internalisation' of the subject matter to take place, hence richer, deeper, and more meaningful learning takes place.[13] Using graphic fiction characters brings their worlds and the constitutional theories closer to home – they are less abstract and indistinct, they can almost be touched and felt, resulting in this 'giraffe effect'.

Graphic fiction in particular, as opposed to other media such as literary fiction, visual arts, film or television, etc, maximises this giraffe effect as the pages can be held and smelt and the narrative and pictures combine to bring the world to life. The medium effectively pauses the story allowing students to look at it, digest it, go back and forth, and contemplate and reflect upon it at their own pace. They can be their own director of the story in a much more overt way than they can with other media, which is what sets graphic fiction apart from a learning and teaching perspective: the active involvement of the reader.[14]

Beard quotes Edward Cell who notes that TS Eliot, 'has suggested that experience is like a partially developed roll of film. As we later reflect upon it, especially as we look back from a new perspective, we may develop it further, bringing out more if its meaning'.[15] Encapsulating Eliot's sentiment, using graphic fiction facilitates this process of looking at our experiences from a new perspective, thereby enhancing critical reflection and learning, helping to challenge and change beliefs. Using graphic fiction offers a completely different perspective from that which law students are used to utilising. This new perspective allows them to break free of the usual mental classroom restraints which Brookfield discusses (see below), thereby facilitating students to challenge previous beliefs (learning) and promote the formation of new ways of thinking. Brew has also discussed the strength of experiential learning to destroy prior learning and in the process thereby create new learning, facilitating transformation.[16] This is critical learning in action. One of the key things is that all of these benefits derive from the fact that a new perspective has been provided to the students – the graphic fiction perspective. That is the power of graphic fiction, and that is why it is such a valuable pedagogical tool – it provides a new perspective, which provides the foundations for a new structure of learning.

13 Beard (n 9).

14 For an excellent overview of the strengths of graphic fiction as a medium, see S McCloud, *Understanding Comics* (William Morrow Paperbacks 2001).

15 Beard (n 9) 247, quoting Edward Cell.

16 A Brew, 'Unlearning through Experience' in D Boud, R Cohen and D Walker (eds), *Using Experience for Learning* (Society for Research into Higher Education and Oxford University Press 1993).

Another benefit of experiential learning is that it aids students' abilities to be self-learners. This can be explained with reference to Vygotsky's zone of proximal development. His thesis was that development is closely linked to instruction.[17] For example when children learn, they perform better when instructed by and copying from adults when they are present together. When they are on their own, they do not learn as effectively. This gap in performance, or learning, between what our abilities are independently and what they could be through instruction is what he calls the zone of proximal development. Effective instruction bridges this gap. Providing students with the methodology of using graphic fiction to conceptualise theories is a useful tool to allow them to learn more effectively independently, thereby reducing the gap in their zone of proximal development.

Vygotsky also explored in depth exactly what is meant by 'development'. He says the following about development, 'What is changed and modified are the relationships, the links . . . New constellations emerge which were unknown in the preceding stage'.[18] This accurately describes the development and enhanced learning that the suggested process aims to achieve. Students are able to make those new connections through the process of using graphic fiction to conceptualise the abstract theories. Some 'dots' or stars representing knowledge already existed, but new connections are seen between these dots, hence new constellations formed.

A further significant benefit of using experiential learning is that it improves knowledge acquirement; the epistemological dimension. One aspect of this theory is the difference between two different forms of knowledge: apprehension and comprehension.[19] These two concepts are a way of examining how knowledge is structured. One simplified way to describe the difference between these two concepts is that apprehension is when we are aware of a matter, in the here-and-now, and comprehension is when we understand a matter and are able to conceptualise it, to help define future activity. The assertion is that both apprehension and comprehension are required for the most effective learning to take place. A concept is needed to be able to understand abstract matter. Using graphic fiction to characterise constitutional theories provides the concept allowing students to conceptualise the otherwise abstract theories and attain a more holistic knowledge of them by achieving comprehension. In short, deeper and more meaningful learning takes place by using graphic fiction

17 See H Daniels, M Cole and J Wertsch (eds), *The Cambridge Companion to Vygotsky* (Cambridge University Press 2007).

18 Ibid 308.

19 Many theorists have looked at this interaction. For a useful overview see Kolb (n 5) 100.

as it helps students to apprehend and comprehend by conceptualising the theories enhancing their fundamental understanding. It is the immersive, non-threatening and enjoyable qualities of graphic fiction as a medium that provide the experiential element allowing this to happen. Kolb summarises this phenomenon well when he states:

> The interactionism of experiential learning theory places knowing by apprehension on an equal footing with knowing by comprehension, resulting in a stronger interactionist position, really a transactionalism, in which knowledge emerges from the dialectic relationship between the two forms of knowing.[20]

The impact of using graphic fiction upon critical thought

Transposing individual theories onto the worlds of graphic fiction characters allows us not only to demonstrate what the theory says, but also aids critique of that theory. It does this via the latent quality of either complying or not complying with the theory, which allows a 'way in' to explore the rights and wrongs of this compliance or lack of compliance. It also does it in a way with which students may feel comfortable or find engaging. Perhaps they are more comfortable and relaxed exploring whether the rules in a graphic fiction world are right or wrong, in their opinion, as opposed to considering whether academic leviathans such as Albert Venn Dicey are right or wrong. It promotes a safe way for students to have an opinion - something which some first year law students in particular can find challenging due to the black letter nature of much of the law they study.[21] The informality provides a safe methodology for students to start to get into the mindset of critiquing what they are being presented with. It is then a much shorter step up to critiquing the academic theories themselves.

Brookfield says the following about critical thinking, 'When we think critically, we come to our judgments, choices and decisions for ourselves, instead of letting others do this on our behalf'.[22] As for how we can tell when critical thinking is happening, according to Brookfield, two main

20 Kolb (n 5) 101.

21 For further discussion of students' critical thinking skills, see L Niu, LS Behar-Horenstein and CW Garvan, 'Do Instructional Interventions Influence College Students' Critical Thinking Skills? A Meta-Analysis' (2013) 9 *Educational Research Review* 114.

22 S Brookfield, *Developing Critical Thinkers: Challenging Adults to Explore Alternative Ways of Thinking and Acting* (Oxford University Press 1997) x.

tasks are taking place: identifying and challenging assumptions, and exploring alternative ways of thinking.[23] Both of these are encouraged when using graphic fiction to teach law and this is demonstrated in the case studies below.

Brookfield discusses different traits that promote critical thinking.[24] One component is having a critical teacher. He refers to Freire's work, when he said that liberated classrooms become unique spaces, akin to separate worlds, where normal consciousness is altered, allowing students to free themselves of their usual thought processes and patterns and see their worlds in different ways.[25] Using graphic fiction will liberate the classroom for students and academics alike. Brookfield quotes Shor when he says, 'by identifying, abstracting and problematising the most important themes of student experience, the teacher detaches students from their reality and then re-presents the material for their systematic scrutiny'.[26] By positing students in the alternate reality of a graphic fiction world, the constitutional theories are re-presented to them and analysed. This fresh approach gets students to challenge and explore alternate ways of thinking, thereby aiding critique, and giving a fresh perspective, allowing greater depth of knowledge and meaning.

Graphic fiction as experiential learning: two case studies

Judge Dredd and the separation of powers

As a graphic fiction fan, I was struck one day by the similarities between the world of Judge Dredd and the theory of the separation of powers.[27] Theories of the separation of powers involve ideas about the relationship between three different branches of the state: the executive, the legislature and the judiciary.[28] Some theories favour a complete separation of the personnel and functions of these three branches, whilst others prefer a more diluted or blended relationship. The purpose of the separation theory is to provide a system which prevents too much power being concentrated

23 Ibid 71.

24 Brookfield (n 22) 80.

25 See P Freire, *Pedagogy of the Oppressed* (Continuum 1973).

26 Brookfield (n 22) 80, citing Shor.

27 For an introduction to Judge Dredd, see J Wagner and others, *Judge Dredd: The Complete Case Files 01* (Rebellion 2012).

28 Any public law textbook will give an overview of the theory. One good example is A Le Sueur, M Sunkin and J Murkens, *Public Law: Text, Cases and Materials* (2nd edn, Oxford University Press 2013) 114. Montesquieu is often credited for the modern theory, see C Montesquieu, *The Spirit of the Laws* (first published 1748, Cambridge University Press 1989).

in the hands of too few, thereby preventing the potential for power to be abused. The UK constitution undoubtedly does not comply with a strict separation of powers and there are those who argue to what extent it does and should do so.[29] In order to gain a good critical understanding of the UK constitution, students need to engage with these theories to understand not only what the position is in the UK, but to consider whether that position is desirable or could be improved.

In the world of *Judge Dredd*, we see a civilisation's legal solution to a high-crime, high-population world. Judges have created a Book of Law and that law governs absolutely. The judges enforce that law by policing the streets of mega-cities. When they apprehend criminals they can charge them with an offence and sentence them on the spot. If we reflect upon this for a moment, we see that the judges are performing the role of the legislature (by creating the Book of Law), the executive (by policing the streets) and the judiciary (by sentencing offenders). This is a fantastic example of a complete blurring of the separation of powers. However, there is more complexity to this position. This solution has been taken in good faith. It is seen as the only viable solution to a high-crime, high-population world. If we imposed our justice system onto a mega-city, then it would grind to a halt. This raises questions about what values a justice system holds most highly. In *Judge Dredd*'s world, the speed of 'justice' is of paramount importance due to the sheer volume of criminal activity. This prioritisation exposes the way constitutional systems value different approaches in the context of their own individual needs. This reflects the real world debate about criminal justice models, and in particular the tension between a 'crime control' model and a 'due process' model.[30] Packer states the crime control model holds repression of crime as the most important factor in a criminal justice system. The due process model is not diametrically opposed to the values of the crime control model, as it too values repression of crime, but it places much more value on the structure and formalities of the law, believing that errors are inevitable, and where the stakes are so high, there need to be rigorous safeguards in the system to prevent miscarriages of justice. The world of *Judge Dredd* therefore offers a valuable case study to explore what the separation of powers is and what it should be; it is a vehicle to allow good critical understanding.

29 See eg, H Phillips, 'A Constitutional Myth: Separation of Powers' (1977) 93 *Law Quarterly Review* 11; cf C Munro, 'The Separation of Powers: Not Such a Myth' [1981] *Public Law* 19.

30 For a good introduction to this debate, see HL Packer, 'Two Models of the Criminal Process' (1964) 113 *University of Pennsylvania Law Review* 1.

Separation of powers case study

To demonstrate the utility of using *Judge Dredd*, let us examine the very first story-line as a case-study.[31] The story introduces Dredd and gives readers some background information about the judges and their role in society. We are told that in order to bring down the high crime rate, judges have been appointed to deliver instant justice. In it we see Dredd responding to an instruction by Law Control to attend a bank robbery in Manhattan. We see Dredd set off to the scene, with his first words being, 'No one can escape justice!'. When Dredd finds the 'law breakers', a fight ensues, during which Dredd gives some narrative of his own. He says, 'This city's a jungle - crawling with crime. Law breakers like these running wild. Somebody's got to stamp it out! That's my job, I'M A JUDGE!'. Dredd wins the fight, of course, and he says to the perpetrator, 'I find you guilty of bank robbery and murder - and hereby terminate you!', at which point Dredd then shoots the offender dead. A bystander cheers in celebration. Dredd says to this person, 'I take no pleasure in terminating law breakers'. Dredd then finds this bystander guilty of stepping off the pavement and onto the road, and sentences him to 400 days in jail. The offender tries to bribe Dredd to let him off, for which Dredd finds him guilty of the further offence of trying to bribe a judge. The offender then tries to escape, at which point Dredd shoots this person dead. Dredd leaves us with the words, 'Only those who break the law have anything to fear from me. I am the law and you'd better believe it!'.

There are a number of important elements in this story illustrating the characteristics of Dredd and the values of his society. The justification for instant justice, and what seems to us extremely harsh rules and sentences, is a society which has high-population and high-crime. Dredd's society is very much at the crime control end of the spectrum of a criminal justice model as described earlier. Also, the remark made by Dredd that somebody has to stamp it out suggests that there is no one else, no other body or group that can ensure justice, thereby giving legitimacy to the judges in this crime control model, and thereby justifying the fusion of powers into one body.

When Dredd says to the bystander that he does not enjoy killing people, this illustrates the characteristic of Dredd being a professional as opposed to a thug; he is merely carrying out his duty rather than abusing his powers for personal gratification. To bolster this further, we see Dredd refusing

31 The first Dredd story appeared in 'Prog 2' of *2000AD* in 1977, but some of the original material was cut out; that which demonstrated Dredd's role as executioner. The complete original story can be found as an appendix in Wagner and others (n 27).

to be bribed. This illustrates Dredd's integrity and his ability to carry out the letter of the law efficiently, although it may appear ruthless. To try to appeal to readers and reassure us that he is on the side of good as opposed to evil, his final remark that only law-breakers have to fear him provides this reassurance. This, again, instils trust in the judges having so much power.

This story is fascinating from a separation of powers perspective. We see a complete fusion between the three different branches of government in operation. Dredd is a judge, and the judges produced the Book of Law. We see Dredd executing this law in this story. He attends a bank robbery in order to apprehend the perpetrators, thereby performing executive actions. He passes judgment upon the perpetrators and sentences them, and then carries out that sentence on the spot, thereby performing judicial actions. The judges in this society get their legitimacy from its adherence to the crime control model of criminal justice. There are no issues from this society about the separation of powers not being adhered to, rather, a complete fusion helps them achieve their crime control model of justice. The characteristics of Dredd illustrated in this first story help to reassure us that this fusion of powers in the judges is not a negative issue due to their legitimacy and integrity.

This allows us to question the *value* of the separation of powers theory. If a society can function better without it, does it render the theory worthless? If this story took place in the UK, we would see the police performing the executive actions of enforcing the law by attending the scene and apprehending the criminals. The police would be executing the law passed by Parliament, the legislative branch of the state. The suspects (not criminals) would then enter the criminal justice system, which upholds many of the values of the due process model, and if sufficient evidence is found by the executive to present to the courts, the courts would perform the judicial role of finding guilt and if so sentence the offenders accordingly. The separation of powers theory is accorded with to a large extent in the UK's approach. Separate bodies have made the law, enforced it, and then examined guilt. This approach ensures there are deliberate hurdles in place to make sure that a satisfactory threshold has been reached at each stage before we can proceed to the next. This due process style of approach maximises the potential for mistakes to be identified at each stage, thereby trying to minimise oppression and injustice. This lets students question which approach is better, in their opinion, and why. Do the hurdles put in place in the UK system work effectively?[32] In

32 In his initial form, Dredd was envisaged as an anti-hero, a satirical figure used to critique punitive law and order policies in the Thatcher era. This leads to good critique of the UK system and whether it does what it is supposed to or whether certain offices have too much power. For more on this 'satirical' reading of Dredd, see Chapter 12.

Dredd's world, due to Dredd's characteristics, in particular his integrity and ability to perform the letter of the law without hesitation and without questioning it, he is able to perform each of his roles with integrity, so he is, essentially, able to separate his powers within himself, thereby abiding by the theory of the separation of powers *internally.* It is his apparent ability to do this which makes him such a fascinating case study to introduce the separation of powers doctrine to students. This story therefore sows the seeds in students' minds to think critically about the separation of powers theories. It is a good starting point from which to then go into and explore the theories themselves in greater depth and detail.

Judge Dredd and the rule of law

The rule of law is of paramount relevance and importance to the UK constitution. What exactly it means, though, is still debatable, which makes teaching the subject challenging. Traditional teaching of the rule of law starts with Albert Venn Dicey's tripartite theory from the late 19th century which spans: the supremacy of regular law (no separate constitutional law); equality before the law; and the special role the courts play in espousing constitutional principles in the absence of a written constitution.[33] After this has been digested, attention may then turn to more recent theories, such as those of Joseph Raz and Tom Bingham, with recourse to the difference between 'formal' and 'substantive' doctrines.[34] Joseph Raz highlighted eight principles that, for him, the rule of law contained as a minimum - these principles are 'formal' principles, insofar as they relate to the form that laws take and how they are enforced.[35] They are, briefly: (a) laws must be prospective, open and clear; (b) they should be stable; (c) the systems for creating laws should be open, clear and stable; (d) the judiciary must be independent; (e) procedural fairness must be observed by decision-makers; (f) courts should have review powers over the other principles; (g) courts should be easily accessible; and (h) discretion of crime-preventing agencies should not pervert the law. These are all formal requirements - they do not dictate what the *content* of laws should be.

Some people argue that for the rule of law to be meaningful it must have something to say about the content of law. Tom Bingham was one such advocate, and his theory also elucidated eight principles as a minimum: (a) law must be accessible and so far as possible intelligible, clear and predictable; (b) questions of legal right and liability should ordinarily

33 AV Dicey, *An Introduction to the Study of the Law of the Constitution* (first published 1885, 10th edn, MacMillan 1967).

34 For a discussion of this debate, see P Craig, 'Formal and Substantive Conceptions of the Rule of Law: An Analytical Framework' [1997] *Public Law* 467.

35 Joseph Raz, 'The Rule of Law and its Virtue' (1977) 93 *Law Quarterly Review* 195.

be resolved by application of the law and not the exercise of discretion; (c) the laws of the land should apply equally to all, save to the extent that objective differences justify differentiation; (d) ministers and public officers at all levels must exercise the powers conferred on them in good faith, for the purpose for which the powers were conferred, without exceeding the limits of such powers and not unreasonably; (e) the law must afford adequate protection of fundamental human rights; (f) means must be provided for resolving, without prohibitive cost or inordinate delay, bona fide civil disputes which the parties themselves are unable to resolve; (g) adjudicative procedures provided by the state should be fair; and (h) the rule of law requires compliance by the state with its obligations in international law as in national law.[36] Whilst most of these principles bear a striking resemblance to those of Dicey and Raz, there are some key differences. For example, Bingham included a principle that the law must afford adequate protection of fundamental human rights. This concerns the *content* of laws, and as such his theory can be said to include *substantive* elements. This brief overview highlights one of the academic debates about the rule of law that students are expected to engage with - whether it is a formal or a substantive theory.

Even with detailed analysis of case law, the rule of law can still seem an abstract concept to students. Using *Judge Dredd* as a reference point may help bring the theory to life. In the same way as the elements of the separation of powers theory, the individual elements of the different theories of the rule of law outlined above can also be applied to Dredd's world.

Rule of law case study

A good story to use to introduce theories of the rule of law is 'The Return of Rico'.[37] In this story we see Dredd's brother, Rico, return to Mega-City One after spending 20 years in prison on Titan. Rico has only one thing in mind: to take revenge upon the person who sent him to prison - his brother Judge Dredd! Rico makes his way to Dredd's apartment and waits for him to return. When they meet, the narrative gives us the back-story about Rico and Dredd. We are told that they were both clones, so not brothers, but duplicates. Throughout their time at the judge training academy, Rico was better than Dredd at everything. Once they became judges, Rico strayed from the path of law. He started a protection racket and began bribing people. Rico killed someone who refused to pay him and Dredd witnessed it. Rico tried to persuade Dredd that they could make it look

36 Tom Bingham, *The Rule of Law* (Penguin 2010).

37 See 'Prog 30' of *2000AD*; 'The Return of Rico' is reprinted in Wagner and others (n 27).

like an accident. Dredd refused to do so without any hesitation at all, saying to Rico, 'No way Rico, I'm taking you in!'. The sentence Dredd gave to Rico was 20 years on the penal colony on Titan. The story returns to the present with Rico telling Dredd that he is going to exact revenge and kill him. Dredd tries to persuade Rico to give up but he refuses to do so. A Western-style quick-draw then takes place that Dredd wins. Rico always used to be faster but his time in prison had slowed him down allowing Dredd to win.

We can see Dicey's theory of the rule of law manifested in this story. Dicey's first component is the supremacy of regular law. Mega-City One has only one type of law: the Book of Law. There are no different types of law, such as constitutional laws, private laws, or public laws, and there are no different laws for judges; the judges have to abide by the very laws which they created. Rico was breaching this Book of Law with his activities and Dredd was enforcing this law. We therefore see the supremacy of this one type of law, which is what Dicey was referring to and was an advocate of. He believed having different systems of law resulted in complexities, overlaps, and gaps; defects which can be prevented by only having one system of law.[38]

Dicey's second component is equality before the law. For a country to comply with the rule of law, the same regular law Dicey discussed in his first component must apply to all citizens in the same way, regardless of their position in society. It would be unfair for some classes of people to be bound by some laws and not others. In particular, Dicey was referring to agents of the state being bound by the law, and the case of *Entick v Carrington*[39] was very influential upon him in this regard. In 'The Return of Rico' we see this principle very clearly illustrated in two ways. First, Rico has been holding himself above the law, flouting it for his own personal advantage. This type of corruption is exactly the kind of behaviour that Dicey wanted to avoid, and a country could only be said to comply with the rule of law if this kind of behaviour did not take place. Second, we see Dredd refusing to turn a 'blind-eye' and allowing his own brother to evade justice. If Dredd did this, he also would be putting himself above the law. Rather, he complies with Dicey's principle and upholds the law, again illustrating the integrity of his character.

Dicey's third component highlights the special role played by the courts in upholding the first two principles. In this story, we do not see a court performing this role, rather, we see Dredd performing this role in his judicial capacity. Dredd has judicial powers and he found Rico guilty of his

38 Dicey (n 33) 406.
39 (1765) 19 St Tr 1030.

crimes, upholding the first two principles. This illustrates the role of the judiciary within a country and stresses the importance of their independence and integrity. The independence referred to means independent from executive decisions in particular, and here we see Dredd able to perform his judicial role without being susceptible to external interests, such as family ties.[40]

This story is a good way to introduce theories of the rule of law to students to get them to appreciate the substance and subject matter of the theories. After this, students may be better equipped to start to look at the theories themselves in greater depth and detail. Just like with the separation of powers case study described above, this is a good way to get students started, and it is not suggested that this replaces any content or examination of the theories themselves.

The theories of Raz and Bingham (or others) can also be explored in this same way. Raz emphasised the independence of the judiciary from the executive branch. This is clearly violated by Dredd, as he performs both an executive and a judicial role, but what is the impact of this? Bingham emphasised laws must protect human rights - it would be interesting to hear Dredd's opinion as to whether citizens of Mega-City One have human rights! An authoritarian figure such as Dredd sees the contents of his Book of Law as the pinnacle of perfection and no interference with its contents is allowed. To suggest that principles such as individual rights should be inserted into it or may trump or interfere with the application of the content of his Book of Law would seem alien. For Dredd, individual rights would arguably prevent the quick, clean and certain application of the Book of Law.[41]

Summary

Using graphic fiction in the way I have suggested accords with experiential learning theory and yields the benefits of such an approach. These benefits are due to the way knowledge is acquired. It enhances and balances apprehension and comprehension of the constitutional theories to allow a holistic and deeper knowledge acquirement. Using graphic fiction is a valuable pedagogical tool which offers a fresh perspective for knowledge structure, and law, like other disciplines, should embrace it.

40 This story also has relevance to the separation of powers case-study. Rico is the perfect example of the dangers of fusing too much power in the hands of the judges.

41 Dredd would perhaps agree with Jeremy Bentham when he said that the notion of natural or human rights is 'nonsense upon stilts'. See P Schofield, C Pease-Watkin and C Blamires (eds), *Rights, Representation, and Reform: Nonsense upon Stilts and Other Writings on the French Revolution* (Oxford University Press 2002).

Whilst this approach may not be universally applicable for all constitutional law students, the potential benefits described above demonstrate that using graphic fiction to characterise abstract theories is worth exploring from both pedagogical and epistemological perspectives - we all learn in different ways and for some abstract theory comes easily, not so for others. The approach outlined in this chapter will be most useful for students who struggle to embark upon the journey of learning about constitutional theory. This approach may also invigorate academics to explore their subjects from a different perspective and to utilise the medium of graphic fiction as an aid to do so. It also offers an additional fun element to introduce onto a course whilst aiding learning and teaching at the same time. As Kenneth Eble said, 'If there is no place for pleasure in teaching, surely our learning has failed us altogether'.[42] I wonder whether Judge Dredd would have approved of such an approach while he was at Law School?

Case

Entick v Carrington (1765) 19 St Tr 1030

Bibliography

Allan TRS, *Law, Liberty, and Justice: The Legal Foundations of British Constitutionalism* (Clarendon Press 1994).

Beard C, *The Experiential Learning Toolkit: Blending Practice with Concepts* (Kogan Page 2010).

Bingham T, *The Rule of Law* (Penguin 2010).

Brew A, 'Unlearning through Experience' in Boud D, Cohen R and Walker D (eds), *Using Experience for Learning* (Society for Research into Higher Education and Oxford University Press 1993).

Brookfield S, *Developing Critical Thinkers: Challenging Adults to Explore Alternative Ways of Thinking and Acting* (Oxford University Press 1997).

Craig P, 'Formal and Substantive Conceptions of the Rule of Law: An Analytical Framework' [1997] *Public Law* 467.

Daniels H, Cole M and Wertsch J, *The Cambridge Guide to Vygotsky* (Cambridge University Press 2007).

Dewey J, *Experience and Education* (Kappa Delta Pi 1938).

Dicey AV, *An Introduction to the Study of the Law of the Constitution* (first published 1885, 10th edn, Macmillan 1967).

Freire P, *Pedagogy of the Oppressed* (Continuum 1973).

Kayes C, 'Institutional Barriers to Experiential Learning Revisited' in Reynolds M and Vince R (eds), *The Handbook of Experiential Learning and Management Education* (Oxford University Press 2007).

42 Ramsden (n 8) 233.

Kolb D, *Experiential Learning: Experience as the Source of Learning and Development* (Prentice-Hall 1984).
Laws J, 'Law and Democracy' [1995] *Public Law* 72.
Le Sueur A, Sunkin M and Murkens J, *Public Law: Text, Cases and Materials* (2nd edn, Oxford University Press 2013).
McCloud S, *Understanding Comics* (William Morrow Paperbacks 2001).
Montesquieu C, *The Spirit of the Laws* (first published 1748, Cambridge University Press 1989).
Munro C, 'The Separation of Powers: Not Such a Myth' [1981] *Public Law* 19.
Niu L, Behar-Horenstein LS and Garvan CW, 'Do Instructional Interventions Influence College Students' Critical Thinking Skills? A Meta-Analysis' (2013) 9 *Educational Research Review* 114.
Packer HL, 'Two Models of the Criminal Process' (1964) 113 *University of Pennsylvania Law Review* 1.
Phillips H, 'A Constitutional Myth: Separation of Powers' (1977) 93 *Law Quarterly Review* 11.
Ramsden P, *Learning to Teach in Higher Education* (RoutledgeFalmer 2003).
Raz J, 'The Rule of Law and its Virtue' (1977) 93 *Law Quarterly Review* 195.
Savin-Baden M and Howell Major C, *Foundations of Problem-based Learning* (Society for Research into Higher Education and Oxford University Press 2004).
Schofield P, Pease-Watkin C and Blamires C (eds), *Rights, Representation, and Reform: Nonsense upon Stilts and Other Writings on the French Revolution* (Oxford University Press 2002).
Wagner J and others, *Judge Dredd: The Complete Case Files 01* (Rebellion 2012).

Chapter 5

Not foresighting, not answering: using graphic fiction to interrogate social and regulatory issues in biomedicine

Shawn HE Harmon

Introduction

We live in a society dependent on science. Science has been a key instigator of technical and social change, not only encouraging instrumental changes in the way we interact with the natural world, but also paradigm shifts in how we understand the world and our place in it. That change can be accelerated or slowed, facilitated or hindered, entrenched or reshaped, through regulation.[1] This intimate regulation-science-change relationship - which is not always appreciated - means that both science and law are only justified when they have been subject to socio-ethical considerations. Importantly, that assessment must include many publics; Susan Greenfield, former head of the Royal Institution, once suggested that the engagement of the public in science, and the expression of scientific ideas in ways that can be understood, is a key *scientific* challenge.[2] Of course, the same observation is applicable to law, and, importantly, to the law relating to science.

In this chapter, I consider the communication of, and engagement around, law and science within the context of the 'Graphic and Novel Project',[3] an interactive, interdisciplinary science/regulation communication project undertaken at the University of Edinburgh ('the Project'). First, I trace the troubled history of public engagement around science and its governance with a particular focus on the ambiguous/contested relationship that science has had with science fiction (SF) as a communicative media. Second, I articulate the ambition of the Project, which is to use speculative graphic fiction to facilitate education and enrich public engagement

1 Regulation means that collection of norms, rules and practices that influence actor behaviour in a given field, and it includes law and legal instruments.

2 M Brake and R Thornton, 'Science Fiction in the Classroom' (2003) 38 *Physics Education* 31, quoting Greenfield at 34.

3 *Graphic and Novel: Law, Bioethics and Medical Futures* <http://masoninstitute.org/our-research/#G&N> accessed 23 May 2014.

with the ultimate aim of encouraging meaningful social discourse. Third, I outline the process by which we crafted the Project's primary output – a near-future, illustrated SF novel called *Fever Medicine* – and how such a project might be undertaken differently the next time round.

Public engagement – arts opportunities

Public participation in the development of science and its governance is a relatively new phenomenon. For a long time, interactions with publics were viewed by policymakers and scientific authorities as a means of 'educating' the public about science. While education around, and excitation for, science is almost certainly vital to the sustained pursuit of knowledge, it was incorrectly believed that this unidirectional transfer of information would suffice, and that it would alleviate any public ambiguity around science.[4] This approach guided authorities during the controversial attempt to introduce genetically modified foods to Europe, and it was met with criticisms that communicative processes were impoverished and used as an *ex post facto* means of legitimating already-made decisions around science and its regulation.[5]

These criticisms, which turned in part on concerns for transparency, led to calls for a more 'decentred' regulation of science, with an increased role for public participation in policymaking and trajectory-setting; a more active public engagement characterised by information exchange was demanded.[6] While strides were made, criticisms continued to the effect that processes remained narrow and risk-based, leaving deeper questions about the values, visions, and vested interests that motivate science underexplored.[7] Thus,

4 That it would relieve the 'crisis of trust' that threatened to swallow science, and specifically the biosciences, see M Jones and B Salter, 'The Governance of Human Genetics: Policy Discourse and Constructions of Public Trust' (2003) 22 *New Genetics and Society* 21.

5 C Stewart Jr and others, 'Transgenic Plants and Biosafety: Science, Misconceptions and Public Perceptions' (2000) 29 *Biotechniques* 832; G Gaskill and others, *Ambivalent GM Nation? Public Attitudes to Biotechnology in the UK, 1991–2002* (London School of Economics 2003); Commentary, 'Going Public' (2004) 431 *Nature* 883, which reported that the UK government held a public debate on genetic modification and ignored the results.

6 For more on 'governance' and 'decentred regulation', which express a pattern of rule characterised by increased networks of influence between civil society and the state and an increased role for non-government actors, see J Black, 'Decentring Regulation: The Role of Regulation and Self-Regulation in a "Post Regulatory" World' (2001) 54 *Current Legal Problems* 103; M Bevir and others, 'Comparative Governance: Prospects and Lessons' (2003) 81 *Public Administration* 191; C Lyall, T Papaioannou and J Smith (eds), *The Limits to Governance* (Ashgate 2009).

7 DEMOS, *See-Through Science: Why Public Engagement Needs to Move Upstream* (Demos 2004) 18.

stakeholders tried (and continue to try) to move engagement activities further 'upstream', before key development decisions are made and stakeholder positions entrenched.[8]

While this policy struggle continues,[9] the shifts that *have* occurred in the science/regulatory engagement sphere have opened up new opportunities for designing academic communication relating to innovation and its governance. In particular, it has opened space for scientists and lawyers who see value in using the arts to engage in new ways with a wider range of publics, and to potentially *learn from* publics in more creative ways. There is a growing number of examples of graphic fiction being used to reflect (or augment) reality so that complex or technical information is more manageable or comprehensible. In this regard, see *Hope Beyond Hype*,[10] which endeavours to make more comprehensible stem cell research and its uses. And there are manifold examples of graphic fiction being used to give greater depth to the transfer of personal experiences or observable phenomena.[11] There are also important web-based resources being developed, such as Graphic Medicine,[12] Graphic Storytelling and Medical Narratives,[13] and the Literature, Arts and Medicine Database.[14] There are much fewer graphic depictions of contemporary *law*, although one should note *Bound by Law*,[15] which explores copyright law in a graphic context.

8 The Royal Society, *Nanoscience and Nanotechnologies: Opportunities and Uncertainties* (Royal Society 2004); S Jasanoff, *Designs on Nature: Science and Democracy in Europe and the United States* (Princeton University Press 2005).

9 S Harmon, 'From Engagement to Re-Engagement: The Expression of Moral Values in Patenting Proceedings, Present and Future' (2006) 31 *European Law Review* 642; F Huzair and others, 'An Interdisciplinary and Developmental Lens on Knowledge Translation' (2013) 40 *Science and Public Policy* 1.

10 K MacLeod and E Ross, *Hope Beyond Hype: A Story of Stem Cells from Discovery to Therapy* (EuroStemCell 2012).

11 See eg, Ampersand, *Fat Monologue* <http://amptoons.com/blog/> accessed 24 January 2014; David B, *Epileptic* (Jonathan Cape Ltd 2006); A Davison, *The Spiral Cage* (Active Images 2003); S Fatah, J Eng and R Boyd, *Drawing The Line* (Fengsuli Press 2004); B Feis, *Mom's Cancer* (Abrams Books 2006); M Green and R Rieck, 'Missed It' (2013) 158 *Annals of Internal Medicine* 357; J Hall and E Ross, *Parasites* (Wellcome Trust 2010); *Prozacville* <http://prozacville.blogspot.co.uk/> accessed 24 January 2014; S Seagle, *It's A Bird* (Vertigo 2004); G Trudeau, *The Long Road Home* (Andrews McMeel 2007). See also C O'Luanaigh, 'Comics Put Patients in the Picture' (*The Guardian*, 14 July 2010) <www.guardian.co.uk/science/blog/2010/jul/14/medical-comics-patients> accessed 12 February 2013.

12 *Graphic Medicine* accessed 24 January 2014. This site explores the interaction between comics and healthcare discourse.

13 *Penn State University*< www2.med.psu.edu/humanities/for-medical-students/research-opportunities/graphic-storytelling-medical-narratives/> accessed 24 January 2014. Penn State was the first humanities department in a US medical school.

14 *NYU* <http://litmed.med.nyu.edu/Main?action=aboutDB> accessed 24 January 2014.

15 K Aoki, J Boyle and J Jenkins, *Bound by Law* (Duke U Press 2006).

Even rarer than graphic explorations of the legal, and somewhat more challenging, are examples of the use of graphic SF to elucidate science and regulatory boundaries and encourage discourse. While one must acknowledge such benchmark works as *Appleseed*,[16] and *The Ghost in the Shell*,[17] both of which explore social consequences of technology convergence through action-genre SF stories, they do not articulate any existing regulatory frameworks or encourage dialogue around prevailing issues or values so as to encourage better or more engaging exchanges between 'expert' and 'lay' publics. A question that remains to be answered, therefore, is whether graphic SF can be used effectively for this objective. However, before exploring the Graphic and Novel Project, positioning it in the SF and science relationship is important.

SF and public understanding of science

Although described as one of the most important ways of popularising and disseminating scientific ideas, and one which has helped shape public attitudes toward scientists and scientific activities,[18] SF has an ambiguous relationship with science, and an all-too-often ignored relationship or utility to law. Like other mass media elaborations of science - which are often grounded on imperfectly understood reports, or outcomes whose position along the innovation pathway are unknown - science proponents often complain that SF characterisations of science are sensationalist and negative, casting science and scientists in a poor light, and encouraging public disquiet. A common assumption is that, '[F]iction, particularly dystopian science fiction, can have a very powerful, and inevitably *negative*, impact on an ignorant public, driving "the masses" to dread the potential of science and technology'.[19]

Thus, proponents 'routinely express intense frustration about a public made fearful of scientific advances through "science fiction scare-mongering".'[20] Indeed, many stories *are* bound up in the destructive potential of science and technologies, and many suggest a trend toward the instrumentalisation and/or marginalisation of humans. The film industry in particular has caricatured scientists as single-minded, obsessive social outcasts and arrogant meddlers in a fragile nature, or, alternatively, as single-minded, saintly interlocutors

16 M Shirow, *Appleseed* (Kodansha Comics 1985–1989).

17 M Shirow, *The Ghost in the Shell* (Kodansha Comics 1989–1997). For analysis of philosophical issues of human-machine integration in this work, see Chapter 5 of this book.

18 Researchers and space agencies have scoured SF for inspiration and ideas, see Brake and Thornton (n 2) 32.

19 J Kitzinger, 'Questioning the Sci-Fi Alibi: A Critique of How "Science Fiction Fears" are Used to Explain Away Public Concerns about Risk' (2010) 13 *Journal of Risk Research* 73, 74.

20 Ibid 74.

between us and an indifferent or unkind nature.[21] This imposes on scientists a myopia of hopes and fears, making them the unwarranted targets of vociferous polemics and the unearned benefactors of overly-positive propaganda, and it encourages within publics unsupported suspicions about, and expectations for, science.[22]

While there is substance to this lament, it rests on an inaccurate understanding of how people use popular or cultural expressions of science, and how they form their opinions about the value of science (and its regulation).[23] Lay publics do not misunderstand science as often or as fundamentally as assumed by scientists, and they are not led to the misunderstandings they *do* have by fictional depictions.[24] They can and do have rather sophisticated and nuanced views about science, and those views are shaped by a range of factors, many of them outside popular portrayals.[25]

21 Film often relies on less nuanced approaches than literature. The best SF, film or otherwise, tackles deep philosophical or ethical issues and widens the audience's perceptions of our reality. Consider the work of Wells, Asimov, Clarke, Dick, LeGuin, Vonnegut, Gibson, Baxter, and Banks, and films such as: *Twelve Monkeys* (1995) and *Contagion* (2011) (pathogens and virology); *The Stepford Wives* (1975), *The Boys from Brazil* (1978), *Blade Runner* (1982), *Jurassic Park* (1993), *Gattaca* (1997), *Alien: Resurrection* (1997) and *Splice* (2010) (genetics, cloning, hybridisation); *Minority Report* (2002), *Paycheck* (2003) and *Limitless* (2011) (neural sciences); and *Johnny Mnemonic* (1995), *The Matrix* (1999) and *Terminator: Salvation* (2009) (technology convergence and human-machine interfacing).

22 Brake and Thornton (n 2); D Knight, *Public Understanding of Science: A History of Communicating Scientific Ideas* (Routledge 2006).

23 J Turney, *Frankenstein's Footsteps: Science, Genetics and Popular Culture* (Yale Uniersity Press 1998); D Kirby, 'The New Eugenics in Cinema: Genetic Determinism and Gene Therapy in *Gattaca*' (2000) 27 *Science Fiction Studies* 1; M Barker and J Petley (eds), *Ill Effects: The Media/Violence* (2nd edn, Routledge 2001); D Kirby, 'Cinematic Science' in B Trench and M Bucchi (eds), *Handbook of Public Communication of Science and Technology* (Routledge 2008); E Hughes, J Kitzinger and G Murdoch, 'SCARR Working Paper 27: Media Discourse and Framing of Risk' (2008) <www.cardiff.ac.uk/jomec/resources/KitzingerWkPaper27.pdf> accessed 14 February 2013; F Coyle, C Chekar and J Kitzinger, 'Comparative Analysis of "Public Discourse" and "Discourses About the Public" in Relation to Stem Cell Research' (2008) <www.cardiff.ac.uk/jomec/resources/ProjectSummaryPublicsCoyleetal.pdf> accessed 14 February 2013; J Haran and J Kitzinger, 'Modest Witnessing and Managing the Boundaries between Science and the Media: A Case Study of Breakthrough and Scandal' (2009) 18 *Public Understanding of Science* 634.

24 T Gieryn, *Cultural Boundaries of Science: Credibility on the Line* (University of Chicago Press 1999); M Michael and S Carter, 'The Facts about Fictions and Vice Versa: Public Understandings of Human Genetics' (2001) 10 *Science as Culture* 5.

25 A Kerr and others, 'The New Genetics and Health: Mobilizing Lay Expertise' (1998) 7 *Public Understanding of Science* 41; B Bates, 'Public Culture and Public Understanding of Genetics: A Focus Group Study' (2005) 14 *Public Understanding of Science* 47; G Haddow and others, 'Tackling Community Concerns about Commercialisation and Genetic Research: A Modest Interdisciplinary Proposal' (2007) 64 *Social Science and Medicine* 272.

SF *reflects* rather than *shapes* concerns and debates about science and what they might mean for human identity, dignity, and autonomy.[26] In other words, it highlights, in easily accessible shorthand form, both concerns that have endured and evolved over long periods of time, and concerns that are perhaps only beginning to emerge in response to specific technologies - but it does not *generate* those concerns or encourage negative responses to them.

Science proponent complaints are rendered rather less sympathetic by their own widespread deployment of wholly positive imaginaries to *promote* science and technologies; they regularly craft utopian visions which are no less speculative than those dystopian ones they bemoan, using powerful positive cultural and popular images and metaphors in the process.[27]

What can we take from this? First, despite a rather fractious relationship with science proponents, SF and (to a lesser extent) graphic literature are intimately connected with science and (to a much lesser extent) its regulation. Second, SF has been used by antagonists, agnostics/neutrals, and proponents in pursuit of very different ends. Third, when discursive space has been marginalised in science governance settings, SF has provided the deliberative space for discussing the implications of science and technology.[28] Fourth, it is generally accepted, and academics are increasingly aware, that SF and graphic literature can be a useful tool for disseminating information about science and law.[29]

The role of graphic science fiction in the graphic and novel project

Given the popularity, perceived utility, and versatile nature of non-academic media like graphic literature for disseminating knowledge

26 D Kirby and L Gaither, 'Genetic Coming of Age: Genomics, Enhancement and Identity in Film' (2005) 36 *New Literary History* 263.

27 Note references to the 'Holy Grail' and 'language of God' in relation to genetics, aimed at suggesting the fundamental nature of this work: A Hessenbruch, 'Beyond Truth: Pleasure of Nanofutures' (2005) 8 *Techné* 34. Note the frequent demand-creating use of metaphors of urgency and speed: Kitzinger (n 19).

28 Note criticisms of the ELSI component of the Human Genome Project and others: J Evans, *Playing God? Human Genetic Engineering and the Rationalisation of Public Bioethical Debate* (University of Chicago Press 2002); M Huijer, 'Reconsidering Democracy: History of the Human Genome Project' (2003) 24 *Science Communication* 479; L McCain, 'Informing Technology Policy Decisions: The US Human Genome Project's Ethical, Legal and Social Implications Programs as a Critical Case' (2003) 24 *Technology and Science* 111; N Brown, 'Hope Against Hype: Accountability in Biopasts, Presents and Futures' (2003) 16 *Science Studies* 3.

29 M Tatalovic, 'Science Comics as Tools for Science Education and Communication: A Brief Case Study' (2009) 8 *Journal of Science Communication* 1.

to new audiences,[30] the Graphic and Novel Project sought to use it for disseminating knowledge about science and law, but also for *encouraging discussion* about the social context from which science and law emerge and into which they ultimately embed. Invariably, two questions are asked about the Project:

(a) Why use SF to talk about ethico-legal research around the governance of science?
(b) Why use graphic literature?

A general answer is that some people might not care about the issues, but might still enjoy the graphic narrative, and some people might not care for the story (or the art), but might have an interest in the issues which are implicated, so a vehicle that might appeal on some level to both camps is useful, and in any event would be interesting and fun to pursue. But a more detailed answer is warranted, and this answer elucidates the ambitions of the Project.

The first question – why use SF – is answered with reference to the elements and objectives of (good) SF literature. It has been argued that the essence of SF is the introduction of a set of imaginary or inventive changes into a background of 'known facts' to create an environment in which the responses and perceptions of the characters can reveal something about technologies, society, and/or character(s).[31] It is a means of examining science and law, and of critiquing their relationship, with the added element (burden?) of positing outcomes of observed trajectories. Importantly, the outcomes posited need not come to pass, nor even be particularly plausible, for the exercise to be valuable; one should not allow doubts about the viability of literary technologies to obscure one's understanding of the issues meant to be raised.[32] Ultimately, it is the act of thinking about

30 Graphic fiction has been used for autobiography and journalism, see A Spiegelman, *Maus: A Survivor's Tale* (Pantheon Books 1996); J Sacco, *Palestine* (Fantagraphic Books 2001); R Glass and D Turbitt, *Dougie's War* (Freight 2010). See Chapter 14 in this book for a discussion of the merits of such 'graphic reporting'. And graphic SF has been used for social/political commentary, see A Moore and D Lloyd, *V for Vendetta* (Quality Comics 1982–89); A Moore and D Gibbons, *Watchmen* (DC Comics 1987); N Gaiman, *The Sandman* (Vertigo 1988–96).

31 See J Merill, *SF – The Best of the Best* (Hart-Davis 1971), who argues that SF is an application of the scientific method (eg observation, hypothesis, experimentation) to examine some approximation of reality.

32 It has similarly been argued that we should not allow controversies over the viability of certain speculated technologies or futures to obscure the similarities that exist between how SF narrative elements are used to negotiate the gap between current techno-scientific capabilities and their future development, see J Lopez, 'Bridging the Gaps: Science Fiction in Nanotechnology' (2004) 10 *International Journal for Philosophy of Chemistry* 129.

the relationship, and its desirable/undesirable components, that gives the exercise value.

While getting technical and legal information out to wider audiences is an aim of the Project, the more important (and questionably achievable) ambition is to use SF to encourage people to think critically about the biosciences and their regulation through an informal medium and informal exchanges. This might then *generate* knowledge by bringing a wider range of perspectives into reflective activities; more engaging dialogues around socio-ethical issues thrown up by the biosciences could improve science/innovation governance decisions (by enriching the thinking of all parties involved). Importantly, the Project is not an exercise in technological or ethical 'foresighting'. Recognising the difficulty of technology foresighting,[33] and the concerns around ethical foresighting,[34] it is intended as a vehicle for highlighting *current* ethico-legal issues and instruments in an interesting/provocative way. Hence we postulated social/technical potentialities, which was interesting for the team, but used them to raise contemporary legal and ethical issues, which satisfied the academic component.

The second question - why use graphic literature - is answered with reference to the increasingly recognised strengths of graphic narrative. It is claimed that:

- the visual aids learning,[35] particularly where science is implicated;[36]
- graphic narratives can promote literacy and critical-thinking through a variety of story-types;[37]
- literature is a useful and interesting platform for engaging with publics about socio-ethical issues around innovation.[38]

33 R Williams, 'Compressed Foresight and Narrative Bias: Pitfalls in Assessing High Technology Futures' (2006) 1 *Science as Culture* 327; Nuffield Council on Bioethics, *Emerging Biotechnologies: Technology Choice and the Public Good* (NCB 2013).

34 A Nordmann and A Rip, 'Mind the Gap Revisited' (2009) 4 *Nature Nanotechnology* 273.

35 G Yang, 'Graphic Novels in the Classroom' (2008) 85 *Language Arts* 185. See also Chapter 4 in this book.

36 J Trumbo, 'Visual Literacy and Science Communication' (2000) 21 *Science Communication* 379.

37 M Mooney, 'Graphic Novels: How They Can Work in Libraries' (2002) 21 *Book Report* 18; G Schwarz, 'Graphic Novels for Multiple Literacies' (2002) 46 *Journal of Adolescent and Adult Literature* 262; L Grossman, 'Singing A New Toon' *Time* (New York, 25 August 2003) 56; S Krashen, *The Power of Reading: Insights from the Research* (Libraries Unlimited 2004).

38 M Stern, 'Jurassic Park and the Moveable Feast of Science' (2004) 13 *Science as Culture* 347; R Berne, 'Science Fiction: A Portal to the Ethics of Nanotechnology' in L Pin and others (eds), *Nanoethics: Examining the Societal Impact of Nanotechnology* (Wiley 2007) 10.

Accepting these claims, graphic narratives might also be used to promote an appreciation of science and law and their intertwined trajectories, and to do so for audiences not normally reached by traditional academic publications. The Project accepts that different media have different grammars and literacies, and different competencies for carrying certain messages.[39] It also accepts that there are multiple 'publics' and therefore the need for multiple narratives through multiple mediums so that different publics can be effectively engaged.[40] Lastly, the graphic narrative format is characterised by a 'visual permanence' (ie the rate of information-transfer is within the reader's control[41]) that is not present in typical academic presentations to 'publics'. The Project can ultimately be viewed as part of the movement (since the late 1970s) towards a more 'contextualised' approach to the study of law, which has included increased engagement with literature, film and popular culture.

The development of *Fever Medicine*

Fever Medicine - the near-future illustrated SF novel that is the primary output of the Project (see Figure 5.1) - seeks to highlight *existing* or *contemporary* cultural values and legal rules, including issues of justice and morality, while also helping people to appreciate the fact that science is a cultural activity in which everyone has a stake. The underlying belief is that a more authentic partnership amongst stakeholders might result in better regulation of the scientific enterprise. *Fever Medicine* emerged from an exercise in scenario-building in two multidisciplinary encounters. The first was a roundtable workshop attended by Edinburgh-based experts from science, industry, social science, ethics, law and illustration. Using an open format, we explored current scientific capabilities, trajectories and ambitions, technical hurdles, business models and industry challenges, ethical concerns, and the role of regulation. The second encounter was a tour of the new MRC Regenerative Medicine Centre, where we talked informally with scientists and science communicators. The insights gleaned from those events informed the scenario/world-building and imagery produced by the Project team.

In crafting the world of Edinburgh 2050, existing scenario-building scholarship from the field of synthetic biology was drawn upon.[42] Consideration was given to 'driving forces', which are those social and technical phenomena that are in flux and rapidly advancing as at the time

39 J Meyrowitz, 'Multiple Media Literacies' (1998) 48 *Journal of Communication* 96.
40 J Kitzinger, 'Researching Risk and the Media' (1999) 1 *Health, Risk and Society* 55.
41 Yang (n 35).
42 S Aldrich, J Newcomb and R Carlson, 'Scenarios for the Future of Synthetic Biology' (2008) 4 *Industrial Biotechnology* 39.

Figure 5.1 The cover of S Harmon and others, *Fever Medicine* (Edinburgh University Press 2012). © 2012 Shawn HE Harmon. Used with permission.

of writing. Such phenomena were necessarily implicated in the story and helped shape the characters' perspectives and experiences. Driving forces taken into consideration were:

- *Technology convergence*: DNA sequencing and synthesis technologies will advance, and will increasingly integrate with information and communication technologies.
- *Popularisation and commercialisation*: bioscientific knowledge will progress and pressure around associated commercial activities will increase.
- *Consumption*: energy demands will rise, resources will dwindle, and human-generated environmental stress and climate change will impact on living arrangements and food security.
- *Growth*: growing and aging populations, combined with growing infectious disease threats and sharper social divisions will create untenable pressures on national health systems.

Consideration was also given to 'major uncertainties', which are phenomena of uncertain trajectory at time of writing, and so permitting larger scope for creativity. Whether regenerative medicine and synthetic biology would fulfil their promise was considered a major uncertainty, as was the developmental trajectory and ultimate capabilities of these sciences.[43] Other uncertainties were: (a) the role of intellectual property and whether it would shift and transform approaches to science; (b) the level of control that would be assumed around biotechnologies and whether access to certain of them would be restricted; and (c) the prevailing geopolitical realities and whether they would realign and dramatically alter security concerns.[44]

Lastly, consideration was given to who would emerge as 'primary actors' (first-movers) in 2050. In this regard, a conservative approach was adopted: national governments were assumed to be unevenly subservient to private multinational entities, including research institutions; open science researchers would be more strident; and bio-activists and bio-terrorists would be relevant. One can see from this that the three currently recognised categories of actors - science proponents, policymakers, citizens - were considered to remain relevant.[45] The caveat is that it would be impossible to accurately predict the evolving preferences of these first-movers. This again offered scope for creativity.

43 M Hopkins and others, 'The Myth of the Biotech Revolution: An Assessment of Technological, Clinical and Organisational Change' (2007) 36 *Research Policy* 566; L Orsenigo and J Tait, 'Special Issue on Evolution of the Life Science Industries' (2008) 10 *International Journal of Biotechnology* 404.

44 J Mittra, 'Impact of the Life Sciences on Organisation and Management of R&D in Large Pharmaceutical Firms' (2008) 10 *International Journal of Biotechnology* 416.

45 D Wield and others, 'Twenty-First Century Bioeconomy: Global Challenges of Biological Knowledge for Health and Agriculture' (2013) 40 *Science and Public Policy* 17.

Consideration was also given to the role of the graphic element. Graphic novels might be viewed as a method which relies on text and sequential graphics in fluctuating priority, but the balance, like this definition itself, is contested. Some argue that deliberate sequencing of images is mandatory and that text is not.[46] Others argue that sequencing is not necessary,[47] and others that text is essential.[48] Some argue that equal priority must be given as between the text and graphics.[49] All of this debate around the fundamentals lends weight to the claim that the field has neither grasped its object nor posed its project.[50] In any event, some synergy between word and image must be present such that the combined effect is greater than, or different from, what might have been in the absence of both;[51] both should represent a narrative track of some utility to the 'story'.[52]

The text/image interaction in *Fever Medicine* was shaped by the time the artists could invest and our (in)experience with comic design/layout, both of which pushed us toward an 'illustrated' rather than a 'graphic' novel, though one with more images than is common.[53] In keeping with the medium, the text preceded the images, specifying the story world and giving direction to the imagery. While the illustrated representations were largely faithful to the text, there was scope for the artists to build beyond the text and to codetermine the story world, a power they exercised sparingly (although some 'canonical' images, such as the biohazard image and the binary code tartan, were not story-dependent). Ultimately, the images were meant to make the story and its characters come to life; by depicting the world and its people rather than abstract ethical or legal issues, the images give greater context to the city, the characters, and their (augmented) capabilities. And while some of the scientific kit was faithfully depicted, the imagery is more in the nature of 'art-science' than 'science-art'.[54]

46 S McCloud, *Understanding Comics: The Invisible Art* (Kitchen Sink Press 1993).
47 H Chute, 'Comics and Literature? Reading Graphic Narrative' (2008) 123 *PMLA* 452.
48 R Harvey, *The Art of the Comic Book: An Aesthetic History* (University Press of Mississippi 1996).
49 T Wartenberg, 'Wordy Pictures: Theorising the Relationship Between Image and Text in Comics' in A Meskin and R Cook (eds), *The Art of Comics: A Philosophical Approach* (Blackwell Publishing 2012) 88.
50 Chute (n 47).
51 C Gibbons, 'Introduction' in R Varnum and C Gibbons (eds), *The Language of Comics: Word and Image* (University Press of Mississippi 2001).
52 Chute (n 47).
53 For more on their differences, see Wartenberg (n 49).
54 'Science-art' increases the accessibility of complex or technical information, or gives greater depth to the transfer of personal experiences or observable phenomena. The art is expected to reflect or augment reality so that it is more comprehensible, aiding rather than challenging the audience. 'Art-science' is science that is subordinate to art. The primary driver is creativity or provocation as opposed to accuracy; the art need not reflect, and the artist is not constrained by, technical realities.

The result is a magnificently illustrated SF story about illness, ambition, ambivalence, exclusion, injustice, and reconciliation. Within the context of a richly rendered postmodern dystopia characterised by darkness, uncertainty, and morally ambiguous characters, however, it tries to articulate risks and highlight conflicting values and expectations. It engages current ethico-legal issues such as access to medicines, regulatory burden, uncertainties around regulatory demands, and the role of commercialisation in biomedical science, while explaining in an accessible manner the scientific method and the current state of regenerative medicine.

While socio-ethical issues and values are woven into the narrative, and are framed by specific character dialogues and thoughts, they are also captured in text boxes placed throughout the story (ethics boxes). Boxes are also used to explain the technical state-of-the-art (science boxes) and the current regulatory landscape (regulation boxes). The latter articulate key regulatory concepts such as consent, privacy, or risk, and their role in legal instruments, while others explain the content of specific instruments and convey the legal complexity and normative fragmentation that prevails in this setting. Each chapter is also supplemented by question boxes which contain questions raised directly or indirectly by the plot, such as:

- Should we be seeking international consensus on the boundaries of science in regenerative medicine? Is consensus a realistic objective? What normative rules would you erect in relation to the conduct of science?
- How would you define 'normal'? How would you defend that definition?
- Is it possible to use technologies (or pharmaceuticals) to 'morally enhance' someone (ie to negate the possibility of certain immoral decisions or actions)?
- Legal responsibility follows mental capacity, but what happens when cognitive ability is enhanced? Will enhancing technologies require the law to recognise different types of responsibility?
- Do you think the law has an important role to play in identifying and then operationalising core values? Which values would you identify as the most important to questions that arise in clinical and research practice?

These questions demonstrate how *Fever Medicine* is an exercise in 'Mode 2' knowledge production whereby the arts are not used to transmit science to publics for the purpose of assembling those publics for the benefit of science, but rather to *contextualise* science and to render it more accessible and so more *accountable.*[55]

55 A Barry and G Born, 'Logics of Interdisciplinarity' (2008) 37 *Economy and Society* 20; G Born and A Barry, 'ART-SCIENCE: From Public Understanding to Public Experiment' (2010) 3 *Journal of Cultural Economy* 103.

Whereas the development of *Fever Medicine* was largely internal-facing in its knowledge exchange, it is our hope that it might be used by secondary and post-secondary educators interested in exploring techno-ethico-legal issues,[56] or interested stakeholders desiring a tool to assist in their deliberations, or science communicators in bespoke participative events. To this end, a range of classroom and public uses will be designed in cooperation with knowledge-exchange practitioners and users, the ultimate purposes of which are to:

- expose different cultures to one another in 'controlled' engagement environments;
- encourage the sharing of ideas and the examination of assumptions; and
- open up minds and debates around science trajectories and decisional frameworks.

In this respect, the Project draws inspiration from a range of art-science experiments.[57]

Conclusion: from discourse, to book, to discourse

Despite claims of urgency, it is imperative to reflect. Given the pace of scientific change and the uncertainties around how the biosciences might develop, it is critical to interrogate values, interests, and perceptions of, and tolerances for, risk. Only by *persistently* doing so might we avoid 'locking in' the more unhelpful characteristics of the prevailing milieu (eg ultra-individualism, consumerism, subservience to commercial sensibilities) at the expense of more positive ones that might find greater purchase if broader value-based social discourses are undertaken. Sociotechnical imaginaries like *Fever Medicine* offer a space in which we can consider dignity, solidarity, conformity, reciprocity, risk, transparency, and more. They permit us to play out the implications of decisions, to question who has been cut out of decision-making, and to query whether sufficient effort has been expended in considering any given course. While *Fever Medicine* might be described as 'dystopian' (and open to well-rehearsed complaints), this is of no significance: the idea was simply to create something that was beholden to neither law nor science, and that might be used to explore social, technological, and legal possibilities with publics not normally reached by academia. It is a deliberative tool aimed at posing and discussing questions, not generating answers to be offered to publics – *publics*

56 It will be used in a new course for the LLM Medical Law and Ethics at the University of Edinburgh.

57 *ACE Program* <http://escholarship.ucop.edu/uc/ace>; *Art/Science Fusion Program* <http://artsciencefusion.ucdavis.edu/MissionStatement.html>; *ASCUS Art Science Collaborative* <http://ascus.org.uk/>; SymbioticA all accessed 1 December 2013.

must come up with the answers. Obviously, it is hoped that *Fever Medicine* will have some salutary 'impact', but we are not yet in a position to report on any measurable impact. The project facilitated the formation of a growing network of individuals interested in combining the arts and humanities and sciences, and *Fever Medicine* enjoyed a positive reception at its launches,[58] at LonCon 3,[59] and from the academics in both the UK and North America. It has been the subject of increasing requests for hardcopies and downloads,[60] and, as noted, it will be used in a new course at Edinburgh.

Acknowledgements

The author would like to acknowledge with thanks the valuable support received from the University of Edinburgh (through the Challenge Investment Fund and Knowledge Exchange Fund), the School of Law, the Mason Institute, and the ESRC Innogen Centre.

Bibliography

Aldrich S, Newcomb J and Carlson R, 'Scenarios for the Future of Synthetic Biology' (2008) 4 *Industrial Biotechnology* 39.

Aoki, K, Boyle J and Jenkins J, *Bound by Law* (Duke U Press 2006).

B D, *Epileptic* (Jonathan Cape Ltd 2006).

Barker M and Petley J (eds), *Ill Effects: The Media/Violence* (2nd edn, Routledge 2001).

Barry A and Born G, 'Logics of Interdisciplinarity' (2008) 37 *Economy and Society* 20.

Bates B, 'Public Culture and Public Understanding of Genetics: A Focus Group Study' (2005) 14 *Public Understanding of Science* 47.

Berne R, 'Science Fiction: A Portal to the Ethics of Nanotechnology' in L Pin and others (eds), *Nanoethics: Examining the Societal Impact of Nanotechnology* (Wiley 2007).

Bevir M and others, 'Comparative Governance: Prospects and Lessons' (2003) 81 *Public Administration* 191.

Black J, 'Decentring Regulation: The Role of Regulation and Self-Regulation in a "Post Regulatory" World' (2001) 54 *Current Legal Problems* 103.

Born G and Barry A, 'ART-SCIENCE: From Public Understanding to Public Experiment' (2010) 3 *Journal of Cultural Economy* 103–19.

Brake M and Thornton R, 'Science Fiction in the Classroom' (2003) 38 *Physics Education* 31.

Brown N, 'Hope against Hype: Accountability in Biopasts, Presents and Futures' (2003) 16 *Science Studies* 3.

58 *Fever Medicine* was launched at Pulp Fiction, Edinburgh, 24 January 2014, and at 'The Art and Science of Science (and Law) Communication Through Arts', Playfair Library, University of Edinburgh, 27 January 2014.

59 72nd World Science Fiction Convention, London, 14–18 August 2014.

60 Available from <http://masoninstitute.org/graphic-novel/>.

Chute H, 'Comics and Literature? Reading Graphic Narrative' (2008) 123 *PMLA* 452.
Commentary, 'Going Public' (2004) 431 *Nature* 883.
Coyle F, Chekar C and Kitzinger J, 'Comparative Analysis of "Public Discourse" and "Discourses About the Public" in Relation to Stem Cell Research' (2008) <www.cardiff.ac.uk/jomec/resources/ProjectSummaryPublicsCoyleetal.pdf> accessed 14 February 2013.
Dahl K, *Monster* (Secret Acres 2009).
Davison A, *The Spiral Cage* (Active Images 2003).
DEMOS, *See-Through Science: Why Public Engagement Needs to Move Upstream* (Demos 2004).
Evans J, *Playing God? Human Genetic Engineering and the Rationalisation of Public Bioethical Debate* (University of Chicago Press 2002).
Fatah S, Eng J and Boyd R, *Drawing the Line* (Fengsuli Press 2004).
Feis B, *Mom's Cancer* (Abrams Books 2006).
Gaiman N, *The Sandman* (Vertigo 1988–96).
Gaskill G and others, *Ambivalent GM Nation? Public Attitudes to Biotechnology in the UK, 1991–2002* (London School of Economics 2003).
Gibbons C, 'Introduction' in Varnum R and Gibbons C (eds), *The Language of Comics: Word and Image* (University Press of Mississippi 2001).
Gieryn T, *Cultural Boundaries of Science: Credibility on the Line* (University of Chicago Press 1999).
Glass R and Turbitt D, *Dougie's War* (Freight 2010).
Green M and Rieck R, 'Missed It' (2013) 158 *Annals of Internal Medicine* 357.
Grossman L, 'Singing A New Toon' *Time* (New York, 25 August 2003) 56.
Haddow G and others, 'Tackling Community Concerns about Commercialisation and Genetic Research: A Modest Interdisciplinary Proposal' (2007) 64 *Social Science and Medicine* 272.
Hall J and Ross E, *Parasites* (Wellcome Trust 2010).
Haran J and Kitzinger J, 'Modest Witnessing and Managing the Boundaries between Science and the Media: A Case Study of Breakthrough and Scandal' (2009) 18 *Public Understanding of Science* 634.
Harmon S, 'From Engagement to Re-Engagement: The Expression of Moral Values in Patenting Proceedings, Present and Future' (2006) 31 *European Law Review* 642.
Harvey R, *The Art of the Comic Book: An Aesthetic History* (University Press of Mississippi 1996).
Hessenbruch A, 'Beyond Truth: Pleasure of Nanofutures' (2005) 8 *Techné* 34.
Hopkins M and others, 'The Myth of the Biotech Revolution: An Assessment of Technological, Clinical and Organisational Change' (2007) 36 *Research Policy* 566.
Hughes E, Kitzinger J and Murdoch G, 'SCARR Working Paper 27: Media Discourse and Framing of Risk' (2008) <www.cardiff.ac.uk/jomec/resources/KitzingerWkPaper27.pdf> accessed 14 February 2013.
Huijer M, 'Reconsidering Democracy: History of the Human Genome Project' (2003) 24 *Science Communication* 479.
Huzair F and others, 'An Interdisciplinary and Developmental Lens on Knowledge Translation' (2013) 40 *Science and Public Policy* 1.

Jasanoff S, *Designs on Nature: Science and Democracy in Europe and the United States* (Princeton University Press 2005).
Jones M and Salter B, 'The Governance of Human Genetics: Policy Discourse and Constructions of Public Trust' (2003) 22 *New Genetics and Society* 21.
Kerr A and others, 'The New Genetics and Health: Mobilizing Lay Expertise' (1998) 7 *Public Understanding of Science* 41.
Kirby D, 'Cinematic Science' in Trench B and Bucchi M (eds), *Handbook of Public Communication of Science and Technology* (Routledge 2008).
Kirby D, 'The New Eugenics in Cinema: Genetic Determinism and Gene Therapy in Gattaca' (2000) 27 *Science Fiction Studies* 1.
Kirby D and Gaither L, 'Genetic Coming of Age: Genomics, Enhancement and Identity in Film' (2005) 36 *New Literary History* 263.
Kitzinger J, 'Questioning the Sci-Fi Alibi: A Critique of How "Science Fiction Fears" are Used to Explain Away Public Concerns about Risk' (2010) 13 *Journal of Risk Research* 73.
Kitzinger J, 'Researching Risk and the Media' (1999) 1 *Health, Risk and Society* 55.
Knight D, *Public Understanding of Science: A History of Communicating Scientific Ideas* (Routledge 2006).
Krashen S, *The Power of Reading: Insights from the Research* (Libraries Unlimited 2004).
Lopez, J, 'Bridging the Gaps: Science Fiction in Nanotechnology' (2004) 10 *International Journal for Philosophy of Chemistry* 129.
Lyall C, Papaioannou T and Smith J (eds), *The Limits to Governance* (Ashgate 2009).
MacLeod K and Ross E, *Hope beyond Hype: A Story of Stem Cells from Discovery to Therapy* (EuroStemCell 2012).
McCain L, 'Informing Technology Policy Decisions: The US Human Genome Project's Ethical, Legal and Social Implications Programs as a Critical Case' (2003) 24 *Technology and Science* 111.
McCloud S, *Understanding Comics: The Invisible Art* (Kitchen Sink Press 1993).
Merill J, *SF - The Best of the Best* (Hart-Davis 1971).
Meyrowitz J, 'Multiple Media Literacies' (1998) 48 *Journal of Communication* 96.
Michael M and Carter S, 'The Facts about Fictions and Vice Versa: Public Understandings of Human Genetics' (2001) 10 *Science as Culture* 5.
Mittra J, 'Impact of the Life Sciences on Organisation and Management of R&D in Large Pharmaceutical Firms' (2008) 10 *International Journal of Biotechnology* 416.
Mooney M, 'Graphic Novels: How They Can Work in Libraries' (2002) 21 *Book Report* 18.
Moore A and Gibbons D, *Watchmen* (DC Comics 1987).
Moore A and Lloyd D, *V for Vendetta* (Quality Comics 1982–89).
Nordmann A and Rip A, 'Mind the Gap Revisited' (2009) 4 *Nature Nanotechnology* 273.
Nuffield Council on Bioethics, *Emerging Biotechnologies: Technology Choice and the Public Good* (NCB 2013).
O'Luanaigh C, 'Comics Put Patients in the Picture' *The Guardian* (London, 14 July 2010).

Orsenigo L and J Tait, 'Special Issue on Evolution of the Life Science Industries' (2008) 10 *International Journal of Biotechnology* 404.
Royal Society, *Nanoscience and Nanotechnologies: Opportunities and Uncertainties* (Royal Society 2004).
Sacco J, *Palestine* (Fantagraphic Books 2001).
Schwarz G, 'Graphic Novels for Multiple Literacies' (2002) 46 *Journal of Adolescent and Adult Literature* 262.
Seagle S, *It's A Bird* (Vertigo 2004).
Shirow M, *Appleseed* (Kodansha Comics 1985-1989).
Shirow M, *The Ghost in The Shell* (Kodansha Comics 1989-1997).
Spiegelman A, *Maus: A Survivor's Tale* (Pantheon Books 1996).
Stern M, 'Jurassic Park and the Moveable Feast of Science' (2004) 13 *Science as Culture* 347.
Stewart C and others, 'Transgenic Plants and Biosafety: Science, Misconceptions and Public Perceptions' (2000) 29 *Biotechniques* 832.
Tatalovic M, 'Science Comics as Tools for Science Education and Communication: A Brief Case Study' (2009) 8 *Journal of Science Communication* 1.
Trudeau G, *The Long Road Home* (Andrews McMeel 2007).
Trumbo J, 'Visual Literacy and Science Communication' (2000) 21 *Science Communication* 379.
Turney J, *Frankenstein's Footsteps: Science, Genetics and Popular Culture* (Yale University Press 1998).
Wartenberg T, 'Wordy Pictures: Theorising the Relationship Between Image and Text in Comics' in Meskin A and Cook R (eds), *The Art of Comics: A Philosophical Approach* (Blackwell Publishing 2012).
Wield D and others, 'Twenty-First Century Bioeconomy: Global Challenges of Biological Knowledge for Health and Agriculture' (2013) 40 *Science and Public Policy* 17.
Williams R, 'Compressed Foresight and Narrative Bias: Pitfalls in Assessing High Technology Futures' (2006) 1 *Science as Culture* 327.
Yang G, 'Graphic Novels in the Classroom' (2008) 85 *Language Arts* 185.

Chapter 6

Law and the machine: fluid and mechanical selfhood in *The Ghost in the Shell*

Thomas Giddens

> Why should our bodies end at the skin, or include at best other beings encapsulated by skin?[1]
> ... humans are always changing, and I want to be able to change too.[2]

Where is the boundary between human and machine? This is an important question for law, and one this chapter fails to answer. Indeed, the aim in the following pages is emphatically not to produce answers, but to provoke thought and reflection. My concern is not with delineating the human, but with showing the deep uncertainty that haunts the human's boundaries in our contemporary and increasingly technologised world. This provocation begins with an initial overview of the growing integration of technology into our human lives and the impact this has, in terms of human-machine boundaries, on fundamental legal concepts. We then dive headlong into the fluid conceptual landscape of Shirow Masamune's classic manga work *The Ghost in the Shell*, examining first the complex line between human and machine represented by the cyborg threshold and the role the eponymous 'ghost' plays in solidifying that line, before moving on to examine the fluid self that emerges through philosophical engagement with this work. The chapter closes with a pondering upon the role of law's regulation as a bringer of certainty in the face of the radical *un*certainty found in the boundary between human and machine.

Law, self, technology

Over 20 years ago, Donna Haraway painted an intimate picture of the way developing science and technology and its suffusion throughout culture and society was breaking down traditional boundaries, including

1 D Haraway, 'A Cyborg Manifesto: Science, Technology and Socialist-Feminism in the Late Twentieth Century' in D Bell and BM Kennedy (eds), *The Cybercultures Reader* (first published 1991, Routledge 2000) 314.
2 Shirow M, *The Ghost in the Shell* (FL Schodt and T Smith trs, Kodansha 1991) 343.

that between human and machine.[3] Since then, technology and its use has become increasingly widespread. Late modern life is underpinned by technology, giving it structure and articulation.[4] Our already heightened 'sense of connection to our tools'[5] has become even more intimate. Mobile phones, for example, enable the expansion of our individual selves through the storage of personal data and augment our capacity for communication and integration with other similarly connected humans; moreover, our interactions are increasingly mediated through technological devices on a general level. Whereas historically simple mechanical devices such as pens enabled alternative means of human engagement, today our interactions are layered in a multifaceted range of communications protocols, from face-to-face interaction, telephone conversations, and video-conferencing, to texting, email and instant messaging.[6] This is culminating currently in the sophisticated development and maintenance of virtual presentations of self in the form of visually and verbally captured experiences, collected in multi-media formats and made accessible and interactive via a multitude of social networking gateways - Facebook, Tumblr, Wordpress, Twitter. The navigation of contemporary life, for many, involves not just the traditional socio-corporeal interactions of biologically limited human beings, but is blended with electronic data transfer protocols and augmented by increasingly complex and sophisticated digital experiences - experiences bound up with our interaction and integration with machines.

This integration of the human and mechanical raises complex questions when it comes to delimiting the human. The significance of this difficulty goes beyond our ontological identities, and stems into what is arguably the most fundamental structure of law and legal theory - for law, in terms of its creation, application and critique, rests upon the human. On one level law is a product of human activity, and is applied by humans to other humans. But the question of the human is also of critical substance in various areas of law and legal theory, shaping their application and content. Consider the following: one must know if something is

3 See Haraway (n 1) 300–4, 313.

4 For more on the legal issues involved in the general increase in the technological nature of human life, see eg, J Goldsmith, 'How Cyber Changes the Laws of War' (2013) 24 *European Journal of International Law* 129; LB Moses, 'Agents of Change: How the Law "Copes" with Technological Change' (2011) 20 *Griffith Law Review* 763; LB Moses, 'The Legal Landscape following Technological Change: Paths to Adaptation' (2007) 27 *Bulletin of Science, Technology and Society* 5, 408. See also Chapter 5 in this book.

5 Haraway (n 1) 313.

6 For some thoughts on the shift from hard and quintessentially 'modern' technologies, such as the motor car, to the softer 'digital' technologies represented by mobile phones, see K Tranter, 'Materiality and Memory: Motor Cars and Mobile Phones' (2013) 22 *Griffith Law Review* 532.

'human' before the destruction of that something can count as 'murder'; thus we need to explore 'the human' to enable both the application of the rules of murder and the conceptualisation and critical examination of those rules. Consider more generally: if we are to develop and apply rules at all, we need to know who or what is the subject of those rules. What types of entity are included under law's protection and restraint? What entities *should* be included, and how should they be understood? And, of course, how should the 'we' developing these rules be defined in the first place?

Concerned with precisely these questions, Ngaire Naffine tackles the issue of personhood directly, invigorating our concern with the often unasked question, 'Who is law for?'.[7] She observes the tendency for strict legalists to dismiss the issue of personhood as 'a pure abstraction, a technical device within the great apparatus or machinery of law'.[8] The legal person is the bearer of rights and duties, constituted purely by law for legal purposes;[9] it is arguably a legal fiction. But this approach not only (deliberately[10]) overlooks broader philosophical, scientific, and religious debates on selfhood, it ignores the real role that such 'extra-legal' understandings play in legal determinations of what counts as a 'person'.[11] There is undoubtedly a conceptual dimension to the structures of law - including its model of the person - but that is not the *only* dimension there is. And as already mentioned, the law applies to and is applied by humans. Accordingly, the complex and multi-disciplinary question of 'the human' is a crucial issue for law, both in terms of its practical application (Does or should this rule apply to this entity?) and its conceptual foundations (How do or should we understand the entity to which law applies?).

In our contemporary technological contexts, this 'human' question is of literally *vital* importance - and is also deeply complex. One key area of difficulty rests at the boundary between human and machine: if elements of our identities and experiences are becoming stored within or mediated through mechanically enabled electronic environments, if medical technologies are substituting our organs with engineered replacements, at what point - if ever - do these 'machines' start to become integrated with our human selves? This is an issue, particularly in a technological context, that can be symbolised by the idea of the cyborg. A deeply unresolved being, the cyborg models in-betweenness in a way that Donna Haraway famously argued disrupts and derails the attainment of monolithic,

7 N Naffine, *Law's Meaning of Life: Philosophy, Religion, Darwin and the Legal Person* (Hart 2009).
8 Ibid 31–32.
9 See generally ibid ch 3.
10 'The possession of any of these [physical, spiritual, or metaphysical] attributes would be extra-legal and so necessarily extraneous to any definition of law's person', ibid 34.
11 See ibid ch 4.

unitary understandings of selfhood. Wholeness is resisted by the cyborg; it is partial, fractured, divided:

> The machine is not an it to be animated, worshipped and dominated. The machine is us, our processes, an aspect of our embodiment ... There is no drive in cyborgs to produce total theory, but there is an intimate experience of boundaries, their construction and deconstruction.[12]

Haraway's analysis of our developing relationship with technology suggests a kind of digitally gothic vision of humanity. We are cyborgs, lacking unity and cohesion, made up of multiple, pluralistic dimensions. Our various elements are still us, and machines are important parts of our embodiment and experience. Globally, human life is shaped and mediated by code, binary number systems, and nexuses of programmes and subroutines; by operating systems, visual display units and haptic feedback, not to mention the bio-medical integration of artificial and bio-engineered organs and prostheses into somatic humans. Amidst this complex and multiplying technological environment, classic understandings of our selves are threatened. We are emerging as – 'becoming' – a species in symbiosis with technology. Whilst this may not necessarily always be on the somatic level, technology suffuses our living humanity.[13] The pluralistic challenges that Haraway's conceptual cyborg feeds into our streams of discourse are symbolic of this wider ontological mess. Accordingly, the concept of the cyborg can be used to model many of the issues in delineating the human in the face of technological integration. The complexity of the cyborg challenges personic boundaries, opening up pluralistic understandings of life and identity.[14] For law, this means challenging our ability to distinguish between what is and is not a 'person', between what can and cannot be the subject of regulation, between what 'owns' and what can be 'owned'. My task in this chapter is to highlight some of the difficult issues for legal philosophy that abound in such boundary disintegrations, through engagement with a work of graphic fiction, a medium itself uniquely 'in-between'.[15]

12 Haraway (n 1) 315–16.

13 Richard Sherwin's concept of the 'digital baroque' taps into related concerns: the near-infinite proliferation of images in late-modern culture challenges, through its complexity and promulgation, our capacity to distinguish between 'real' and 'imaginary', threatening the existence of meaning itself. See RK Sherwin, *Visualizing Law in the Age of the Digital Baroque: Arabesques and Entanglements* (Routledge 2011). Similarly, the vast spread of technology and our increasingly intimate relationship(s) with it challenges, through its complexity and proliferation, our capacity to distinguish between 'human' and 'machine', threatening to rob 'humanity' of meaning and value.

14 See Haraway (n 1), notably 310–16.

15 See T Giddens, 'Comics, Law, and Aesthetics: Towards the Use of Graphic Fiction in Legal Studies' (2012) 16 *Law and Humanities* 85. See also Chapter 1 in this book.

The cyborg threshold

Shirow Masamune's manga *The Ghost in the Shell* (hereafter, *Ghost*) depicts complex challenges to the traditionally sealed idea of selfhood. Its pages and narrative streams are populated with beings whose 'humanity' is unclear. The main protagonists are nearly all 'cyborgs', beings created from highly sophisticated technology but with a bio-human core - a human brain and brainstem housed in a 'prosthetic body'.[16] The physical bodies of these cyborgs are almost entirely mechanical, constructed from electronic devices and engineered substances. Yet it is these bodies that interact with the inhabited world - at least partly: these cyborgs are also able to directly interface with mechanical devices, communicate through networks, and infiltrate computer programmes as well as the minds/brains of others. They can patch into others' consciousness and 'brain dive' into other minds to communicate or extract information. Whilst our current levels of integration may not be so developed, like us the characters in *Ghost* inhabit a virtual as well as a physical world. In such an existence, the boundaries and limits of the 'self' become profoundly unclear, on both a somatic and a conceptual level.

Yet the blurring of the limits of self is not unique to technology: it can be seen in the phenomenon of procreation. Like *Ghost*, Christine Battersby in *The Phenomenal Woman*[17] deeply problematises the concept of the somatic container, and undermines any understanding of the self's boundaries as simply coinciding with those of the body. Battersby takes as her starting point the rather mundane observation that it is 'normal' to be a woman. More specifically, that it is normal (although far from essential) for women to get pregnant and give birth. Indeed, the fact of pregnancy and birth is ubiquitous throughout human history, involving the potential for physiological females to grow 'others' within themselves and birth those beings as 'separate' individuals. Despite this, one of the most influential philosophies of the self in Western philosophy is that of Immanuel Kant, in which the self processes the mass of empirical data we gain through experience, synthesising it into knowable structures and concepts, such that self and world emerge in symbiotic union, dependent upon each other for definition and form.[18] The phenomenal world is a product of our experience and, importantly, our capacity to order that

16 Shirow (n 2) 101–6.

17 C Battersby, *The Phenomenal Woman: Feminist Metaphysics and the Patterns of Identity* (Polity Press 1998).

18 See I Kant, 'Foundations of the Metaphysics of Morals', *Foundations of the Metaphysics of Morals and What Is Enlightenment?* (first published 1785, LW Beck tr, Bobbs-Menil 1959); I Kant, *Critique of the Power of Judgment* (first published 1790, P Guyer and E Matthews trs, Cambridge University Press 2000). See also Battersby (n 17) 61–63.

experience under concepts; it exists in dynamic tension with our selves that emerge as sharply delineated from the world.[19] But concomitant with this self/other divide, as Battersby points out, is Kant's distinction between our ability to experience *ourselves* ('inner sense') and to experience the *external world* ('outer sense'). Outer sense relies on our imposition of a spatial framework over sensory data, whilst inner sense is purely introspective and has no such spatial dimensions; the spatial limits of our bodies become the limits of our phenomenal selves. The body becomes a somatic container, housing the self.[20] Thus, Battersby argues, Kant's metaphysics is unable to conceive of internal bodily spaces - most notably the existence of a potential self within someone's womb.[21] In light of the wider point that neither women nor childbirth are an exception, Battersby highlights a critical and profound issue in Kant's classical system.[22]

From the classical Kantian perspective, machines are not human: they are outside the body, and hence not-self. But through this Kantian lens we are unable to think about internal bodily spaces, which may or may not be inhabited by mechanical devices - such as cochlear implants or artificial hearts - let alone understand their metaphysical relationship with our selves. Similarly, if aspects of ourselves may be located within a mechanical setting outside the body - housed in or mediated through a virtual environment, for example - in Kant's metaphysics we remain unable to 'think' these as still part of the human. Against the idea of the somatic container, and through her analysis of 'alternative' philosophies,[23] Battersby puts forward a model of the self in a dynamic state of restless stability, patterned through a symbiotic flux with an interpenetrating otherness: the self is never sealed off from the world, never settled or stable or static: we are not in a state of 'being', but are constantly 'becoming':[24]

19 The Kantian concept of autonomy rests on this division, requiring us to be the source of our behaviour as rational beings rather than succumbing to the influences of the phenomenal world beyond the self. The distinction between the noumenal and phenomenal is crucial to Kantian autonomy, as in order to be autonomous we must act as if we are noumenal beings-in-ourselves rather than phenomenal, contingent beings. See CM Korsgaard, introduction to I Kant, *Groundwork of the Metaphysics of Morals* (first published 1785, M Gregor tr, Cambridge University Press 1998) notably xxviii–xxix.

20 See also Naffine (n 7) 146–47.

21 See Battersby (n 17) 70–71.

22 For her extended discussion on Kantian metaphysics when faced with the existence of women, see Battersby (n 17) ch 4.

23 Notable amidst Battersby's 'alternatives' are Nietzsche's *Beyond Good and Evil* and *Thus Spoke Zarathustra*, where the self emerges as a collection of flowing energies (see Battersby (n 17) 54–57), and Kierkegaard's *Stages on Life's Way*, where the self is seen as emerging from interplay between past and present, self and other (see Battersby (n 17) ch 8).

24 For Battersby's extended development of this model, see Battersby (n 17), particularly chs 9–10.

> That which is the self's 'essence' or identity emerges through patterns of flow, and cannot simply be ascribed to ... [the rational self's] decision or 'will' to produce itself ... Neither fully autonomous nor completely determined, the self is produced relationally: in the resonance between self and other; in a 'present' that is a generative caesura between future and past.[25]

Although focused on the 'human' otherness represented by the foetus, such an analysis is useful for thinking about the problems of human-machine integration, allowing us greater insight into the complex and shifting threshold between human and machine, that hazy line where living selfhood ends and inert objecthood begins.

The bodily self of Kusanagi, the main protagonist of *Ghost*, is predominantly depicted as fleshly and human.[26] The engineering that creates Kusanagi's prosthetic body is so intricate and mimetic that her body appears organic. But at times this 'humanity' is disrupted in the visual narrative, when Kusanagi's mechanical entrails are exposed (either through injury[27] or somatic interfacing[28]). Her robotic nature ruptures the seemingly human skin. Yet it is clear from the world of *Ghost* that Kusanagi and her cohort *are* human - as opposed to being mere robots powered by artificial intelligence (AI). Under Battersby's metaphysics of becoming, our bodies are not integrally or coincidentally our selves, nor are we static, unchanging beings. We are not only in a constant state of flux, but this flux is a dynamic symbiosis with the external world. Like the engineered corporeal self of Kusanagi, we can be reconfigured through experience and interplay with the world 'outside'. Incorporating some machine or other into one's physical body, or developing aspects of one's self outside the body in a machine, does not, in Battersby's model, necessarily undermine our selfhood or our ability to understand selfhood. Our new configuration can be patterned into our phenomenal experience of ourselves; our selves can (repeatedly) shift and adapt to new arrangements:

> On such a model, 'self' grows out of 'otherness', and 'sameness' is gradually patterned out of 'difference' ... 'identities' are fluid and might be transformed - or dispersed or metamorphosed into new structures

25 Battersby (n 17) 184.

26 Although beyond the scope of this chapter, the gendered aspects of *Ghost* are significant. For instance, Kusanagi is often sexualised, giving a sensual dimension to her mechanical body, further problematising where her humanity ends and her mechanics begin. (This chapter also puts aside the boundary between humans and animals, but see Naffine (n 7) 119–42.)

27 See eg, Shirow (n 2) 224.

28 See eg, Shirow (n 2) 278.

> and propensities – as the configurations are subject to further historical change.[29]

Read in this way, Battersby's model gives an open and inclusive approach to mechanical selfhood, permitting multiple (re)configurations of humanity beyond traditional flesh. The limits of the self are accepted as changing and uncertain – the human threshold is rendered permeable. But there is more to this threshold than the physical aspects of the body. Whilst on one level it is the incorporation of key biologically human parts (that is, brain and brainstem[30]) that maintains Kusanagi's humanity, more significantly this humanity is grounded by the eponymous phenomenon known as the 'ghost'. And the concept of the ghost is distinct from the self's essence in Battersby's metaphysics of becoming: while Battersby's metaphysics involves a constantly shifting 'essence', something that is patterned through our complex, living interaction with the world of otherness,[31] the 'ghost' represents a stable human core sealed off from the outside.

A ghost is encoded into the mind of the cyborg, existing within the mechanical *shell* of the engineered body, animating it as a living entity. It is what separates a mere tool from a living machine, a robot from a cyborg – property from person. Indeed, the ghost is seen as the seat of criminal responsibility: whilst reporting on a cyborg's criminal activity, a newscaster states that 'an investigation will . . . determine whether this crime was committed by his [the suspect's] ghost, or . . . was a mechanical malfunction'.[32] And as another character states, observing the lack of humanity of merely AI robots, 'Something sad about these ghostless 'bots . . .'.[33] This 'ghost' is housed within software and hardware architecture, and importantly is sealed away and protected by layers of security protocols. The ghost is not coincidental with the 'body' or shell in the manner of the somatic container; rather, it is portrayed as the essence of the human, that which maintains a being's humanity despite deeply radical physiological reconfiguration and complex interfacing of consciousness with other beings and devices. It is not a shifting essence, as Battersby's metaphysics would have it, but a static core within a shifting architecture of self.

Such a concept suggests that there is something deep inside us that delineates the ultimate boundaries of the human. A similarly essentialist position has recently been argued by Alaric Kohler in the context of

29 Battersby (n 17) 209.

30 The importance of the brainstem in identifying humanity is also implied in law's definition of the end of life, which according to *R v Malcherek and Steel* [1981] 2 All ER 422 occurs with the death of the brainstem.

31 See quotation at n 29.

32 Shirow (n 2) 146.

33 Shirow (n 2) 36.

scientifically modelling the human.[34] Kohler opposes the organic with the mechanical, asserting that only the organic is capable of attaining personhood, based on the assumption that machines cannot have subjective experience or autonomy.[35] Whilst Kohler makes some moves towards conceptualising 'organic' as only containing those features needed for humanity (namely 'the core idea about having an inner life'[36]) and divorcing it from its fleshly origins, he retains a biological essentialism which means no being, no matter how much subjective experience or autonomy it may achieve, can ever be a person unless it is also biological. Susan Stuart takes a more nuanced stance, arguing that a phenomenal experience or 'sense' of an agent's embodied situation 'in the world' is necessary for true consciousness, due to the need for sensory data to be meaningfully differentiated for the mechanism to function as a decision-making agent,[37] regardless of the material physically constituting that agent. However, this model shares much with Kant's synthesis of space-time data in order to separate a unified 'self' from the world it inhabits, sharing also its problematically strict distinction between self and world.

Like Stuart, *Ghost* demonstrates an inclusive concept of humanity that goes beyond any requirement of biology. As Kusanagi muses, 'Sometimes I wonder if … what I think of as "me" isn't really just an artificial personality comprised of a prosthetic body and a cyberbrain'.[38] On the same page, it is expressly suggested that if a machine were made that was so close to human as to be indistinguishable, it would cease to be a 'robot' but would be 'human', and thus worthy of treatment as a human.[39] As already seen, it is the existence of the ghost that makes something human, which may seem to represent a simple 'essentialist' argument about human nature.[40] However, the ghost is not defined; this essence of life is not tabulated and conceptualised in any certain or quantifiable way. Rather, the ghost is a device that delimits the human, that marks out what is unique and 'living' in a being - an ineffable *something* that makes a cyborg 'alive' and a robot or a calculator not.

34 See A Kohler, 'To Think Human out of the Machine Paradigm: *Homo Ex Machina*' (2010) 44 *Integrative Psychological and Behavioural Science* 39.

35 Ibid 44–49.

36 Ibid 43.

37 See SA Stuart, 'Conscious Machines: Memory, Melody and Muscular Imagination' (2010) 9 *Phenomenology and the Cognitive Sciences* 37.

38 Shirow (n 2) 106. A cyberbrain is a mechanically engineered brain, as opposed to the biological ones typically used to create cyborgs.

39 Even phrase 'don't discriminate against robots' is used, see Shirow (n 2) 106. There is also an undertone throughout *Ghost* of 'cyborg rights' and the ethics of how to treat cyborg beings as opposed to mere robots, protecting their rights in a similar way to how human rights are protected today. See, for example, Shirow (n 2) 94, 104, 140.

40 Cf Naffine (n 7) 99–118.

More than a metaphor for the soul,[41] on a symbolic level the ghost represents the instinctual need to distinguish humans from machines without collapsing the two together, a collapse that would either rob our existence of meaning or value, or extend 'humanity' to clearly non-human devices and objects. The instinctual need for this 'something' is brought into focus when the mechanical nature of the traditional human is exposed. The biological self, the fleshly human body, can be reduced to a large extent to its mechanical functions, its electro-chemical processes, a complex system of valves and pressures and articulation points and forces and flows and circuitry and the physical, bio-chemical encoding of sensory data. The self, on this understanding, becomes a product of this intricate mechanical system. The human body becomes a machine, articulated and 'brought to life' by *something*: a soul - a *ghost* - that inhabits its bio-mechanical shell.

The fluid self

When Kusanagi encounters the Puppeteer - a being that was 'spontaneously created from the sea of information'[42] and became 'a self-aware life-form - a ghost'[43] with life beyond its original AI programming - *Ghost*'s narrative delves into the question of what animates the ghost and gives it human lifehood. The interaction and negotiation between Kusanagi and the Puppeteer takes place in a virtual environment, through the blending of their minds, articulated through visualisations of their selves and the networks that constitute them (accompanied by verbal narration and speech).[44] The ultimate nature of life is described by the Puppeteer as he transcends his physical form, 'And in me, a giant network that includes me . . . is now connected to me'; he continues, 'We are part of it . . . our collective totality. . . '.[45] *Ghost* thus imagines our place in the world as part of a great, universal network. Our selves are complex networks of systems that we are integrated into. Brain, heart, memories, thoughts, lungs - these are all parts of our personal networks, our mechanical selves. But this network includes 'us'; our 'selves' are connected into this nexus, both separate and integrated. We are more than our connected parts, but our connected parts are all (interconnected and integrated) elements of our selves. Our bodies, memories, thoughts, hopes - each is merely one dimension of our complex selves, a self that can be reconfigured and patterned through experience. As the Puppeteer's speech explains, we are also integrated as a 'collective

41 Note the religious associations made with the ghost, see Shirow (n 2) 277. And for discussion of religious approaches to personhood and the sanctity of life, see Naffine (n 7) 99–198.
42 Shirow (n 2) 249.
43 Shirow (n 2) 248.
44 See generally Shirow (n 2) 266–77.
45 Shirow (n 2) 276–77.

totality' into a universal network much larger than ourselves, a network of 'otherness' that helps produce us. As part of this larger system, we living beings become 'fruit' on the bifurcating branches of a complex and interconnected universal network.[46] In *Ghost*, we are a product of the general system of the universe into which our own personal systems are integrated.

This integrated systems model has overt similarities to Battersby's metaphysics of becoming, contextualising the 'static' core of the ghost seen above within the wider complexity of the universal system, thus suggesting something far less stable than first perceived. The unsettling connotation of this universal connectivity is represented in *Ghost*'s dénouement, the crux of which can be found in Figure 6.1. Here we see Kusanagi and the Puppeteer merging, their ghosts combining into a single being. The one element of Shirow's cyborgs that might have approached the status of essence (whether static or not) is violated, ruptured, challenged. The new combined being that emerges is not a hybrid, not a 'multiple personality', but a single being. It is Kusanagi's and the Puppeteer's life forces, their ghosts, that merge, not their fractured and complex personal systems. Hence the result is not a unified being, but a 'new' cyborg of

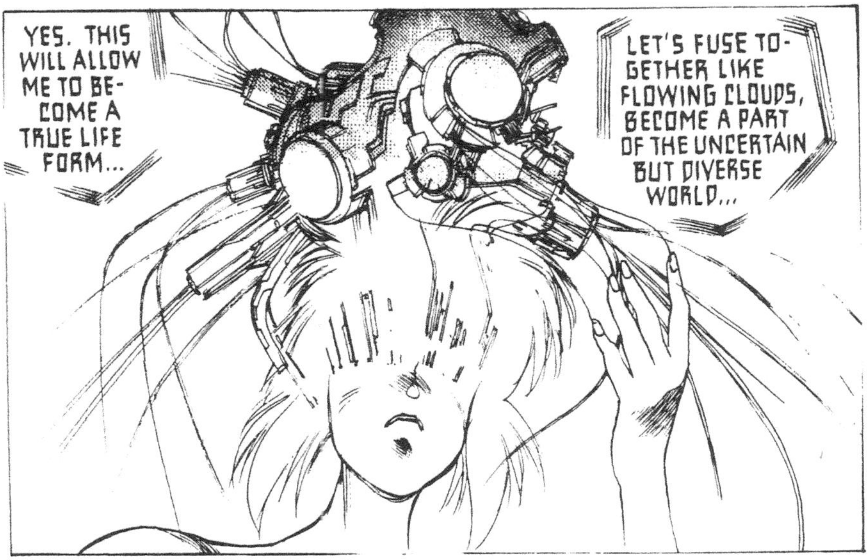

Figure 6.1 Excerpt from page 138 of M Shirow, *The Ghost in the Shell* (Kodansha 1991). *The Ghost in the Shell* © 1991 Shirow Masamune / KODANSHA LTD. All rights reserved.

46 See Shirow (n 2) 337–38.

somewhat uncertain identity, neither Kusanagi nor Puppeteer. The fact this new being has to be integrated into a new prosthetic body highlights the change; the fact this new body is transsexual serves to foreground the uncertainty or 'in-betweenness' of the new being's identity in relation to traditional categories of being.[47]

The visual depiction in Figure 6.1 highlights the seemingly obvious difference between the mechanical and the organic, with the Puppeteer's form being mostly constituted by angled, technical and mechanical lines, and Kusanagi by flowing, organic ones. The Puppeteer's claim that fusing with the 'human' Kusanagi will enable him to become a 'true life-form' initially seems to confirm this opposition (that organic means life, whilst mechanical does not). Yet this is at odds with the generally expansive understanding of lifehood throughout *Ghost*. This claim derives from the Puppeteer's loss of significant aspects of himself earlier in the narrative. When Kusanagi first interacts with the Puppeteer, large swathes of his personal network (or self) were lost. As he notes during that experience, 'The totality of my "self" is being radically simplified, but for some reason my true self is not changing . . .'.[48] This event undermines the Puppeteer's capacity to sustain his existence as a stable being, removing any 'slack' or 'play' in his system that would give him 'protection against catastrophe',[49] but without destroying his ghostly lifehood. It is by merging with Kusanagi, a fully complex and diverse being, that the Puppeteer hopes to overcome this problem - and thus become a 'true life-form'. True life, on this reading, is not so much organic as wildly complex and adaptable, changeable. As the Puppeteer clarifies, 'humans are always changing, and I want to be able to change too'.[50]

The visual distinction between organic and mechanical in Figure 6.1 highlights the radical uncertainty and fluidity that *Ghost*'s engagement with selfhood brings about. Indeed, it is precisely this 'certain' distinction that the work profoundly undermines, and by juxtaposing the visual depiction of a clear difference between human and machine with an event where that difference is completely broken down, Figure 6.1 foregrounds the blurring of the human threshold. Through *Ghost* we see a fluid self, a concept of the human that is deeply unsure, with no certain boundary or essence. The work moves from a seemingly solid concept of the ghost - protected and sealed off, a static essence of humanity - to an expansive breaking down of the human's boundaries. Traversing this narrative, a self emerges that is able to be deeply reconfigured, that is an intricate and restless blend of organic and mechanical. Although 'ghosts' may delineate

47 See Shirow (n 2) 346.
48 Shirow (n 2) 271.
49 Shirow (n 2) 341.
50 Shirow (n 2) 343.

lifehood, ultimately there remains an intractable doubt as to their stability, as to where our own systems end and 'other' systems begin, and as to what constitutes a 'ghost' anyway. This is not a simple return to the shifting essence of Battersby, where our core selves are 'there' but are constantly changing through our engagement with the world; rather, it is an acceptance that life itself cannot be codified - that there is no 'essence', no sacred core, not even a changing one, patterned through experience. Even ghosts can be taken apart and manipulated, re-organised and re-configured, the same as a biological or mechanical body. By diving into the ghost in order to explore its nature and conceptualise its essence, we do not find answers - but mysteries. The ghost slips away beyond grasp and dissipates into the background, back along the bifurcated pathways of the universal network that constitutes it; it is ineffable, a flowing cloud in the uncertainty of the diverse system of the universe.

Regulating the ghost

Nikolas Rose has argued that technologies surrounding our somatic biology (medicine, genetics, biotechnology, psychiatry) have been reconfigured from the eugenics of the 19th and 20th centuries: whilst those approaches judged and manipulated the individual for the good of the nation, the public health justifying the private intervention, our contemporary methodologies are focused on the individual level. It is the health of the individual that is paramount, Rose claims, and that underpins intervention; at the same time medical technologies have become 'molecular' - drugs, microscopes, X-rays, brain mapping, genes - enabling greater levels of intervention and manipulation of the self towards an ideal 'healthy' or 'normal' sate. And these technologies, due to their prolific scope, challenge understandings of 'normal'; what is normal becomes shaped more in terms of our context or social values, and the technologies being used to normalise. In short, our individual selves and bodies are judged good or bad - broken or healthy - in relation to what technology can do to us.[51] The development of virtual networking and communication environments, and their integration into our social lives and personal interactions, may also shape the contours of human life, and similarly do so in relation to the capacities of our developing technologies. The associated question - as to what those technologies are *permitted* to do - means law's regulation of technology is also implicated in the shifting concept of 'humanity'.

In the world of *Ghost*, a humanity is imagined where technology has taken over not only our everyday lives, but our physiological make-up and our psychic experiences of ourselves and others. The nature of the

51 See N Rose, 'The Politics of Life Itself' (2001) 18 *Theory, Culture and Society* 1.

human, its limits and capacities, become defined in relation to the available technology; being a cyborg does not preclude being a human. Indeed, it is worth noting that the main protagonists of *Ghost* are law enforcement officers: in Shirow's future, legality has advanced alongside technology such that cyborgs both enforce and are subject to the law. But the model of the universal network raises the problem of distinguishing personal and universal systems, distinguishing what is 'self' and 'other'. The merging of two living ('ghostly') beings into a new, single being challenges not only the stability of self over time, but also the uniqueness of individuals. The ghost may represent our human 'essence' or 'soul', no matter how hazily, but if our 'souls' can merge and reconfigure as thoroughly as our bodies, this does not return us to classically stable understandings selfhood or even of the self as a dynamic essence. Rather, it solidifies the fact that such neat concepts are no longer available. The work suggests that as science and technology develop more and more sophisticated ways of mimicking and mediating life, of repairing or augmenting diverse human capacities, as the boundaries of knowledge are pushed back and more of the secrets of the universe, of life, are revealed to us - the more difficult the defining of that life will become. Humanity is emerging today as already integrated into a world suffused with technology - in the 'in-between' manner of a cyborg. The sophisticated hybrid beings present across the panels and pages of *Ghost* may not yet exist in our contemporary reality, but this speculative concept is symbolic of many of the complex interactions of human and machine that are taking place today. The unresolved meeting of human and machine in the concept of the cyborg symbolises the developing reliance upon technology for significant aspects of our daily experience, the mediation of human communication and presence through electronic environments, and the use of increasingly sophisticated medical technologies to augment and repair the physical body. *Ghost*, in its intricate navigation of the human threshold in a world populated by cyborgs, suggests that as new forms of technology, new modes of understanding, and new disciplinary techniques develop, so our 'selves' will develop beyond any traditionally stable categories. If we add to this the recognition of the wide complexity involved in developing regulatory structures for technology,[52] the task of pinpointing humanity - either in terms of the entity law regulates today, or how that entity is manifested and protected in legal regulation - seems unattainable.

There are references throughout *Ghost* to various rules and regulations pertaining to ghosts and cybernetic technology. There are references to 'cyberbrain ethics', and also the need for heavy security and 'ghost keys' to protect people's ghosts from infiltration and injury. One major example

52 See N Priaulx, 'Governance: Creating an Ethical Architecture' in N Priaulx and A Wrigley (eds), *Ethics, Law and Society: Volume V* (Ashgate 2013).

is the prohibition on 'ghost dubbing'. Like most of the regulation, this is only referred to in passing. Ghost dubbing essentially involves making copies of a cybernetic individual; it can be seen taking place in Figure 6.2. The ghost dubbing process explicitly demonstrates both the replicability and mechanical permeability of the self in the world of *Ghost.* All the beings present in Figure 6.2 are radically integrated into their mechanical surroundings, the central original particularly so. The complex interfacing of the ostensibly human flesh of the cyborg with multitudes of wires and connective devices undermines any simple somatic understanding of self-hood, but this also reflects the wider difficulties present in *Ghost.* It is not just that the bodies of these beings are integrated into mechanical devices and circuitry, their systems are interlinked: the one feeding off and replicating the other; the memories and capacities of the one being transferred and imprinted into the other; the ghost, the defining life-force of the one being duplicated, mapped and 'dubbed' into the replicant software and hardware architecture of the other. The one literally *becoming* the other.

This ghost dubbing system, in all its intricacies and complexes, its subroutines and automations, represents the core problematics of cyborg life in the context of retaining or understanding the concept of the self in the face of advancing technology. Such activities undermine the very notion of an individual, of a unique being or self. Humans become replicable, able to be

Figure 6.2 Excerpt from page 344 of M Shirow, *The Ghost in the Shell* (Kodansha 1991). *The Ghost in the Shell* © 1991 Shirow Masamune / KODANSHA LTD. All rights reserved.

formatted, wiped, copied, reprogrammed - like a machine. This is perhaps the more troubling side of the human-machine coin: the problem is not just that of where machines take on lifehood and the concomitant rights and duties of law, but also, 'When do humans become mere machines?' If we develop machines so complex that they become 'human', it could also be said that they remain machines - since they were developed as such - and thus those factors that were traditionally 'human' become simply products of mechanical systems, and worthy of the same respect and value as those systems: that is, as property. Contemporarily, similar concerns can be raised in relation to such bio-technologies as transplants, stem cells, and artificial organs. Transplants radically challenge any stable identification of self with body;[53] stem cells suggest the ability of technology to manipulate the physical body and create (organic) mechanisms that can be patched into existing personal systems;[54] whilst implanting mechanical parts into the human body effectively gives rise to a nascent bio-mechanical cyborg.

Ghost dubbing may represent the thick end of the wedge, but symbolically we can see in it the wider issues of our relationship(s) with technology, and the suggestion of a terrible fear at the heart of the in-betweenness of human-machine integration: that we humans may be nothing more than machines. In one sense, prohibiting ghost dubbing tries to stop such issues arising and uses law to maintain some degree of certainty at the boundaries of life. But regardless, it challenges the existence of humans as being more than (albeit complex) mechanical objects, hinting that underneath all our assertions on the distinction between human and machine, beneath all our technological regulation - we are really just sad, ghostless 'bots.

Acknowledgements

I would like to extend my cordial thanks to Christine Battersby, Stephen Skinner and Melanie Williams (as well, of course, as the mysterious reviewers) who provided invaluable and constructive comments on earlier drafts of this chapter.

Case

R v Malcherek and Steel [1981] 2 All ER 422

53 For examination on how transplants challenge the boundaries of life, see MM Lock, *Twice Dead: Organ Transplants and the Reinvention of Death* (University of California Press 2002).

54 See eg, J Pearlman, 'Kidney Grown from Stem Cells by Australian Scientists' (*The Telegraph*, 16 December 2013) <www.telegraph.co.uk/news/worldnews/australiaandthepacific/australia/10520058/Kidney-grown-from-stem-cells-by-Australian-scientists.html> accessed 13 March 2014.

References

Battersby C, *The Phenomenal Woman: Feminist Metaphysics and the Patterns of Identity* (Polity Press 1998).

Giddens T, 'Comics, Law, and Aesthetics: Towards the Use of Graphic Fiction in Legal Studies' (2012) 6 *Law and Humanities* 85.

Goldsmith J, 'How Cyber Changes the Laws of War' (2013) 24 *European Journal of International Law* 129.

Haraway D, 'A Cyborg Manifesto: Science, Technology and Socialist-Feminism in the Late Twentieth Century' in Bell D and Kennedy BM (eds), *The Cybercultures Reader* (first published 1991, Routledge 2000).

Kant I, 'Foundations of the Metaphysics of Morals' in *Foundations of the Metaphysics of Morals and What Is Enlightenment?* (first published 1785, LW Beck tr, Bobbs-Menil 1959).

Kant I, *Critique of the Power of Judgment* (first published 1790, P Guyer and E Matthews trs, Cambridge University Press 2000).

Kohler A, 'To Think Human Out of the Machine Paradigm: *Homo Ex Machina*' (2010) 44 *Integrative Psychological and Behavioural Science* 39.

Korsgaard CM, introduction to I Kant, *Groundwork of the Metaphysics of Morals* (first published 1785, M Gregor tr, Cambridge University Press 1998).

Lock MM, *Twice Dead: Organ Transplants and the Reinvention of Death* (University of California Press 2002).

Moses LB, 'The Legal Landscape following Technological Change: Paths to Adaptation' (2007) 27 *Bulletin of Science, Technology and Society* 408.

Moses LB, 'Agents of Change: How the Law "Copes" with Technological Change' (2011) 20 *Griffith Law Review* 763.

Naffine N, *Law's Meaning of Life: Philosophy, Religion, Darwin and the Legal Person* (Hart 2009).

Pearlman J, 'Kidney Grown from Stem Cells by Australian Scientists' (*The Telegraph*, 16 December 2013) <www.telegraph.co.uk/news/worldnews/australiaandthepacific/australia/10520058/Kidney-grown-from-stem-cells-by-Australian-scientists.html> accessed 13 March 2014.

Priaulx N, 'Governance: Creating an Ethical Architecture' in Priaulx N and Wrigley A (eds), *Ethics, Law and Society: Volume V* (Ashgate 2013).

Richardson J, 'The Law and the Sublime: Rethinking the Self and its Boundaries' (2007) 18 *Law and Critique* 229.

Rose N, 'The Politics of Life Itself' (2001) 18 *Theory, Culture and Society* 1.

Sherwin RK, *Visualizing Law in the Age of the Digital Baroque: Arabesques and Entanglements* (Routledge 2011).

Shirow M, *The Ghost in the Shell* (FL Schodt and T Smith trs, Kodansha 1991).

Stuart SA, 'Conscious Machines: Memory, Melody and Muscular Imagination' (2010) 9 *Phenomenology and the Cognitive Sciences* 37.

Tranter K, 'Materiality and Memory: Motor Cars and Mobile Phones' (2013) 22 *Griffith Law Review* 532.

Part II

Graphic criminology

Chapter 7

When (super)heroes kill: vigilantism and deathworthiness in *Justice League*, *Red Team*, and the Christopher Dorner killing spree

Nickie D Phillips and Staci Strobl

Neutralising threats

From Batman serving as 'the world's greatest detective' to Green Lantern thwarting the cosmic forces of evil, themes of crime and justice abound in American comic books. Most notably, this plays out in mainstream superhero comic books featuring heroes engaging in tactics that would otherwise be considered unconstitutional if committed by governmental agents. One of the most interesting facets of the superhero genre is the preoccupation with justice that manifests as an ongoing tension between public safety and individual rights. Reminiscent of Herbert Packer's model of the real-life American criminal justice, the criminal justice system in comic books operates on a continuum between two ideals: crime control and due process. As Packer argued, crime control and its focus on the increased and unobstructed power of law enforcement is at odds with due process, which privileges individual rights and the presumption of innocence.[1]

The formulaic nature of superhero comics allows this tension to be played out *ad infinitum* - the superheroes most commonly incapacitate villains temporarily (rather than kill them outright), until the next battle commences. In most mainstream American comics, the tension between crime control and due process is set against a backdrop of rampant incompetence and corruption within the criminal justice system. Existing authorities are powerless to neutralise the threats posed by villains, often equal in strength and power to the heroes. It is within this perpetual dystopia that the stage is set for extra-legal justice. The hero embarks on a quest to neutralise the threat and return the community perhaps not merely to the status quo, but to an aspired idyllic order. We broadly call this quest - which takes many forms, from extra-legal villain investigations and manhunts to harnessing technology or raising armies against a threat - the 'path to

1 H Packer, *The Limits of the Criminal Sanction* (Stanford University Press 1968).

justice'.[2] It is in this context that the hero(es) must make a determination of deathworthiness - of how far the protagonist may go in violation of the law, and his or her corresponding decision of whether or not to kill those deemed deserving. At times, by stepping outside the bounds of law, the hero moves beyond temporary incapacitation into a determination that the villain must be killed for justice to prevail.

In *Comic Book Crime*, we studied nearly 200 mainstream comic books published between 2002 and 2010, finding that deathworthiness operates on a continuum ranging from the avoidance of killing to the killing of innocents as collateral damage in a larger cosmic battle between good and evil.[3] For the most part, heroes in contemporary mainstream comics fall short of retributive killing favouring what we term 'apocalyptic incapacitation' - an incapacitation of the villain that falls short of death, but that features the rhetorical and graphic drama often associated with retribution such as flashy fight scenes and tough banter.[4]

For readers, we found that the heroes' path to justice, including determinations of deathworthiness, serve as a means of processing anxieties about crime, victimisation, and extra-legal justice. Mainstream American comic books privilege retributive sentiment, even if it is not fully realised, and we suggest that the books serve as an important cultural artefact that reflects and shapes attitudes toward crime, crime causation, and social control.[5]

As a means of focusing more intently on deathworthiness, this chapter outlines the historical basis for the legal concept and its role in American due process. It then explores the theme in two recent comics books, a mainstream superhero title (*Cry for Justice*[6]) and a non-superhero title (*Red Team*[7]). We apply our notion of deathworthiness as a decision-making process to each book with the underlying theoretical orientation that such fictional media contribute to readers' collective consciousness around ideas of crime and justice. Comic books, along with other mass media entertainment, serve as an internalised cultural landscape that individuals may draw upon in their own lived experience as it intersects with crime

2 See ND Phillips and S Strobl, *Comic Book Crime: Truth, Justice, and the American Way* (NYU Press 2013).

3 Ibid.

4 Ibid.

5 Ibid.

6 JD Robinson and others, *Justice League: Cry for Justice #1* (DC Comics 2010).

7 G Ennis and C Cermak, *Garth Ennis' Red Team #3* (Dynamite Entertainment 2013). While deathworthiness is a common theme among mainstream superhero comic books, we chose *Cry for Justice* because the series ignited the passions of the readers and sparked public discussions of the concept. We chose *Red Team* because the book's release coincided with the Dorner shooting spree, both of which involved vigilantism on the part of former and current police officers.

and justice.[8] We conclude by offering an illustration of how popular culture discourse, like those in comic books, mirrors ways in which members of the public process and confront real-life incidents of vigilante justice, such as the public discourse around the Christopher Dorner killing spree that resulted in the deaths of four civilians during the winter of 2013.

Deathworthiness as due process in the American system

In 2013, the death penalty was a legal sentence in 32 states and in federal criminal courts.[9] Deathworthiness is a term used in American jurisprudence when discussing which cases are considered capital crimes and which cases lead to actual sentences of death. The United States implements a bifurcated process, one in which decisions of deathworthiness in the sentencing phase are separate from determinations of guilt at the plea allocution or trial stages. In states that have the death penalty as an option, for an offender to receive it a prosecutor must first charge the defendant with a death-eligible crime. Absent a plea of guilty, the state then holds a jury trial to determine the guilt of the defendant and a separate sentencing phase for the jury to determine whether the punishment for the defendant will be death or a less severe alternative. Even if a sentence of death is received, the process of fulfilling the sentence can be a lengthy one. The defendant is automatically entitled to an appeals process, resulting in an amount of time from conviction to sentence that reaches on average almost 15 years.[10] Because implementation of the death penalty lacks certainty and swiftness, many - including the co-victims (friends and family of the deceased) - have found its enforcement to be a frustrating and less than satisfying process.[11] Moreover, though most Americans support the death penalty, its popularity has been declining over the last decade. The practice itself is also waning.[12]

8 J Ferrell, K Hayward and J Young, *Cultural Criminology: An Invitation* (Sage 2008).

9 'States With and Without the Death Penalty' <www.deathpenaltyinfo.org/states-and-without-death-penalty> accessed 10 January 2014.

10 'Time on Death Row' <www.deathpenaltyinfo.org/time-death-row> accessed 1 September 2013.

11 C Burton and R Tewksbury, 'How Families of Murder Victims Feel Following the Execution of Their Loved One's Murderer: A Content Analysis of Newspaper Reports of Executions from 2006 - 2011' (2013) 1 *Journal of Qualitative Criminal Justice and Criminology* 53; S Vollum, *Last Words and the Death Penalty: Voices of the Condemned and Their Co-Victims* (LFB Scholarly Publishing 2010).

12 'Death Penalty | Gallup Historical Trends' <www.gallup.com/poll/1606/death-penalty.aspx> accessed 10 January 2014; D Garland, *Peculiar Institution: America's Death Penalty in an Age of Abolition* (Belknap Press 2010).

In 2013, only a quarter of the number of executions occurred compared to its peak in 1994, when 315 people were executed.[13]

The notion that the death penalty is implemented in an unfair manner has long been debated among the public and addressed by the US Supreme Court. In their decision that provided guidelines for states to avoid the arbitrary and capricious administration of the death penalty, the Supreme Court ruled that juror determinations of deathworthiness must consider both aggravating and mitigating circumstances.[14] Aggravating circumstances are those factors that are likely to increase severity of the punishment, such as a particularly heinous crime or the commission of a murder during a felony. Mitigating circumstances, such as severe emotional disturbance or a history of severe abuse during childhood, are likely to lessen the punishment.

Legal scholars continue to debate the appropriateness of the death penalty and standards for making deathworthiness decisions.[15] For example, Jules Epstein suggests that prosecutors charge only the 'worst of the worst' offenders by taking into consideration the crime, prior convictions, and the 'negative background of the perpetrator' as well as 'an assessment of deservedness in light of all *mitigating* background'.[16] However, in response, Natali suggests that Epstein's standard is problematic in that prosecutorial discretion is potentially discriminatory and that more objective benchmarks are needed. Ultimately, Natali concludes that 'we cannot balance the gravity of the offense against individual life worthiness'.[17] For legal scholar Phyllis Crocker, a clear distinction between the guilt and punishment phase must be maintained. For Crocker, deathworthiness decisions should remain separate from considerations of guilt, and that culpability for the crime itself should not be conflated with considerations of deathworthiness – factors that may include 'the defendant's character, background, and record, his prior criminal conduct, and his future dangerousness'.[18] As it stands, determinations of guilt and deathworthiness become conflated to the extent

13 E Eckholm, 'In Death Penalty's Steady Decline, Some Experts See a Societal Shift' (*NY Times*, 19 December 2013) <www.nytimes.com/2013/12/19/us/in-death-penaltys-steady-decline-some-experts-see-a-societal-shift.html?_r=0> accessed 10 January 2014.

14 *Gregg v Georgia* (1976) 428 152 (US Supreme Court).

15 HA Bedau and PG Cassell, *Debating the Death Penalty: Should America Have Capital Punishment? The Experts on Both Sides Make Their Best Case* (Oxford University Press 2004).

16 J Epstein, 'Death-Worthiness and Prosecutorial Discretion in Capital Case Charging' (2009) 19 *Temple Political and Civil Rights Law Review* 389.

17 L Natali, 'A Reply to Jules Epstein: Is There an Objective Way to Define the Worst of the Worst' (2009) 19 *Temple Political and Civil Rights Law Review* 421, 427.

18 PL Crocker, 'Concepts of Culpability and Deathworthiness: Differentiating between Guilt and Punishment in Death Penalty Cases' (1997) 66 *Fordham Law Review* 21.

that defendants who are guilty, but not deathworthy, are too frequently sentenced to die (see also Giddens on the wider problem of holding 'living humans' criminally responsible[19]).

Deathworthiness and the heat of passion: *Cry for Justice*

Unlike the real-life American criminal justice system, where police officers, federal agents, and court officials must abide by due process concerns and constitutional mandates, determinations of deathworthiness in comic books are not transparent and not based on any constitutional considerations. In essence, deathworthiness is relegated to the heroes' own informal death penalty determination – a conflation of culpability and punishment that fans ultimately judge as just based largely on the inherent goodness of the hero.

The extra-legal narratives that are common in mainstream comic books bypass the frustration of due process concerns, allowing the hero flexibility to serve as 'judge, jury, and executioner', a process that can be rather satisfying for readers because it likely stands in sharp contrast to their direct experience with the criminal justice system or the experience typically portrayed in news media.[20] Rather than based on the rule of law and bound by constitutional considerations, comic book deathworthiness is based on the heroes' own personal ethics. Acknowledging that what constitutes justice is contested by the reading public, we suggest that what is significant is not necessarily the outcome – that is, whether or not the hero *actually* kills. Instead, we argue that the *path to justice* itself and the *determinations* of deathworthiness are significant in that this process is what invites readers to work through their own anxieties and moral dilemmas that shape their perceptions and attitudes about what it means to achieve justice. For example, when Wonder Woman violently snapped the neck of Max Lord, killing him in response to his mind control over Superman and potentially all heroes,[21] readers were divided in their reaction to her use of deadly force. Some suggested that she was justified in doing what was necessary to stop the villain, including killing. Other readers, in contrast, felt that she had gone too far and Lord should have been incapacitated rather than killed.

19 T Giddens, 'Criminal Responsibility and the Living Self' (2013) *Criminal Law and Philosophy* (DOI: 10.1007/s11572 - 013 - 9212 - 2), <http://link.springer.com/article/10.1007/s11572 - 013 - 9212 - 2>.

20 For discussion of key issues with conflating the roles of judge, jury and executioner into a single person in relation to the constitutional separation of powers, see Chapter 4 in this book. And, on broader issues with the legitimacy of exceptional executive violence, see Chapters 11 and 12.

21 See G Rucka, R Morales and M Bair, *Wonder Woman #219* (DC Comics 2005).

The Wonder Woman story arc provided readers a way to explore, if only vicariously, their own personal moral boundaries as well as those of the larger community. Fan reaction to *Cry for Justice* was similarly explosive, but not quite as divisive given that the consensus among most fans was that Green Arrow's use of deadly force against the villain Prometheus was explicitly criminal.[22]

Cry for Justice begins in the aftermath of *Final Crisis*,[23] a cross-over event in the DC universe that left the heroes shaken at the death of Martian Manhunter at the hands of villain Libra and the presumed killing of Batman by Darkseid (the God of Evil). Green Lantern (aka Hal Jordan) declares that the Justice League's current course of action is inadequate against the new kinds of threats faced by the League. Specifically, the heroes argue for a move to pre-emptive strikes based on deterrent principles:

> **Green Lantern:** . . . we wait for villains to do wrong and then go after them or we wait for them to attack us. Might have worked then. But these aren't the villains of yesterday, and our being 'good' and 'true' isn't scaring them back into the shadows. Not anymore.[24]

Discussions of deadly force and pre-emptive strikes have long been common themes in comic books, but the themes took on particular relevance in the United States and other western democracies after the terrorist attacks on 11 September 2001. These narratives are easily reminiscent of foreign policy discussions that tended to promote a simplified rhetorical dichotomy of 'good versus evil'. The notion that a 'new kind of evil' is present in America and familiar refrains such as 'you're either with us or against us' were used by the GW Bush administration as a means of gaining support for policies that were likely to otherwise be considered unconstitutional.

Ultimately, however, the path to justice in *Cry for Justice* is not one of pre-emptive strikes. Rather, it is a form of retributive justice directed against a single villain, Prometheus, who has brought destruction on a grand scale from Gotham to Metropolis. He is blamed for Batman's absence and Martian Manhunter's death. Most notably, he is responsible for the maiming of Green Arrow's son and the death of his granddaughter Lain, and it is personal vengeance that drives Green Arrow to murder.

The notion of 'justice' is highly contested in the series and is often subject to a team discussion. However, deliberations of deathworthiness tend

22 No legal defence could logically be constructed for Green Arrow in that he single-handedly sought personal revenge on Prometheus in a planned and calculated way. The events do not suggest self-defence, diminished capacity, necessity, nor any other commonly-applied legal defences in the US.

23 G Morrison and others, *Final Crisis* (DC Comics 2009).

24 Robinson and others (n 6) 1.

to occur in the heat of passion - during a violent encounter in which the hero must be reined in from killing the enemy. For example, Congorilla Bill (charged with protecting his African homeland) strikes out against those responsible for the deaths of his clan. Starman restrains him:

> **Starman:** We can't kill them! I mean, yes we can - but we shouldn't. We mustn't! We defeated them - they're our captives. That's enough!
> **Congorilla:** . . . a death is mercy to this scum.
> **Starman:** . . . vengeance isn't justice, Bill. Blood isn't justice![25]

Similarly, Donna Troy has to be restrained from killing by fellow hero, Shade:

> **Shade:** My ardent dear. The last time I checked in the big book of superhero bylaws and whatnot . . . your kind doesn't kill. Unless you want to go down the dark lanes that I amble, I'd stop now . . .[26]

Generally, extreme violence - including torture - is accepted as a just response, while killing is deemed off-limits. As such, the two options are not usually treated as moral equivalents by the heroes. However, even the villains, at times, serve as a check on the heroes' absolute power in making such judgment. For example, Ray Palmer (aka The Atom) threatens Killer Moth with torture. Killer Moth replies, 'You're heroes, you don't act that way'. Palmer responds, '. . . welcome to pain'. Further, Green Arrow calls out Ray Palmer for using torture to gain information. In response, Palmer outlines his criteria for deathworthiness: specifically, that torture is permitted under certain circumstances while death is not.[27]

In *Cry for Justice,* nearly all villains are deemed deathworthy - that is, until the hero is reined in and convinced that incapacitation is a more appropriate and moral response. However, the deathworthiness of any given villain is constantly negotiated. For example, Green Arrow deems those who have personally harmed those he loves as deathworthy, while other heroes hold a more nuanced view. When Congorilla Bill and Starman show up to recruit Animal Man to their team, Animal Man replies:

> **Animal Man:** The way you're describing it, it seems like you intend to murder Prometheus and I simply can't be a party to that.

25 JD Robinson and others, *Justice League: Cry for Justice #4* (DC Comics 2010).
26 JD Robinson and others, *Justice League: Cry for Justice #6* (DC Comics 2010).
27 Robinson and others (n 25). In addition to heroes often having a no-kill moral compass, comic books may often feature torture as a means of showing explicit violence without killing off time-honoured villains, relied upon to keep interest in long-running serial plots, particularly in the superhero genre, see Phillips and Strobl (n 2).

> **Congorilla:** No, I've had a change of heart in that regard. When I say I want justice – I mean I want him brought to justice. Mik [Starman] has shown me the difference.[28]

Upon capturing Prometheus, the heroes must make a deathworthiness determination – to release Prometheus to avoid further death and destruction or to incapacitate or kill him. The decision to kill Prometheus was initially subjected to a team discussion (see Figure 7.1). The team weighs the heinousness of Prometheus's crimes (eg the killing of Green Arrow's granddaughter, the maiming of his son, the 'dead of Star City' and others) and states that the heroes' only choice is to give Prometheus freedom in return for the deactivation codes that will stop the carnage. The time-honoured 'no-killing' code of the heroes was (briefly) honoured. Collectively, at Green Arrow's lead, the heroes granted Prometheus's release for the greater good of the citizens. Despite leading the team, it is soon revealed that Green Arrow harbours doubts about whether they did the right thing. Ultimately, based on his own personal losses and the deaths of tens of thousands of Star City inhabitants, Green Arrow goes rogue and makes his own deathworthiness decision. Green Arrow traces Prometheus to another dimension, fires an arrow into Prometheus's skull killing him, and proclaims 'Justice'.

Ultimately, whether or not determinations of deathworthiness are considered appropriate by the readers has less to do with classical criminological concerns of whether the punishment fits the crime, but more to do with the character of the hero – whether it felt 'true' to the character for them to kill. Much of the discussion among fans around *Cry for Justice* revealed their disappointment in Green Arrow's actions and his behaviour was frequently described as criminal. For example, one blogger reviewing the series writes that Green Arrow 'straight-up murders Prometheus in his Phantom Zone crib'.[29]

Another reviewer taps into the satisfaction of retribution fulfilled, stating:

> my anger was sated by as visceral and cold a murder as any committed by its victim in these seven issues. I can't help but wonder if the sense of vindication I felt at this scene made me as cheap and as garish as the book itself often seemed. . .[30]

28 JD Robinson and others, *Justice League: Cry for Justice #5* (DC Comics 2010).

29 D Uzumeri, 'David Loses His Shit on Justice League: Cry For Justice #7' (*The Savage Critics*, 3 March 2010) <www.savagecritic.com/reviews/david-loses-his-shit-on-justice-league-cry-for-justice-7/> accessed 20 November 2013.

30 G Marston, 'Best Shots Extra: JL: Cry For Justice #7' (*Newsarama*, 3 March 2010) <www.newsarama.com/4834-best-shots-extra-jl-cry-for-justice-7-spoilers-w-poll.html> accessed 20 November 2013.

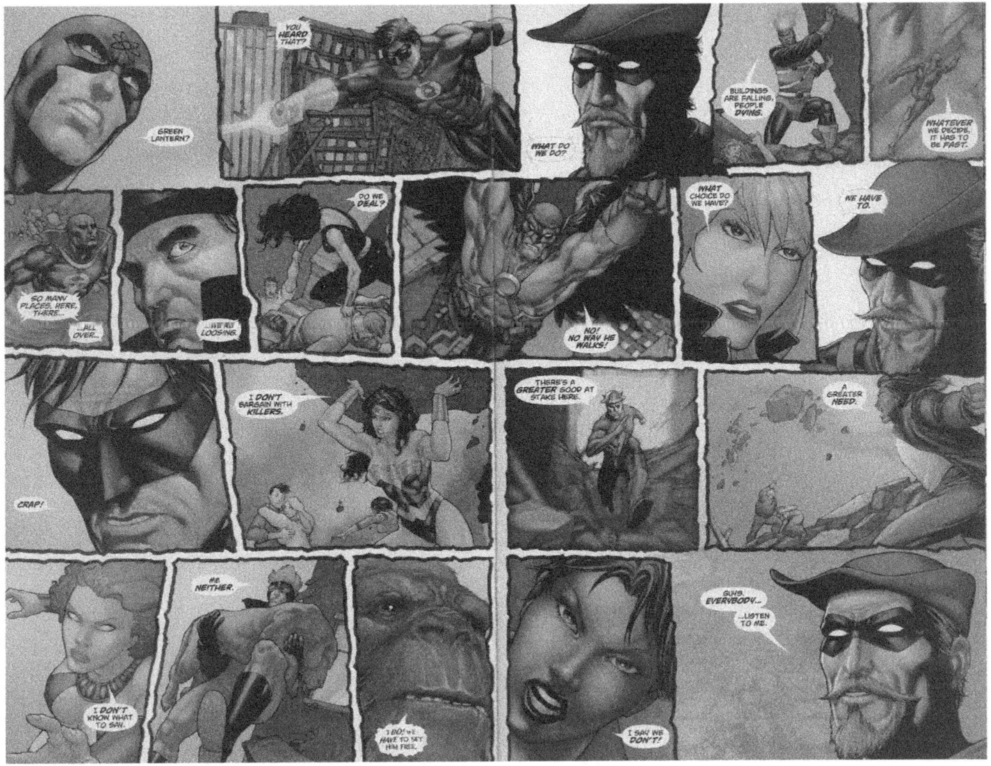

Figure 7.1 In this two-page spread, Justice League team members deliberate deathworthiness. From 'Justice League: Cry for Justice' #7™ and © DC Comics. Available in *Justice League: Cry for Justice* (DC Comics 2011).

Readers are keen to make judgments about the characters' deathworthiness determinations as a means of processing their own attitudes and perceptions of when it is appropriate to kill. For example, one blogger suggested that Prometheus was in fact deathworthy:

> Is it murder to kill a dude who's committed a grand act of terrorism, like partially obliterating an entire city? Like, I'm pretty sure the US government would deem Prometheus an 'enemy combatant' and have no qualms about dropping a bomb from a Predator drone on him.[31]

Vigilante teamwork and deathworthiness: *Red Team*

An alternate portrayal of deathworthiness is presented in *Red Team*, a non-superhero comic focusing on the actions of an elite police unit. The story opens with the interrogation of Detective Eddie Mellinger who is in the midst of a stunning confession. He, and the other members of the major crime unit Red Team, murdered a suspect; the first among many offenders that the team deemed deathworthy and assassinated. The book follows the interrogations of Mellinger and his fellow team member Trudy Giroux, as they recount their descent from well-respected cops intent on following the rule of law to murderous vigilantes. Unlike the determinations of deathworthiness in *Cry for Justice* that most often occur in the heat of passion, the Red Team engages in intense discussions of who is deemed deathworthy and under what circumstances. As a result of these discussions, the team agrees on preset rules that they must abide by in their quest for justice.

First, the team agrees that there must be absolute certainty as to the guilt of the perpetrator. The team makes clear that their goal is to mete out justice to those most deserving – the truly guilty (see Figure 7.2). One member of the team, George, specifies, 'It has to be something where a jury couldn't do anything *but* reach a unanimous verdict'. However, in a poignant moment, Eddie ironically questions the validity of their goal, 'if a jury would convict, why do we need to get involved at all?'.[32] The circular logic emphasises the team's deep crisis of belief in the system they have worked in for years. They are wrestling with an emotional and moral dissatisfaction with the gap between factual guilt and legal guilt that arises within the context of the rule of law. Procedures which safeguard individual rights, allow the public to weigh in symbolically through a jury, and have

31 C Mozzocco, 'Some Questions I Have about Justice League: Cry for Justice' (*Every Day is Like Wednesday*, 4 March 2010) <http://everydayislikewednesday.blogspot.com/2010/03/some-questions-i-have-about-justice.html> accessed 20 November 2013.

32 G Ennis and C Cermak, *Garth Ennis' Red Team #2* (Dynamite Entertainment 2013).

Figure 7.2 The Red Team outlines one of their rules for deathworthiness: certain guilt. From G Ennis and C Cermak, *Garth Ennis' Red Team #2* (Dynamite Entertainment 2013). *Red Team*™ Copyright © 2014 Spitfire Productions Ltd. All Rights Reserved. RED TEAM, all characters the distinctive likenesses thereof and all related elements are trademarks of Spitfire Productions Ltd.

complicated evidentiary requirements, can sometimes thwart the convictions of defendants who have actually committed the crimes alleged. Red Team ultimately doubts that such a system captures the truly guilty in the net of the legally guilty often enough for them to feel their life's work is worthwhile and meaningful.

Next, the team outlines their remaining guidelines. They must go to great lengths to avoid detection. For example, they must 'think like cops', and be aware of leaving incriminating patterns behind and an obvious *modus operandi*.[33] They must avoid targeting offenders that only the police know about. Their determinations of who is deathworthy must not be personal and efficiency must be paramount. When executing the offenders, there must be no speeches – they will kill, then get out. And finally, as Eddie states, in determining who is deathworthy, 'they'd have to be truly evil', 'killing them would have to make a difference', and 'they'd have to be real monsters'.[34]

Mirroring official investigations, the vigilante team carefully vets each potential target and decides that each matches the deathworthiness criteria set out in the rules. In the first issue, kingpin Clinton Days is executed for his myriad of violence crimes – from human trafficking to

33 Ibid.
34 Ibid.

drug-running to child pornography to multiple murders. Subsequently, a paedophile priest and a Russian mobster are vetted and killed. In fact, none of them appears to offer many mitigating factors for the team to consider, but instead overwhelming criminal culpability and poor character. The child-rapist clergyman may not have murdered anyone, but as one team-member put it, 'If anyone can tell me a bigger crime than fucking someone's life up before they even get started, I'm all ears'.[35] All three criminals managed to go unpunished by the criminal justice system, contributing to the notion that due process had failed and without Red Team there would be no consequences.

Red Team's actions provide the reader a twist on the theme of deathworthiness so common in mainstream superhero comics. There are no superheroics here, just a team of cops intent on punishing the truly deserving, even as they violate the law they are sworn to uphold. In police studies literature, this phenomenon is known as 'noble cause' corruption, wherein police officers prioritise the ends over the means. Crank and Caldero define noble cause corruption as corruption committed in the name of good ends, corruption that happens when police officers care too much about their work. It is corruption committed in order to get the bad guys off the streets, to protect the innocent and the children from the predators that inflict pain and suffering on them.[36]

Red Team writer Garth Ennis explains that the 'starting point for *Red Team* was, essentially, what if someone tried to be the Punisher for real?'[37] This notion of 'for real' - a *real* superhero, a *real* vigilante - problematises 'super'-heroic justice as we move from the pages of the comic book to 'real life' vigilantism, and is a theme that comic book creators and fans are eager to explore.[38] We suggest that the narratives of deathworthiness in comic books resonate with readers and contribute to collective notions of the appropriateness of vigilante justice. Mass media contextualises violence, providing vocabularies of motive for determining when and against whom violence is appropriate.[39] Readers' processing of deathworthiness determinations in these books informs their perceptions of circumstances in which

35 Ennis and Cermak (n 7).

36 JP Crank and MA Caldero, *Police Ethics: The Corruption of Noble Cause* (3rd edn, Elsevier 2010). See also RJ Kane and MD White, *Jammed Up: Bad Cops, Police Misconduct, and the New York City Police Department* (New York University Press 2012).

37 K Phegley, 'Garth Ennis Details His "Red Team"' (*Comic Book Resources*, 11 February 2013) <www.comicbookresources.com/?page=article&id=43697> accessed 21 October 2013.

38 For discussion on examples of 'real life' superheroes, see Chapter 10 of this book.

39 J Young, 'Constructing the Paradigm of Violence: Mass Media, Violence and Youth' (2003) <www.ukobservatory.com/downloadfiles/Paradigm of Violence.pdf> accessed 20 November 2013.

violence is rejected and/or condoned and accepted in the real world. We offer the following analysis as an illustration of the ways in which determinations of deathworthiness – made by a self-appointed 'real-life' vigilante – are processed by members of the public.

Deathworthiness: justifications for real world violence

Issue number one of *Red Team* hit the stands on 6 February 2013, the same week that Christopher Dorner went on the run from law enforcement, setting the Los Angeles Police Department (LAPD) on a major manhunt that ended in a shootout and ultimately Dorner's death six days later.[40] Dorner, a rogue (former) cop, turned his anger on members of the LAPD whom he accused of being corrupt; he also attacked their families. Dorner alleged that he was unjustly terminated from the LAPD for reporting a fellow officer's excessive use of force against a suspect and relays incidents of racial harassment, dishonesty and other incidents of excessive use of force by fellow officers.[41] He is believed to have killed four people, including the daughter of a police captain and her fiancé, and injured three others. The manhunt for Dorner ended with his death from a self-inflicted gunshot wound in a burned-out mountain cabin after exchanging fire with authorities.

For a brief period, Christopher Dorner captured the public's imagination as the archetypal American anti-hero often valorised in fictional media. A hyper-masculine former military man who believed himself wronged by the system, he became a lone wolf on-the-run and used violence in the hope of clearing his name and holding his alleged 'wrongdoers' accountable.

In his final days, Dorner posted a manifesto online that detailed the motivations for his actions that he described as a 'last resort'. The manifesto is

40 Dorner joined the LAPD in 2002, but was fired in 2008 after falsely accusing an officer of excessive use of force, though he maintained that his account was truthful. His appeal of his case was rejected in 2011. See S Bernstein and others, 'Timeline: Revenge Plot Events' (*NBC Southern California*, 16 February 2013) <www.nbclosangeles.com/news/local/Timeline-Ex-LAPD-Officer-Suspected-in-Shooting-Spree-Had-Sued-The-Department-190206031.html> accessed 30 September 2013.

41 N Allen, 'Christopher Dorner "Killed in Cabin Blaze"' (*The Telegraph*, 13 February 2013) <www.telegraph.co.uk/news/worldnews/northamerica/usa/9866733/Christopher-Dorner-killed-in-cabin-blaze.html> accessed 30 September 2013; KTLA, 'Christopher Dorner's Manifesto (Disturbing Content and Language)' (*KTLA 5*, 12 February 2013) <http://ktla.com/2013/02/12/read-christopher-dorners-so-called-manifesto/> accessed 30 September 2013; Miguel Marquez, 'San Bernardino County Sheriff: "This Investigation is Over"' (*CNN*, 14 February 2013) <www.cnn.com/2013/02/13/us/lapd-manhunt/index.html> accessed 30 September 2013.

a mixture of self-delusional bravado peppered with popular culture references. In addition to detailed descriptions of mistreatment and corruption by his fellow officers that led to his reluctant but self-described 'drastic and shocking' spree murder, Dorner's manifesto includes a list of targets that he deemed deathworthy, or those which he felt deserving of death as a direct consequence of their, or their family members', past behaviour, including allegations of police corruption.[42] Envisioning himself as the real-life Punisher, he menacingly proclaims to those on the target list, 'You will now live the life of the prey'.[43]

Some of those Dorner specifically mentions as targets include 'Caucasian officers' whose 'sole intent [is] to victimize minorities who are uneducated, and unaware of criminal law, civil law, and civil rights', lesbian officers who 'degrade male officers', and those who lack courage to fundamentally change the department, including 'Asian officers' who witness malfeasance and 'say nothing, stand for nothing and protect nothing'. He proclaims to each, 'You are a high value target'.[44]

Dorner's manifesto may be read as evidence of mental illness and paranoia and his statement that the 'only thing that changes policy and garners attention is death' is chilling in its cynicism.[45] Still, Dorner's case quickly entered the public's consciousness and serves as a barometer of just how far the public is willing go in accepting deadly force as an acceptable form of vigilante violence. The range of responses on social media to Dorner's actions mirror reactions to the continuum of deathworthiness that we see playing out in comic book narratives. As the incident in early 2013 unfolded, various pages were created on Facebook, such as the 'I Support Christopher Jordan Dorner' page.[46] Some members of the public also expressed that deadly force is never justified – no matter the circumstances (eg 'Anyone who kills to prove his point is a terrorist. People make me sick'[47]). Others were more accepting that Dorner's rage might be directed at those who directly wronged him, but were outraged that he targeted peripheral victims. For example:

42 KTLA (n 41).
43 KTLA (n 41).
44 KTLA (n 41).
45 S Abram, 'Christopher Dorner's Manifesto Reveals an Unraveled Mind, Experts Say' (*Daily News*, 6 February 2013) <www.dailynews.com/20130207/christopher-dorners-manifesto-reveals-an-unraveled-mind-experts-say> accessed 5 October 2013.
46 S Musil, 'Fan Pages Pop up on Facebook to Support Fugitive Ex-LAPD Cop' (*CNET*, 8 February 2013) <http://news.cnet.com/8301 – 1023_3 – 57568311 – 93/fan-pages-pop-up-on-facebook-to-support-fugitive-ex-lapd-cop/> accessed 14 January 2014. See, eg, 'I Support Christopher Jordan Dorner' (*Facebook*) <www.facebook.com/IsupportCJD> accessed 20 November 2013; 'We Are All Christopher Dorner' (*Facebook*) <www.facebook.com/WeAreAllChrisDorner> accessed 13 February 2013.
47 Post on 'I Support', ibid.

> … it's not revenge when a person kills someone not involved, it's a[n] act of [an] insane cold blooded murderer. You seek revenge on those who wronged you, not the innocent. Related to them or not. Only a lunatic thinks in that way.[48]

Interestingly, for the above commenter justice rests on not harming the innocent, and considerations such as being personally wronged (Green Arrow) or objective engagement (Red Team and their guidelines) are not viewed as important. In contrast, some members of the public felt that, although his methods were extreme, Dorner was courageous in exposing the corruption and institutional discrimination that he personally experienced and have long plagued policing organisations, specifically the LAPD.

A review of the posts by commenters revealed a range of responses from the sarcastic (eg in response to the site offering Christopher Dorner-related merchandise, one commenter responded, 'Nothing says "I'm a fucking PSYCHO!" quite like "I Support A Murderer of Innocent People" Chris Dorner swag!'[49]) to more measured statements, providing evidence that most who comment are working through their own understanding of deathworthiness and incomprehensible acts of violence while contemplating the appropriate social response.[50] Comments addressed concerns such as, 'Can we claim to understand actions that are a response to institutional discrimination while simultaneously disagreeing with them and finding them morally reprehensible?'. Or, 'Why, and how, could someone support a spree murderer?' (eg 'We support him because he's trying to bring awareness to the corruption in LAPD not for murder. By the way[,] he is innocent until proven guilty in a court of law or have [yo]u forgotten the constitution and American laws.'[51]). And, 'Is vengeance ever justified?'.[52]

Some commenters made a utilitarian comparison between the number of victims that Dorner harmed versus the number of innocents killed by the LAPD, implying that the LAPD is 'more guilty' than Dorner, 'We as a country kill more innocents supporting war!!'.[53] Others were horrified at the overzealousness of police action, particularly in response to reports that the police 'blasted at least 100 rounds' at two women in a truck, erroneously believing the truck was driven by Dorner. In another case of mistaken identity, police also opened fire on another truck driven by a

48 Ibid.
49 Ibid.
50 Ibid.
51 Ibid.
52 Ibid.
53 Ibid.

surfer.[54] In response to these incidents, the meme 'Don't Shoot, I'm not Dorner' quickly flooded the internet, along with memes of Christopher Dorner as Batman.[55]

Many commenters disagree that Dorner's vigilante actions can serve as an appropriate condemnation of greater harms done by a racially discriminatory institution, 'His message will be lost in his own evil deeds. Any credibility he once had is now gone . . . his wrongs far out weigh those he has brought to lite [sic]'.[56] Most notably, the comments reveal how readily members of the public filter real-life criminal events through popular culture representations of justice. In response to the report of the LAPD using drones in their search for Dorner, one commenter stated, 'This reminds me of Rambo when the sheriffs sent out the chopper for him! Power to you CJD!'.[57]

In a further nod to how seamlessly prominent vigilante fantasies in popular culture feed into real-life perceptions of justice, the Facebook page ('Chris-Dorner') borrowed the script from *The Dark Knight*, the second of the Batman film trilogy, to describe Dorner:

> Chris Dorner is the hero LA deserves, but not the one it needs right now. So we'll hunt him, because he can take it. Because he's not the hero. He's a silent guardian, watchful protector against corruption, he's our Dark Knight.[58]

In his article untangling the intersections of race, gender, authority, and state power, Chauncy DeVega suggests that Dorner may serve as a 'symbol that speaks to our collective subconscious' and part of our 'American

54 Associated Press, '2 Women Get $40,000 Compensation for Pickup Truck Shot up by LAPD Officers during Dorner Hunt' (*Fox News*, 14 March 2013) <www.foxnews.com/us/2013/03/14/2-women-get-40000-compensation-for-pickup-truck-shot-up-by-lapd-officers-during/> accessed 27 January 2014.

55 R Broderick, 'How Chris Dorner's Manhunt Became A Meme' (*Buzzfeed*, 13 February 2013) <www.buzzfeed.com/ryanhatesthis/how-chris-dorners-manhunt-became-a-meme> accessed 27 January 2014; D Romero, 'Christopher Dorner Memes Hit The Internet (PHOTOS)' (*LA Weekly*, 8 February 2013) <http://blogs.laweekly.com/informer/2013/02/christopher_dorner_memes_internet_photos.php> accessed 27 January 2014.

56 Post on 'I Support' (n 46).

57 A Abad-Santos, 'Are Spy Drones Being Used to Find Fugitive Christopher Dorner?' (*The Wire*, 11 February 2013) <www.thewire.com/national/2013/02/are-we-using-drones-find-ex-cop-christopher-dorner/61987/> accessed 20 November 2013.

58 K Miles, 'Christopher Dorner Fans on Facebook, Twitter Call Alleged Cop Killer a "Hero," Citing Police Brutality' (*Huffington Post*, 8 February 2013) <www.huffingtonpost.com/2013/02/08/christopher-dorner-fans-facebook-twitter_n_2647754.html> accessed 30 September 2013.

cultural mythos'.[59] We too suggest that the Dorner case speaks to our collective subconscious so readily because it relates so strongly to violent narratives and images that circulate in popular culture, including comic books. These narratives and images contribute to larger cultural scripts that function as a basis for symbolic action and responses to vigilante justice.

Discussion

In our previous research, we found that comic book readers are very invested in how the path to justice plays out. Part of the enjoyment of reading, a rather solitary endeavour, is to engage with fellow readers about the impact of the storylines, the trajectory of the heroes' path, and the consequences of their actions. The act of reading becomes social, whether through in-person communication at comic book stores or through online communication, and the moral messages resonate throughout our collective consciousness. In fact, the most talked about narratives in mainstream comic books feature the heroes' path to justice and the ethical boundaries that are breached. Rather than setting out to find a consensus among readers as to the 'right' or 'correct' path to justice, we are more interested how these narratives and images circulate and inform perceptions of justice in the real world and feedback into popular culture representations of justice as moral messages.

The heightened media attention given to Dorner's case, as well as the release of fictional material such as *Red Team*, are continuing evidence of our cultural fascination with vigilante justice in both popular culture and mass media. As with the Dorner case, it is often through popularised narratives that people engage in and process the realities of vigilante violence and the consequences of victimisation.

Further, the transgressive nature of consuming punitive narratives – whether comic books, the Dorner saga, or something similar – is not without its moral conundrums. We have previously argued that the sensationalist crime drama in comic books acts as a kind of virtual transgression in which readers can experience the world in a more ideologically punitive and violent way than perhaps they would in everyday life.[60] Whereas Dorner supporters are unlikely to ever embark on a vengeful killing spree, they can imagine themselves as overt vigilantes – due process be damned – as they cheer him on. Such cheering also serves as a deviance of distinction while mainstream news outlets, through displaying the spectacle, are busy performing moral outrage. Similarly, the first three issues of *Red Team* found fans delighting in the fantasy of swift and justified (in the eyes of

59 C DeVega, 'How Do We Interpret Christopher Dorner?' (*alternet.org*, 11 February 2013) <www.alternet.org/speakeasy/chaunceydevega/how-do-we-interpret-christopher-dorner> accessed 13 February 2013.
60 Phillips and Strobl (n 2).

the characters) extra-legal justice, but subsequent issues show the team confronted with the impossibility of the perfect system of vigilantism they thought they created. When a team member spontaneously kills a man threatening to sexually assault a young woman, the necessary cover-up operations are less than ideal given the unplanned nature of the kill. And, when an investigation into another potential target leads the team to witness a horrifying criminal massacre, they balk at calling for help because they would be unable to satisfactorily explain having witnessed the violence first hand. Ultimately, one team member surmises that despite their noble intentions, Red Team 'has been a criminal conspiracy from the beginning'.[61]

In these deathworthiness narratives, the due process and crime control dichotomy is less of a choice than a paradox – they are opposites that are fated to coexist in a democratic society. Although American vigilante narratives have long played with the thrill of a clear-headed and capable hero or group of heroes who can control crime without the fetters of due process, in the narratives we analysed here, the limitations of human capabilities – to control every circumstance or to know every relevant factor – undermines the path to justice. Further, vigilantism is lonely and alienating: Green Arrow loses many friends and the trust of the Justice League in the events of *Cry for Justice*, while Dorner, holed up in a mountain cabin for days, his company, a silencer-equipped Remington sniper rifle with the word VENGEANCE written on it, dies at his own hand. In the end, part of the transgressive thrill could be the unravelling of the transgression itself, the ensuing moral warning, and the return to the notion that due process may indeed have its benefits.

Case

Gregg v Georgia (1976) 428 152 (US Supreme Court)

Bibliography

Abad-Santos A, 'Are Spy Drones Being Used to Find Fugitive Christopher Dorner?' (*The Wire*, 11 February 2013) <www.thewire.com/national/2013/02/are-we-using-drones-find-ex-cop-christopher-dorner/61987/> accessed 20 November 2013.

Abram S, 'Christopher Dorner's Manifesto Reveals an Unraveled Mind, Experts Say' (*Daily News*, 6 February 2013) <www.dailynews.com/20130207/christopher-dorners-manifesto-reveals-an-unraveled-mind-experts-say> accessed 5 October 2013.

61 Ennis G and Cermak C, *Garth Ennis' Red Team #6* (Dynamite Entertainment 2013).

Allen N, 'Christopher Dorner "Killed in Cabin Blaze"' (*The Telegraph*, 13 February 2013) <www.telegraph.co.uk/news/worldnews/northamerica/usa/9866733/Christopher-Dorner-killed-in-cabin-blaze.html> accessed 30 September 2013.

Associated Press, '2 Women Get $40,000 Compensation for Pickup Truck Shot up by LAPD Officers during Dorner Hunt' (*Fox News*, 14 March 2013) <www.foxnews.com/us/2013/03/14/2-women-get-40000-compensation-for-pickup-truck-shot-up-by-lapd-officers-during/> accessed 27 January 2014.

Bedau HA and Cassell PG, *Debating the Death Penalty: Should America Have Capital Punishment? The Experts on Both Sides Make Their Best Case* (Oxford University Press 2004).

Bernstein S and others, 'Timeline: Revenge Plot Events' (*NBC Southern California*, 16 February 2013) <www.nbclosangeles.com/news/local/Timeline-Ex-LAPD-Officer-Suspected-in-Shooting-Spree-Had-Sued-The-Department-190206031.html> accessed 30 September 2013.

Broderick R, 'How Chris Dorner's Manhunt Became A Meme' (*Buzzfeed*, 13 February 2013) <www.buzzfeed.com/ryanhatesthis/how-chris-dorners-manhunt-became-a-meme> accessed 27 January 2014.

Burton C and Tewksbury R, 'How Families of Murder Victims Feel Following the Execution of Their Loved One's Murderer: A Content Analysis of Newspaper Reports of Executions from 2006 - 2011' (2013) 1 *Journal of Qualitative Criminal Justice and Criminology* 53.

Crank JP and Caldero MA, *Police Ethics: The Corruption of Noble Cause* (3rd edn, Elsevier 2010).

Crocker PL, 'Concepts of Culpability and Deathworthiness: Differentiating between Guilt and Punishment in Death Penalty Cases' (1997) 66 *Fordham Law Review* 21.

'Death Penalty | Gallup Historical Trends' <www.gallup.com/poll/1606/death-penalty.aspx> accessed 10 January 2014.

DeVega C, 'How Do We Interpret Christopher Dorner?' (*alternet.org*, 11 February 2013) <www.alternet.org/speakeasy/chaunceydevega/how-do-we-interpret-christopher-dorner> accessed 13 February 2013.

Eckholm E, 'In Death Penalty's Steady Decline, Some Experts See a Societal Shift' (*NY Times*, 19 December 2013) <www.nytimes.com/2013/12/19/us/in-death-penaltys-steady-decline-some-experts-see-a-societal-shift.html?_r=0> accessed 10 January 2014.

Ennis G and Cermak C, *Garth Ennis' Red Team #2* (Dynamite Entertainment 2013).

Ennis G and Cermak C, *Garth Ennis' Red Team #3* (Dynamite Entertainment 2013).

Ennis G and Cermak C, *Garth Ennis' Red Team #6* (Dynamite Entertainment 2013).

Epstein J, 'Death-Worthiness and Prosecutorial Discretion in Capital Case Charging' (2009) 19 *Temple Political and Civil Rights Law Review* 389.

Garland D, *Peculiar Institution: America's Death Penalty in an Age of Abolition* (Belknap Press 2010).

Giddens T, 'Criminal Responsibility and the Living Self' (2013) *Criminal Law and Philosophy* (DOI: 10.1007/s11572 - 013 - 9212 - 2), <http://link.springer.com/article/10.1007/s11572 - 013 - 9212 - 2>.

'I Support Christopher Jordan Dorner' (*Facebook*) <www.facebook.com/IsupportCJD> accessed 20 November 2013.

Kane RJ and White MD, *Jammed Up: Bad Cops, Police Misconduct, and the New York City Police Department* (NYU Press 2012).

KTLA, 'Christopher Dorner's Manifesto (Disturbing Content and Language)' (*KTLA* 5, 12 February 2013) <http://ktla.com/2013/02/12/read-christopher-dorners-so-called-manifesto/> accessed 30 September 2013.

Marquez M, 'San Bernardino County Sheriff: "This Investigation is Over"' (*CNN*, 14 February 2013) <www.cnn.com/2013/02/13/us/lapd-manhunt/index.html> accessed 30 September 2013.

Marston G, 'Best Shots Extra: JL: Cry For Justice #7' (*Newsarama*, 3 March 2010) <www.newsarama.com/4834-best-shots-extra-jl-cry-for-justice-7-spoilers-w-poll.html> accessed 20 November 2013.

Miles K, 'Christopher Dorner Fans on Facebook, Twitter Call Alleged Cop Killer a "Hero," Citing Police Brutality' (*Huffington Post*, 8 February 2013) <www.huffingtonpost.com/2013/02/08/christopher-dorner-fans-facebook-twitter_n_2647754.html> accessed 30 September 2013.

Morrison G and others, *Final Crisis* (DC Comics 2009).

Mozzocco C, 'Some Questions I Have about Justice League: Cry for Justice' (*Every Day Is Like Wednesday*, 4 March 2010) <http://everydayislikewednesday.blogspot.com/2010/03/some-questions-i-have-about-justice.html> accessed 20 November 2013.

Musil S, 'Fan Pages Pop up on Facebook to Support Fugitive Ex-LAPD Cop' (*CNET*, 8 February 2013) <http://news.cnet.com/8301 - 1023_3 - 57568311 - 93/fan-pages-pop-up-on-facebook-to-support-fugitive-ex-lapd-cop/> accessed 14 January 2014.

Natali L, 'A Reply to Jules Epstein: Is There an Objective Way to Define the Worst of the Worst' (2009) 19 *Temple Political and Civil Rights Law Review* 421.

Packer H, *The Limits of the Criminal Sanction* (Stanford University Press 1968).

Phegley K, 'Garth Ennis Details His "Red Team"' (*Comic Book Resources*, 11 February 2013) <www.comicbookresources.com/?page=article&id=43697> accessed 21 October 2013.

Phillips ND and Strobl S, *Comic Book Crime: Truth, Justice, and the American Way* (NYU Press 2013).

Robinson JD and others, *Justice League: Cry for Justice #1* (DC Comics 2010).

Robinson JD and others, *Justice League: Cry for Justice #4* (DC Comics 2010).

Robinson JD and others, *Justice League: Cry for Justice #5* (DC Comics 2010).

Robinson JD and others, *Justice League: Cry for Justice #6* (DC Comics 2010).

Romero D, 'Christopher Dorner Memes Hit The Internet (PHOTOS)' (*LA Weekly*, 8 February 2013) <http://blogs.laweekly.com/informer/2013/02/christopher_dorner_memes_internet_photos.php> accessed 27 January 2014.

Rucka G, Morales R and Bair M, *Wonder Woman #219* (DC Comics 2005).

'States With and Without the Death Penalty' <www.deathpenaltyinfo.org/states-and-without-death-penalty> accessed 10 January 2014.

'Time on Death Row' <www.deathpenaltyinfo.org/time-death-row> accessed 1 September 2013.

Uzumeri D, 'David Loses His Shit on Justice League: Cry For Justice #7' (*The Savage Critics*, 3 March 2010) <www.savagecritic.com/reviews/david-loses-his-shit-on-justice-league-cry-for-justice-7/> accessed 20 November 2013.

Vollum S, *Last Words and the Death Penalty: Voices of the Condemned and Their Co-Victims* (LFB Scholarly Publishing 2010).

'We Are All Christopher Dorner' (*Facebook*) <www.facebook.com/WeAreAllChrisDorner> accessed 13 February 2013.

Young J, 'Constructing the Paradigm of Violence: Mass Media, Violence and Youth' (2003) <www.ukobservatory.com/downloadfiles/ParadigmofViolence.pdf> accessed 20 November 2013.

Chapter 8

Extreme restorative justice: the politics of vigilantism in Vertigo's *100 Bullets*

Angus Nurse

DC Comics' Vertigo title *100 Bullets*[1] provides a narrative concerning flaws inherent in contemporary crime control. Justice is the preserve of the wealthy, traditional notions of law and order are shown to be inadequate to deal with crimes of the powerful, and corruption is endemic to criminal justice systems. Retribution and restoration are central concepts in its visualisation of broken criminal justice, in perpetual conflict between the needs of victims and the desires of the powerful. It also depicts the nature of, and extreme measures needed to address, widespread corruption, social control failures and persistent violent crime. Its core protagonists are those who have suffered from a flawed justice system and the actions of powerful actors exerting corrupting influence over criminal justice. *100 Bullets*'s narrative thus functions as a critique of systemic inadequacy in contemporary crime control policy. In particular, it discusses the failure of institutionalised western justice to treat *all* citizens as equal and the inherent unfairness of justice strategies subjugated by political ideologies and Foucauldian power as governance.[2] Criminal justice in *100 Bullets* is cold, impersonal and subjugating, prioritising harsh crime control techniques and aggressive policing tactics over the interests of justice as a tool for uncovering truth and protecting the innocent. The narrative is one of hopelessness, systemic failure and the need for rethinking both theoretical and practical criminal justice priorities to reduce corruption and achieve effective justice. In this respect, *100 Bullets* presents law and order, socially constructed by capitalist society, as inefficient, disproportionately favouring the wealthy, and upholding conventional middle class values.

This chapter conceptualises a notion of *extreme restorative justice*, using the term to reflect the conflict between revenge and restoration in *100 Bullets*'s

1 Azzarello and Risso's *100 Bullets* ran for 100 issues between August 1999 and April 2009 and is collected in 13 trade paperbacks published between 2000 and 2009. As a Vertigo title it was intended for a mature audience.

2 See HL Dreyfus and P Rabinow, *Michel Foucault: Beyond Structuralism and Hermeneutic* (University of Chicago Press 1982).

core justice narrative. Braithwaite argues for 'reintegrative shaming' (disapproval of the crime act within a continuum of respect for the offender) as a means of preventing crime through forgiveness.[3] The term *extreme restorative justice* is demarcated from traditional restorative justice by *100 Bullets*'s focus on victim-offender discourse on the impact of crime and victims' sense of closure as confrontation rather than forgiveness-centred dialogue. Braithwaite identifies restorative conferences as a means through which offender and victim discuss the consequences of a crime and draw out the feelings of those who have been harmed.[4] But in accordance with Foucault's conception that power exists only when it is put into action, one aspect of restorative justice is to give power back to the victim.[5] This approach is central to *100 Bullets*'s exploration of victims' closure and addressing the harmful impact of crime through victim-offender interaction. Accordingly, it represents a *form* of restorative justice, albeit an extreme representation akin to vigilantism, consistent with *100 Bullets*'s normative violent world. While retribution is sometimes the means through which victims restore their harm, this is not always the case and this chapter identifies that victim-offender discussion and mediation significantly influence the outcome and decisions made by victims concerning restoration versus retribution.

This chapter argues that *100 Bullets*, like the best contemporary crime fiction, raises valid concerns about social problems. It does so via its representation of lawlessness, corruption, the failures of criminal justice and inadequacies of law and order agencies, vigilantism and the use of ultimate force to reassert the power of the state and societal values. *100 Bullets* tackles these issues directly, both in its core narratives of revenge and punishment and sub-plots about the consequences of violent force used by law enforcement officers and the public. In doing so, it discusses the conflicting merits of tolerance and force as a last resort over proactive preventative policing. While the use of deadly force is frequently presented as a potential solution to crime problems, *100 Bullets* also discusses the need for anti-corruption monitoring of crime and justice agencies and the potential conflict between revenge and restoration as the ends of justice. First outlining the comics' basic set-up, this chapter then outlines how genre conventions influence *100 Bullets*'s narratives, examining the nature of inner-city criminal justice failures within its law and order context and the series's allegorical intentions. Second, it argues that the concept of a specific notion of law and order is embodied in central protagonist, Agent

3 J Braithwaite, *Restorative Justice: Theories and Worries* (United Nations Asia and Far East Institute For the Prevention of Crime and the Treatment of Offenders 2004).
4 Ibid 1.
5 Dreyfus and Rabinow (n 2).

Graves, as his character attempts to fight perceived social and personal injustice and adapts to suit the changing social context.

This chapter also examines representations of *extreme* restorative justice and vigilantism within *100 Bullets*. It argues *100 Bullets*'s adherence to genre fiction conventions examines social anxiety about crime while simultaneously exploring complex questions about lethal force within criminal justice. In doing so, the chapter examines the roles of both victim and offender as active participants in a justice system which often marginalises them. The chapter then discusses how *100 Bullets*'s narrative subtly shifts in its depiction of widespread lawlessness to integrate a corruption and conspiracy narrative alongside its basic vigilante, restoration and revenge narratives. This serves both as allegory for increased lawlessness in contemporary society and of unequal responses to individualistic and corporate crime. The series also critiques reactive liberal law enforcement via *100 Bullets*'s conclusion that a reactive non-confrontational crime control approach has proved inadequate against contemporary mass lawlessness, endemic corruption and the marginalisation of minorities within criminal justice. Given this failure to either punish offenders or provide 'pure' restoration for victims a more aggressive partial or extreme restorative law enforcement response is required for contemporary crime problems.

The set-up: a case to die for

> Inside this attaché case is irrefutable evidence that what I'm telling you is true. Also in the attaché are a gun and 100 rounds of ammunition. All untraceable, all yours. Do with it as you see fit. If you act on this information you will have carte blanche.[6]

100 Bullets poses a seemingly simple question, 'What would you do if you were given a simple gift – an untraceable gun, a hundred rounds of ammunition and a chance to forcibly confront the individual who has wronged you with the consequences of their (often criminal) actions?'.

The obvious question is whether the convinced 'victim' will turn vigilante (and pull the trigger). However, *100 Bullets* also explicitly discusses more complex questions of morality, regarding: criminal justice failures; retribution versus restoration; and corporate power abuses where wealthy offenders remain unpunished. Discussion of the implied racism, subjugation and marginalisation of working classes inherent in criminal justice also permeates the narrative. Several of those offered the attaché case are from ethnic minorities (Latino, African American); almost all would fall within the

6 B Azzarello and E Risso, *First Shot, Last Call* (DC Comics 2000) 14.

socio-economic definition of 'working' or 'lower' class according to common (western) stratum models designating blue-collar workers, the working poor and the unemployed as 'working class'.[7]

First Shot, Last Call,[8] the opening collection of the series, introduces readers to Dizzy Cordova, a young Latino girl and former gang banger whose husband and son are killed while she is in jail. Dizzy is first shown with a gun to her head while off panel a character asks, 'what's it feel like to be a ghost, Dizzy?'.[9] In a recent flashback, readers see Dizzy's release from prison and her meeting with 'Agent' Graves on the bus ride home. Before offering the attaché case, Graves discusses Dizzy's criminal career, which began with her first arrest aged 11 for shoplifting, continued with a four-year engagement with the juvenile justice system for gang-related activity, and culminated in a 15-year prison sentence for her involvement in a shooting. The narrative thus identifies Dizzy, protagonist in the initial story and integral part of the ongoing narrative, as resident and complicit in an environment where violent crime is normalised. In response to Graves showing her a photograph of the men he claims killed her husband and child, Dizzy counters that the killing was orchestrated by rival gang the Vice Lords 'as payback for what I'd done'.[10] Graves, however, asserts that the killers were crooked cops – a fact shortly confirmed when the two officers subject Dizzy to a potentially illegal search on the street. However, on finding Graves's gun on Dizzy, the two detectives are officially informed that Dizzy has a 'free pass' to carry the gun despite its possession violating her parole. Thus, Graves's offer is confirmed as legitimate and both readers and Dizzy are informed of official sanction for the gun and 100 bullets, the implication being that Graves represents some covert governmental agency.

In one sense *100 Bullets*'s set-up is a traditional 'maverick' cop narrative; Agent Graves, a lone law enforcement officer fed up with the confines/unfairness of the system, seeks to right its flaws by dispensing summary justice. So far, so *Dirty Harry*. Yet across *100 Bullets*'s sprawling narrative, Graves visits a number of individuals making the same offer. Some accept and use the gun and bullets others do not, with variable consequences. The set-up belies *100 Bullets*'s larger social narrative, which incorporates a sprawling conspiracy theory discourse on corporate power and its corrupting influence on the lives of ordinary citizens. A duality exists in the set-up. First, Graves seeks to address a particular crime's impact on

7 EO Wright, *Class Counts: Comparative Studies in Class Analysis* (Cambridge University Press 1997); WL Warner, K Eells and M Meeker, *Social Class in America: A Manual of Procedure for the Measurement of Social Status* (Science Research Associates 1949).
8 Azzarello and Risso (n 6).
9 Azzarello and Risso (n 6) 5.
10 Azzarello and Risso (n 6) 13.

an individual, many of whom have been set-up either to inadvertently commit crimes which have significantly altered their lives or who have unknowingly been the victim of crimes. Second, Graves seeks to enforce his own moral code in order to address both a wider social problem and a personal betrayal.

Crime and the city: graphic noir

100 Bullets's core concepts are revenge, its consequences and the subjugation of the lower classes by an unfair justice system. Crime in *100 Bullets*, as is often the case in contemporary society,[11] disproportionately affects the poor and ethnic minorities who are also routinely viewed as criminals by law enforcement agencies and over-represented in prison populations. Sveinsson for example notes that 'in England and Wales, black people are stopped and searched at seven times the rate of white people', and while only 'accounting for 2.2 per cent of the British population, Black people make up 15 per cent of the prison population'.[12] This picture explicitly represented in *100 Bullets*'s narrative and protagonists is widely replicated; suggesting that western criminal justice at best has a perception of criminality as being inherent in ethnic minorities. Thus *100 Bullets* asks whether those marginalised by societal disadvantage would seek their own justice (by way of violent revenge) if given the means, opportunity, and a reasonable chance to succeed. The basic device of having an untraceable gun, a hundred rounds of ammunition and a chance to forcibly confront your abuser, seemingly with no consequences (discussed further below), serves as a means through which societal unfairness and the poor/rich criminal justice divide are explored and debated.

Gómez Romero and Dahlman identify comics as 'utterly gripped by issues of legality, order and justice'.[13] While superhero comics tend to dominate the industry,[14] Matthews suggests that crime comics, situated within a realistic universe, are becoming the 'hip and edgy alternative in the universe of mainstream American comics'[15] with titles such as *Road to Perdition*, *A History of Violence*, *Criminal*, *Gotham Central* and *The DMZ*

11 JQ Wilson, *Thinking about Crime* (2nd edn, Vintage Books 1985).

12 KP Sveinsson, 'Introduction' in KP Sveinsson (ed), *Criminal Justice v Racial Justice: Minority Ethnic Overrepresentation in the Criminal Justice System* (Runnymede Trust 2012) 3.

13 L Gómez Romero and I Dahlman, 'Justice Framed: Law in Comics and Graphic Novels' (2012) 16 *Law Text Culture* 3.

14 M Putsz, *Comic Books and American Cultural History: An Anthology* (Bloomsbury Academic 2012).

15 K Matthews, '100 Bullets' (*Popmatters*, 31 December 1994) <www.popmatters.com/review/100-bullets/> accessed 24 January 2014.

all enjoying successful runs in the 1990s and 2000s. Such comics' success is explained by the manner in which comics' formal and narrative structures 'tap into the interacting and multiple ways in which we are able to "make sense" of the world and the people, including ourselves, who inhabit it'.[16] Crime is a perennial societal concern, dominating the mainstream news media and significantly impacting on the lives of the young males who consume comics and who are disproportionately victims and perpetrators of violent crime.[17] As a visual medium - employing literary techniques of metaphor, allegory and use of phonetic language[18] - comics are able to explore certain issues of violence, corruption and inequality in ways problematic to other media forms. Young, in discussing how crime images are portrayed in cinema, identifies violence as a cinematic staple frequently presented via the normative view that 'the violence of wrong-doing is wrong, whereas the violence which responds to wrong-doing is *righteous*'.[19] Cinematic crime images are manipulated to ensure that viewers identify with a (mostly) sympathetic protagonist and images recognisably part of their world. Thus, societal norms such as middle-class affluence, adherence to social rules and the validity of law and order systems and their actors are integral aspects of fictional cinematic and television crime storytelling, even exaggerated narratives within the action and crime film genres. Banks and Wein, however, identify that comic books (as fantasy-based literature) 'are a safe and easy place for readers to explore parts of themselves and their sense of spiritualism and search from transcendence, and to examine and experiment with issues that worry or fascinate them'.[20] In this respect, crime comics provide a means through which stories and characters rarely explored in mainstream visual entertainment can be discussed. In particular, issues including persistent failures in criminal justice, the conflict inherent in law and order systems, the endemic corruption of many social structures and the relentless nature of crime problems lend themselves to comics' visual storytelling. The serial nature of comics (usually published monthly and capable of exploiting the medium's juxtaposition of words and pictures to develop a social commentary

16 T Giddens, 'Comics, Law, and Aesthetics: Towards the Use of Graphic Fiction in Legal Studies' (2012) 6 *Law and Humanities* 85, 104.

17 S McCready, K Harland and K Beattie, *Violent Victims? Young Men as Perpetrators and Victims of Violent Crime* (Centre for Young Men's Studies 2006) <www.ulster.ac.uk/sass/files/2014/09/cyms_ru1.pdf> accessed 20 January 2014.

18 H Miodrag 'Narrative, Language, and Comics-as-Literature' (2012) 2 *Studies in Comics* 263.

19 A Young, *The Scene of Violence* (Routledge 2010) 24.

20 AC Banks and EE Wein, 'Folklore and the Comic Book: The Traditional Meets the Popular' (1998) 2 *New Directions in Folklore* <</Date1>http://astro.temple.edu/~camille/comics1.html> accessed 18 August 2013.

on crime over a period of time) also allows for exploration of complex ongoing narratives. Crime comics, historically rooted in mythic themes and situated within a medium dominated by fantastical events, represent a form of escapism unburdened by mass-audience viewer identification needs. Compared with cinema or ratings-dependent serialised television they are also less constricted by the need to entice the casual viewer.

100 Bullets is *graphic noir*, adapting the tropes of crime noir, a distinct genre concerned with ill-fated relationships and themes of alienation and entrapment,[21] to the graphic fiction format. Savage defined *100 Bullets*'s visual noir style as:

> a world of dingy bars and glittering casinos, both lit with omnipresent neon refracted by smoke; street corner drug deals and cross-border smuggling; lowlifes and high rollers both living on the edge and hence living life all the way.[22]

Thus familiar noir genre conventions - femmes fatales, crooked cops, shady private eyes, revenge and retribution and a broken dysfunctional criminal justice system - are all present within *100 Bullets*'s narrative. Punishment-based ideology dominates criminal justice with reparation, restoration and rehabilitation lesser considerations. However, *100 Bullets* combines these issues with discussions of vigilantism, inequality, racism and crimes of the powerful. In particular it shows criminal justice as rooted in ideologies which favour the wealthy and maintenance of existing justice systems which are manifestly unfair.

Moore identifies globalisation, increases in media coverage and wider technology use, as altering our perceptions of ourselves and the society surrounding us so that 'we make different demands upon the art and culture that is meant to reflect the constantly shifting landscape we find ourselves in'.[23] Thus Matozzi identifies that comics have passed through both golden and silver ages where superheroes have been 'transformed, cancelled, revived, killed, deconstructed, reconstructed, revisited' so that contemporary notions of comic fiction differ from those of previous eras.[24]

21 L Horsley, 'The Development of Post-War Literary and Cinematic Noir' (*Crimeculture*, 2002) <http://crimeculture.com/Contents/Film%20Noir.html> accessed 10 January 2014; K Grant (ed), *Film Genre Reader II* (University of Texas Press 1995).

22 B Savage, 'Foreword' in B Azzarello and E Risso, *A Foregone Tomorrow* (DC Comics 2002) 7.

23 A Moore, 'The Mark of the Batman' in F Miller, *Batman: The Dark Knight Returns* (DC Comics 1986).

24 A Mattozzi, 'Innovating Superheroes' (2003) 3(2) *Reconstruction* <http://reconstruction.eserver.org/issues/032/mottazzi.htm> accessed 3 September 2013.

Moore argues changing social perceptions require new themes, new insights and new dramatic situations, which in the comics field resulted in demand for new heroes and new storytelling paradigms aimed at mature audiences ready for more challenging material.[25] Graphic noir is a logical consequence of this societal need to explore more realistic darker law and order themes including racism and social deprivation as both cause and consequence of crime. *100 Bullets* achieves this by presenting an inner-city crime story exploring America's law and order failures. In subverting restorative and retributive discourse it explores the impact of policy failures on a distinct form of underclass: ethnically diverse, drug using, violent and at best engaged in a grey if not black economy. Inherent in its narrative is the implication that this underclass, denied access to the American Dream, must take its own action to redress a capitalist conspiracy that has led to an unequal distribution of wealth and resources. Whether such action should consist of simple revenge or a form of extreme restoration is the dilemma posed by *100 Bullets*.

Restoration, retribution or revenge: expanding the narrative

The second story in *First Shot, Last Call* revolves around Lee Dolan, a man whose promising restaurateur career was ruined by the FBI finding child pornography images on his computer. Before handing him the attaché case Graves reminds Lee, '[you were] labeled a pedophile, your wife divorced you, your kids were terrified of you . . . your business went belly up and you went bankrupt'.[26] When Lee claims he was framed, Graves agrees, showing him a photograph of businesswoman Megan Dietrich, whom Graves claims is responsible for Lee's misfortune. Graves further informs Lee that Dietrich will visit his low class bar workplace later that evening, providing Lee with a revenge opportunity.

While initially sceptical, both Lee and Dizzy eventually accept Graves's evidence as accurate and each act upon it, but with differing consequences. In Dizzy's case, she kills both crooked cops after discovering that her own younger brother Emilio was complicit with the corrupt police in the death of her family. Yet she declines to kill her brother, despite retaining possession of Graves's untraceable gun and bullets, and instead turns him in arguably having already received restoration. When Graves's associate Mr Shepherd tells Dizzy, 'You could have killed him, y'know, you had every right', Dizzy counters Shepherd's assertion that 'you would

25 G Groth, 'The Alan Moore Interview' (2012) 118 *The Comics Journal* <www.tcj.com/the-alan-moore-interview-118/> accessed 5 September 2013.
26 Azzarello and Risso (n 6) 81.

have got away with it' with her own, 'that don' make it right, knowhumsayin?'.[27] By contrast, Lee engineers a meeting with Megan Dietrich, confronts her and threatens her life, seeking further explanation of what happened to him. At gunpoint, Dietrich admits that four years previously she and girlfriends surfing the internet had inadvertently found child pornography images and programmed computers to instantly download the pictures onto sixty nine random males' email accounts. Dietrich neutralises this as a prank; Lee received the photos solely because he was online at the time.[28] She offers him a college fund for his son's medical studies and his own life-changing financial compensation in exchange for her life and Lee's gun and bullets, ostensibly to track down Lee's benefactor (Graves). However, once Lee has accepted Dietrich's pay-off and handed over the gun she kills him having first removed all trace of his existence from computer records.

Lee and Dizzy's contrasting fortunes set-up a key narrative viewpoint explicit in *100 Bullets*'s crime and morality discourse. Extreme sanctions, such as Dizzy's killing of the crooked cops, are justified when serving the interests of justice by punishing the guilty, whereas greed, endemic in the crimes of the powerful exhibited in *100 Bullets*, is shown as undeserving and is itself punished. Police-duty related deaths are a factor of criminal justice and one conception on use of force by peace officers is its perceived necessity when dealing with extreme threats.[29] However, force is only legitimised where it represents exercise of the amount of force necessary to control an incident.[30] Lee's killing of Dietrich, direct architect of his misfortune and rich manipulator unpunished by the justice system, would be conceptualised as justified - legitimate use of lethal force. But his willingness to trade his righteous justice for money ultimately is corrupt in itself and leads directly to his death. Force used for undeserving ends and representing retribution is not traditionally legitimised through criminal justice processes and its use by civilians is rarely sanctioned. The danger of using such force (ie likelihood of death) by *100 Bullets*'s vigilante protagonists reflects this issue of legitimisation.

A secondary consideration explicitly made clear in *100 Bullets*'s narrative is that of crime as a product of rational choice; that is, individuals actively weighing up the likely consequences and rewards of crime, a notion that

27 Azzarello and Risso (n 6) 72.
28 Azzarello and Risso (n 6) 107–12.
29 S Kent (2010) 'Killings of Police in US Cities since 1980: An Examination of Environmental and Political Explanations' 14 *Homicide Studies* 3.
30 GP Alpert and RG Dunham, *Understanding Police Use of Force: Officers, Suspects, and Reciprocity* (Cambridge University Press 2004).

lies at the heart of much western crime control policies.[31] Integral to Graves's offer is not just the moral conundrum of taking another life but the question of whether individuals secure in the knowledge of no consequences are more likely to act on the information provided and whether they will do so via retribution or restoration. Criminological control theory suggests that rather than conformity and law-abiding being the norm, nonconformity such as crime and deviance 'is to be expected when social controls are less than completely effective'.[32] Vold and Bernard's argument is that left to their own devices; individuals gravitate towards behaviour that carries personal benefit even where this might subvert behavioural norms and be unlawful.[33] Thus criminological theory dictates that effective social control is essential to ensure adherence to societal or social environment norms.

In the conflict-laden environment of *100 Bullets*, revenge may be a simple, logical choice, but whether such revenge brings closure or restoration is problematic to assess. Several individuals decline Graves's offer while others achieve restoration without killing, the confrontation with their 'abuser' itself achieving closure. But by ensuring that existing social controls such as investigation, prosecution and punishment are nullified, Graves creates conditions in which the revenge murder is an almost inevitable consequence and is presented as a justified response to the harm caused by crimes of the powerful.

What kind of vigilante? Agent Graves and the Minutemen

100 Bullets is expressly concerned with vigilantism as a solution to crime but also as a form of restoration, reflecting social concern about the failure of liberal law enforcement to resolve crime's harmful effects on citizens. Conventional cinematic vigilante narratives frequently depict law enforcement professionals attempting to apprehend a lone vigilante seen as a threat to the justice system and the wider public. These narratives usually present a 'cultured' victim who has suffered from extreme violence – usually the death or suffering of a loved one – and who has been failed by

31 R Clarke and D Cornish, 'Rational Choice' in R Paternoster and R Bachman (eds), *Explaining Crime and Criminals: Essays in Contemporary Criminological Theory* (Roxbury 2001).

32 JR Lilly, FT Cullen and RA Ball, *Criminological Theory: Context and Consequences* (Sage 1995) 75.

33 G Vold and T Bernard, *Theoretical Criminology* (3rd edn, Oxford University Press 1986) 231.

the justice system.[34] In film and television such narratives typically commence with establishing shots which show the normal world that will later be threatened, typical examples include:

- showing the world of culture and sophistication;
- showing a level of domestic bliss or normality; or
- establishing the normality of law and order, often by showing law enforcement professionals correctly and courteously carrying out their job.[35]

100 Bullets subverts these genre conventions by instead contextualising the 'normal' world of crime and violence inhabited by its lower-class participants as a direct adverse consequence of dominant social values. Notions of vigilantism are socially constructed and potentially become obsolete or flawed where societal norms inhibit the pursuit of a normal life. Thus cinematic vigilante narratives use establishing scenes to presage the showing of a more deviant, brutal crime that confirms the extraordinary nature of threats facing society or the randomness of violence, raising questions about the adequacy of 'normal' policing. But *100 Bullets* shows how crime and the criminal justice system itself perverts the lives of its protagonists, requiring citizens to consider extreme restorative justice to redress ineffective criminal justice.

Lee Dolan's murder and Dietrich's retrieval of his gun and attaché sets off the wider narrative revealing Graves as part of a larger conspiracy plot involving crime syndicate the Trust. Despite his name not being mentioned by Lee, Dietrich (a member of the Trust) identifies Graves as the attaché's custodian. Graves is subsequently revealed not to be a government agency employee but instead the leader of the Minutemen, the Trust's enforcers who were disbanded after Graves refused to commit a crime which would have expanded the Trust's power and influence. Graves's refusal led the Trust to attempt killing both him and the Minutemen; but they survived, retaliating by assassinating a hooded figure in Atlantic City.[36] Subsequently the Minutemen's memories were wiped and they returned to normal lives for their own protection.[37] Six of those offered attaché cases by Graves are later revealed as Minutemen active four years earlier in the events of Atlantic City, two more (Dizzy Cordova and the young African-American Loop Hughes) are being trained as new Minutemen,

34 A Nurse, 'Decoding the Dark Passenger: The Serial Killer as a Force for Justice' in J Silbey and P Robson (eds), *Law and Justice on the Small Screen* (Hart 2012).
35 Ibid.
36 B Azzarello and E Risso, *The Hard Way* (DC Comics 2005).
37 B Azzarello and E Risso, *Strychnine Lives* (DC Comics 2006).

and many of the others have suffered at the hands of the Trust and its associates.[38]

In this context, Graves is not only a vigilante himself, but also facilitator of others' vigilante actions. By reactivating the Minutemen and recruiting new ones, Graves explicitly challenges the established order of corporate power and control over justice and retribution as a preserve of the wealthy, while also identifying the need for individuals to aggressively participate in their own justice system. Outside the wealthy elite, *100 Bullets*'s participants are outsiders or peripheral to a justice system viewed as serving middle class capitalist interests. Thus the young black and Latino street hustlers refer to themselves as 'Gangstas', while the young mothers prevalent in the inner-city society refer to themselves as 'OG' (Old Girls), denoting the manner in which society destroys their life chances and youth by age 25.[39] Young males identify with their perception as criminals by a capitalistic system denying them legitimate opportunity and creating the strains that leave crime as their only option.[40] Violence, gun ownership and gun use are an accepted part of life, self-image and opportunity for advancement. Thus personal vengeance is seen as justified, a means of restoration, and is legitimised both by Graves who provides evidence of corruption, criminal conspiracy, and the corrosive role of outside forces, including the system itself, in directly impacting on an individual's life chances. Corporate forces nullify a system that fails to consider the individual and the human consequences of a corrupt notion of justice. Graves, well dressed, white and seemingly cultured, is regularly mistaken for a senior establishment law enforcement officer and a part of the system he wishes to bring down.[41] In one sense Graves can be seen as the embodiment of the white majority system bringing the hope of justice to the marginalised ethnic community. In another sense Graves is the ultimate vigilante, using the tools at his disposal to pursue his own notion of justice irrespective of the personal consequences of his actions for those whom he empowers.

Vigilantism in *100 Bullets* is thus collective and individualised, both direct and indirect. *100 Bullets*'s 'collective' notion of vigilantism posits that organised crime, and crimes of the powerful more generally, require an organised response. Thus the crime control tactics of infiltration and surveillance routinely used against organised crime[42] are employed by the

38 Ibid; Azzarello and Risso (n 36).
39 Azzarello and Risso (n 6) 38–48.
40 See RK Merton, *Social Theory and Social Structure* (Free Press 1968).
41 See R Collier, *Masculinities Crime and Criminology* (Sage 1998).
42 M Woodiwiss and D Hobbs. 'Organized Evil and the Atlantic Alliance: Moral Panics and the Rhetoric of Organized Crime Policing in America and Britain' (2009) 49 *British Journal of Criminology* 106.

Minutemen, prioritising the use of force as a tool for effective justice. *100 Bullets*'s depiction of extreme vigilante justice in the form of Agent Graves, Shepherd and the other Minutemen identifies the duality of their actions as both agents of law and order and vigilantes, serving as allegory for the increasing lawlessness of contemporary society and a critique of the failures of liberal law enforcement mechanisms to protect society.

Within *100 Bullets* many of the core characters are unsympathetic but are nonetheless victims for whom Graves provides restoration by addressing individual harm. This individualised notion of vigilantism is one that provides for significant levels of violence, envisaging that this will be needed in seeking retribution or reparation. The gift of 100 bullets (for some a curse) implies either considerable collateral damage or, more likely, a considerable need to engage with a number of armed individuals before eventually encountering the required target (themselves likely to be armed). *100 Bullets*'s vigilante/revenge narrative thus also obliquely critiques a culture of widespread gun ownership and, more importantly, gun use. While the American constitution provides a right to bear arms and to use guns in self-defence, Graves knowingly provides for more than defence and arguably invites restoration through private revenge rather than public reparation: a form of extreme restorative justice.

Extreme restorative justice and *100 Bullets*

The intent behind Graves's offer raises questions about the purpose of criminal justice itself. Criminological and socio-legal commentators are locked in a perennial debate about whether criminal justice and its sanctions are intended to protect the public, punish offenders, provide for retribution or provide for reparation.[43] Much western crime control policy is, in reality, less reliant on prevention than on detection, apprehension and punishment.[44] However, victims of crime often remain without a remedy for their harm, although attempts have been made to incorporate (selected) use of restorative justice aimed at 'reparation' or 'mediation'.[45] Central to 'pure' restorative justice is the principle of direct contact between victim and offender.[46]

43 J Lea and J Young, *What is to be Done about Law and Order?* (Pluto Press 1993). See also section 142(1) of the Criminal Justice Act 2003.

44 J Bright, 'Crime Prevention: The British Experience' in K Stenson and D Cowell (eds), *The Politics of Crime Control* (Sage 1993).

45 The statutory footing for restorative justice in England and Wales is provided by section 142(1)(e) of the Criminal Justice Act 2003.

46 J Braithwaite, *Restorative Justice and Responsive Regulation* (Oxford University Press 2002).

The ideal for effective restorative justice is that offenders are held to account for what they have done and realise the harm that they have caused. In successful restorative justice victims are able to confront offenders, make sense of what has happened and move on with their lives. Successful restorative justice also avoids the escalation of legal justice and its associated costs and delays.[47] Marshall describes such restorative justice as, 'a process whereby all the parties with a stake in a particular offence come together to resolve collectively how to deal with the aftermath of the offence and its implications for the future'.[48] Yet there is no 'absolute' definition of restorative justice and, as in *100 Bullets*, its principles are adapted to suit the circumstances of the crime, culture and jurisdiction where it is employed. Criminological restorative justice discourse often concentrates on the meeting between offender and victim, accordingly public perception of restorative justice idealises this issue: victim-offender meetings which encourage the offender's understanding of impact and consequence of their actions. Llewellyn has argued that 'restorative processes are founded on a conception of justice as fundamentally concerned with restoring relationships'.[49]

100 Bullets presents its own solution to crime problems via *extreme* restorative justice: victim and offender meet, and the offender is forcibly confronted both with the evidence of their actions and clear knowledge of their impact on an individual. The morality of forcing a victim to confront their attacker is not directly addressed by Graves, who simply informs his clients of their choice. The effectiveness of Graves's actions are also only minimally debated, although some who receive his offer are undoubtedly worse off for doing so while for others any closure is at best temporary. In this context, revenge often replaces restoration although the Minutemen arguably go on to find a limited form of closure with the restoration of their memories and the resumption of their crime prevention and order maintenance role. This is arguably strengthened with the addition of Dizzy and Loop.

Hang up on the hang low

100 Bullets identifies western criminal justice as inherently flawed, questioning its purpose, effectiveness and whether its victims are served by traditional justice approaches. While *100 Bullets*'s central question is, 'Would you

47 T Marshall, 'The Evolution of Restorative Justice in Britain' (1996) 4 *European Journal on Criminal Policy and Research* 21.

48 As quoted in Braithwaite (n 46) 11.

49 J Llewellyn, 'Dealing with the Legacy of Native Residential School Abuse in Canada: Litigation, ADR and Restorative Justice' (2002) 52 *University of Toronto Law Journal* 253.

pull the trigger?', doing so is not always a solution. After vengeance has been achieved, what then? By exploring this issue *100 Bullets* provides for an examination of the rhetoric of tough crime control policies which have emerged in western criminal justice policy over the last 20 years or so. In this respect *100 Bullets* reveals a society built on retributive justice, beginning with the rhetoric of 'zero tolerance' (no clemency for even minor offences; getting tough with offenders), which represents a form of authoritative populism.[50] The drive for an increased punitive response to crime and anti-social behaviour continues through to the war on drugs and criminalisation of anti-capitalist protests.[51] By showing the full extent of social deprivation and the brutalising effects of the capitalist inspired criminal justice system, *100 Bullets* essentially asks, 'Should retribution be the goal of criminal justice and how can restoration be achieved?' Retributive policies are popular with some sections of the community who see all crime as simply deviance and contrary to social norms; such policies provide for a simplistic solution to persistent crime problems. Yet given the failures of US death penalty policies to measurably impact on crime levels, it seems unlikely that systematic changes to crimes of the powerful would be achieved by Graves's programme of individualised vigilantism; his collective vigilantism directed at one specific crime consortium seems unlikely to fare much better. At best, personal satisfaction might be gained from individualised action, but our social concerns about criminality may not be allayed by seeing extreme restorative justice via private vigilantism carried out.

In summary, *100 Bullets* examines social anxiety about crime and failures of the justice system. At the same time it offers a critique of western criminal justice as being a system in perpetual conflict.[52] Criminal justice marginalises ethnic minorities and the working class while the wealthy dominant classes and corporations frequently go unpunished or receive sentences disproportionately lenient in respect of their harm causation. One reading of *100 Bullets* is that the justice system is working, continuing irrespective of the impact on or actions of its participants. The system perpetuates, protecting its vested interests, while its successful subversion by vigilantes and the Minutemen is at best only a temporary respite.

Bibliography

Alpert GP and Dunham RG, *Understanding Police Use of Force: Officers, Suspects, and Reciprocity* (Cambridge University Press 2004).

50 S Gilmour and M Punch, 'Zero Tolerance Policing' in A Wakefield and J Fleming (eds), *The Sage Dictionary of Policing* (Sage 2009).

51 T Carter, *The Criminalization of Political Dissent in America* (Global Research 2013).

52 See T Bernard, *The Consensus-Conflict Debate* (Columbia University Press 1983).

Azzarello B and Risso E, *First Shot, Last Call* (DC Comics 2000).
Azzarello B and Risso E, *The Hard Way* (DC Comics 2005).
Azzarello B and Risso E, *Strychnine Lives* (DC Comics 2006).
Banks AC and Wein EE, 'Folklore and the Comic Book: The Traditional Meets the Popular' (1998) 2 *New Directions in Folklore* <http://astro.temple.edu/~camille/comics1.html> accessed 18 August 2013.
Bernard T, *The Consensus-Conflict Debate* (Columbia University Press 1983).
Braithwaite J, *Restorative Justice and Responsive Regulation* (Oxford University Press 2002).
Braithwaite J, *Restorative Justice: Theories and Worries* (United Nations Asia and Far East Institute for the Prevention of Crime and the Treatment of Offenders 2004).
Bright J, 'Crime Prevention: The British Experience' in Stenson K and Cowell D (eds), *The Politics of Crime Control* (Sage 1993).
Carter T, *The Criminalization of Political Dissent in America* (Global Research 2013).
Clarke R and Cornish D, 'Rational Choice' in Paternoster R and Bachman R (eds), *Explaining Crime and Criminals: Essays in Contemporary Criminological Theory* (Roxbury 2001).
Collier R, *Masculinities Crime and Criminology* (Sage 1998).
Dreyfus HL and Rabinow P (eds), *Michel Foucault: Beyond Structuralism and Hermeneutics* (University of Chicago Press 1982).
Giddens T, 'Comics, Law, and Aesthetics: Towards the Use of Graphic Fiction in Legal Studies' (2012) 6 *Law and Humanities* 85.
Gilmour S and Punch M, 'Zero Tolerance Policing' in Wakefield A and Fleming J (eds), *The Sage Dictionary of Policing* (Sage 2009).
Gómez Romero L and Dahlman I, 'Justice Framed: Law in Comics and Graphic Novels' (2012) 16 *Law Text Culture* 3.
Grant K (ed), *Film Genre Reader II* (University of Texas Press 1995).
Groth G, 'The Alan Moore Interview' (2012) 118 *The Comics Journal* <www.tcj.com/the-alan-moore-interview-118/> accessed 5 September 2013.
Horsley L, 'The Development of Post-War Literary and Cinematic Noir' (*Crimeculture*, 2002) <http://crimeculture.com/Contents/Film%20Noir.html> accessed 10 January 2014.
Kent S, 'Killings of Police in US Cities since 1980: An Examination of Environmental and Political Explanations' (2010) 14 *Homicide Studies* 3.
Lea J and Young J, *What is to be Done about Law and Order?* (Pluto Press 1993).
Lilly J, Cullen F and Ball R, *Criminological Theory: Context and Consequences* (Sage 1995).
Llewellyn J, 'Dealing with the Legacy of Native Residential School Abuse in Canada: Litigation, ADR and Restorative Justice' (2002) 52 *University of Toronto Law Journal* 253.
Marshall T, 'The Evolution of Restorative Justice in Britain' (1996) 4 *European Journal on Criminal Policy and Research* 21.
Matthews K, '100 Bullets' (*Popmatters*, 31 December 1994) <www.popmatters.com/review/100-bullets/> accessed 24 January 2014.
Mattozzi A, 'Innovating Superheroes' (2003) 3(2) *Reconstruction* <http://reconstruction.eserver.org/issues/032/mottazzi.htm> accessed 3 September 2013.

McCready S, Harland K and Beattie K, *Violent Victims? Young Men as Perpetrators and Victims of Violent Crime* (Centre for Young Men's Studies 2006) <www.ulster.ac.uk/sass/files/2014/09/cyms_ru1.pdf> accessed 20 January 2014.

Merton R, *Social Theory and Social Structure* (Free Press 1968).

Miodrag H, 'Narrative, Language, and Comics-as-Literature' (2012) 2 *Studies in Comics* 263.

Moore A, 'The Mark of the Batman' in Miller F, *Batman: The Dark Knight Returns* (DC Comics 1986).

Nurse A, 'Decoding the Dark Passenger: The Serial Killer as a Force for Justice' in Silbey J and Robson P (eds), *Law and Justice on the Small Screen* (Hart 2012).

Putsz M, *Comic Books and American Cultural History: An Anthology* (Bloomsbury Academic 2012).

Savage B, 'Foreword' in Azzarello B and Risso, E *A Foregone Tomorrow* (DC Comics 2002).

Sveinsson K, 'Introduction' in Sveinsson KP (ed), *Criminal Justice v Racial Justice: Minority Ethnic Overrepresentation in the Criminal Justice System* (Runnymede Trust 2012).

Vold G and Bernard T, *Theoretical Criminology* (3rd edn, Oxford University Press 1986).

Warner WL, Eells K and Meeker M, *Social Class in America: A Manual of Procedure for the Measurement of Social Status* (Science Research Associates 1949).

Wilson J, *Thinking about Crime* (2nd edn, Vintage Books 1985).

Woodiwiss M and Hobbs D, 'Organized Evil and the Atlantic Alliance: Moral Panics and the Rhetoric of Organized Crime Policing in America and Britain' (2009) 49 *British Journal of Criminology* 106.

Wright EO, *Class Counts: Comparative Studies in Class Analysis* (Cambridge University Press 1997).

Young A, *The Scene of Violence* (Routledge 2010).

Chapter 9

Violent lives, ending violently? Justice, ideology and spectatorship in *Watchmen*

James Petty

What happens, then, when we *shatter* these mirrors?[1]

Introduction

When we consume cultural texts, there is a sense that we are the viewing subject and the image or text the object. This is an illusion in which we imagine ourselves as an active and discerning subject, engaged by choice, and always able to disconnect and move on, whole and unchanged. The illusion of a simple, one-way relation between an active self and an inactive, static text is understandable as we experience a sense of control in what we will and will not watch, read and engage with. On some level, we recognise the complexity of our connection to representations and the effects they can have on us – brand marketing, the power of cinema, the difference between seeing a photograph of a famous painting and seeing it in real life and so on. Yet despite this, we are broadly unwilling to conceptualise the act of looking in terms of participation or investment: the notion of 'just looking', as Alison Young points out, is often utilised as a defence against implications of proximity, investment, genuine engagement or participation, as well as a denial of responsibility.[2] Yet for the reader of comic books, looking is fundamental: to witness a comic's captivating imagery, to follow the narrative text and to thrill in the merging of the two ('KAPOW!'), the reader must *look*.

There are times when we acknowledge the power of representation: the term 'propaganda', for example, is often used as a pejorative, functioning

1 I Thomson, 'Deconstructing the Hero' in J McLaughlin (ed), *Comics as Philosophy* (University Press of Mississippi 2005) 100.
2 A Young, 'The Scene of the Crime: Is there Such a Thing as "Just Looking"?' in KJ Hayward and M Presdee (eds), *Framing Crime: Cultural Criminology and the Image* (Routledge 2010) 91.

to deride specific forms of representation (or the motivations behind them) yet simultaneously acknowledging their seductive, manipulative and implicative power. Propaganda entices the viewing subject, drawing them in and - subtly or not - influencing and changing their perspective and understanding; not just of the image, but of the broader world as well. The recognition of a propagandistic element within a text or image may allow the viewers to locate themselves outside the representation's effective and manipulative orbit. Fans of comic books may well be aware of the medium's explicitly propagandistic history, yet they are perhaps unlikely to consider themselves susceptible to coercion by such popular texts. The title of this chapter's subject, *Watchmen*, should make clear the concept of 'looking' cannot remain so simplistically rendered.[3]

With this in mind, when pursuing representations that we find pleasurable we should remember that George Orwell famously said, 'all art is propaganda'. Or put otherwise by Murray, 'all artworks project and legitimise some view of the world'.[4] Artistic representation then, is always political, though often engages us in various non-political or non-intellectual ways: emotional, affective, nostalgic, symbolic and visceral.[5] That art often does not engage us in overtly political ways, instead appealing to us on more implicit and gratifying levels is one of its greatest pleasures. Comic books for example, deal with explicitly political content - routinely concerned with questions of the law, justice, citizenship, the juridical state and vigilantism - yet explicitly political discourse is often either absent from or ancillary to the main narrative. The political contexts that comic book superheroes operate in are usually framed as largely uncontested, or if contested, then morally weighted in the hero's favour - a superhero rarely cedes to political authority and if so, then not for long. This means, however, that when experiencing the pleasures of reading and viewing comics, our critical faculties may be circumvented or countervailed, leaving us susceptible to the ideological and political messages embedded within these popular representations.[6] What happens then when we enjoy representations that valorise violent retribution, or construct society in overly simplistic moral terms, or that promote problematic and unrealistic conceptions of justice? What happens to the spectator when they read a superhero comic?[7]

3 A Moore and D Gibbons, *Watchmen* (DC Comics 1987).
4 C Murray, 'Propaganda: The Pleasures of Persuasion in Captain America' MJ Smith and R Duncan (eds), *Critical Approaches to Comics: Theories and Methods* (Routledge 2012) 129.
5 ND Phillips and S Strobl, *Comic Book Crime: Truth, Justice and The American Way* (New York University Press 2013) 7.
6 Ibid 130.
7 Given the comic medium's inextricable binding of both the literary and the visual, the terms 'reading' and 'spectating' will be used interchangeably, with each also implying the other.

Seduction, nostalgia and retribution

Superhero comics as a popular form of representation are both pleasurable and seductive. Since their inception in the late 1930s they have been replete with ideological, partisan and propagandistic content, both intended and otherwise.[8] Emerging from the socio-cultural context of that era – concerns about a volatile economy, crime and safety, impending war and America's emergence as an international power amidst this – the themes and aesthetics of the golden age of comics mirrored the keenly felt anxieties and insecurities prevalent at the time.[9] For example, the front cover of the first edition of *Captain America* published in 1940, famously featured the eponymous Captain punching Hitler in the face.[10] While contemporary superhero comics have obviously moved on from this particular historical context, the genre's methodology remains the same; subjecting the 'messy and troubling complexities' of the modern world to the 'ancient simplicities of crime and punishment'.[11] The seductions and pleasures of superhero comics are manifold; providing the vicarious – and therefore safe and contained – realisation of various fantasies regarding power (physical, scientific, national, gendered, symbolic), of an easily-navigable, black-and-white world, of the legitimate application of violence against an identifiably 'evil' villain, of the supremacy of the modern democratic nation, the potency of the individual and of a justice achievable solely through these means.[12] The superhero comic is a genre in which the popular and the propagandistic coexist and coalesce easily; the latter concealed indivisibly within the seemingly natural and universal views, values and power structures of the text.[13] Some comics, however, manage to supplant and pervert these nostalgic renderings of the social world, while also remaining faithful to the genre's doctrines and methodology.[14]

Superhero comics usually locate the source of criminality (and therefore injustice) deeply within the individual, often as a result of psychopathy or childhood trauma.[15] Thus, they tend to ignore other arguably more pernicious forms of injustice such as social marginalisation,

8 Murray (n 4) 130. Murray notes that propaganda often mimics popular forms of representation, leading to a resemblance and kinship between popular and propagandistic representation.

9 Phillips and Strobl (n 5) 23.

10 Murray (n 4) 131.

11 R Sparks, 'Dramatic Power: Television, Images of Crime and Law Enforcement' in C Sumner (ed), *Censure, Politics and Criminal Justice* (Open University Press 1990) 123.

12 Phillips and Strobl (n 5) 7.

13 Murray (n 4) 130.

14 See Phillips and Strobl (n 5) 69 for an account of how superhero comics combine the desire for a 'better' future with the nostalgic longing for the past to create their particular utopian ideal.

15 Phillips and Strobl (n 5) 92.

systemic poverty, and the exploitative and often violent activities of corporations and nation states.[16] What does it mean then, when readers of comics desire acts of extreme injustice in order to legitimise their fantasies regarding individualised power, violence and retributive justice? In the act of looking are readers of comic books rendered complicit in representations that describe the world in the conservative yet comforting rhetoric of individualised criminality and retributive justice?[17] Perhaps it is possible that the punitive juridical logics present in superhero comics - which tend to depict retributive violence as the sole vehicle for achieving justice - shape and influence the reader's understanding of society, crime and justice more broadly.[18] In pursuit of answering these questions, this chapter examines a comic book that itself constitutes a sustained consideration of these very issues: Alan Moore's and Dave Gibbons's 1986 classic, *Watchmen*. The radical methodology of *Watchmen*, which is both a faithful rendition and deconstructionist subversion of the superhero comic, offers a negative reflection of the spectator's own fantasies and desires usually found within the genre, revealing them as dark, troubling and politically problematic.[19] The text offers its own account of the encounter between the looking spectator and the looked-at representation, and the former's susceptibility to the ideologies and political values embedded often implicitly within the latter.[20]

This chapter situates itself within a cultural criminological and necessarily post-modern framework that is concerned with the multiplicity of meaning and thus reading. The ways that representation, even when fantastical or mythic, influences and mediates our beliefs and understandings of what is represented are of central concern. Further, I consider superhero comics in relation to the emergence of broader symbolic and semiotic universes in which depictions of crime, violence and in/justice accrue

16 Phillips and Strobl (n 5) 30. Phillips and Strobl note that some comics have addressed social problems such as poverty, drugs and racism, promoting themes of social and legal reform instead of purely retributive justice. See also Chapter 8 in this book for a discussion of powerful corruption and the politics of a failing justice system in *100 Bullets*.

17 Phillips and Strobl (n 5) 86.

18 A Young, *Imagining Crime: Textual Outlaws and Criminal Conversations* (Sage 1996) 6.

19 AJ Skoble 'Superhero Revisionism in *Watchmen* and *The Dark Knight Returns*' in M Morris and T Morris (eds), *Superheroes and Philosophy: Truth, Justice and the Socratic Way* (Carrus Publishing 2004) 29.

20 See K Wynter 'Of Depths and Surfaces: Notes on *Watchmen* and other (Non)Reflections on Phenomenological Film Experience' (2009) 77 *CineAction* 68 for an account of the relationship that exists between spectator and image in relation to *Watchmen* and a comparative analysis of the comic and the 2009 live action film based on it.

and produce political meaning.[21] That is, while superhero comics are works of fiction, the issues and themes they explore generate symbolic meaning beyond the fictional worlds they describe, resonating with genuine desires and fantasies regarding community, safety, social order and utopian homogeneity.[22] This chapter examines the concept of spectatorship in relation to superhero comics, specifically how the spectator may become implicated or entangled within the often fascistic political ideologies that underpin a comic's depictions of violence and justice. I do not seek to produce an exhaustive account of spectator implication, but rather to examine how a specific comic, *Watchmen*, assists us in confronting potentially uncomfortable facets of comic spectatorship. I acknowledge that post-modern epistemologies allow for multiple readings and mutable meanings (something that *Watchmen* itself acknowledges).[23] However, my approach also takes into account the extreme constructedness of any comic representation: that, while a comic text may well be interpretable, it is nonetheless constructed around an intended or preferred reading. Even an interpretation that subverts or resists this must, by doing so, also acknowledge and thus affirm the original intention.[24]

The world of *Watchmen*

Watchmen takes place in an alternative 1985 America, one where the central fantasy of superhero comics - superheroes actually existing - has become a reality. What sets this particular rendering of a commonly imagined fantasy apart from other comparable examples is that the broad socio-cultural consequences of this are realised in acute detail in a noticeably altered socio-political and cultural landscape.[25] In this uncanny social backdrop, the United States has emerged victorious in Vietnam, Richard Nixon was never impeached and has entered an unprecedented third Presidential term and the violent culmination of the Cold War between the United States and Russia is imminent, threatening global annihilation by nuclear holocaust. The existence of Dr Manhattan, a bright blue, preternatural superman who possesses the power to manipulate matter at an atomic level (and the world's only genuinely super-powered being) is, counter-intuitively, an exacerbating and contributory factor in this dark and uncertain socio-political milieu and the central catalyst in the impending

21 See J Ferrell, 'Cultural Criminology' (1999) 26 *Annual Review of Sociology* 395, 397.
22 See Phillips and Strobl (n 5) 70 for an account of the utopian ideals and ambitions within superhero comics.
23 Thomson (n 1) 100.
24 I am indebted to the work of Alison Young - see Young (n 2) 86 - for this approach to textual analysis.
25 Thomson (n 1) 105.

nuclear war. The text leaves no doubt that Dr Manhattan's existence, as well as that of the other 'heroes', has altered the course of history, however it remains thoroughly unclear whether they have done so for the better.

The morally bleak and ambivalent character of the narrative world in *Watchmen* is not an uncommon trope in the superhero genre; early crime comics from the post-Second World War period and the superhero comics emerging in the 1970s often had dark themes and grim, troubling settings.[26] Historically, such dystopic renderings have often been used to legitimise the existence and behaviour of masked vigilantes, framing their violent actions as redemptive and necessary in the face of a corrupt and morally stagnant society.[27] By describing the social world within largely black-and-white moral terms, justice becomes a (visually) identifiable and objective solid: no longer subject to the murky complexities of ideology, instead, a limited and achievable set of criteria.[28] The kind of justice found within the pages of superhero comics is, as Phillips and Strobl point out, often framed as being contingent upon violent retribution.[29] In a medium that favours the visual, the witnessing of this retribution becomes a requisite for the realisation of justice: it must be *seen* to be done.[30] However, in superhero comics justice is counter-intuitively premised upon something that itself tests various legal and moral boundaries: violent vigilantism. The figure of the superhero – and our idolisation of it – reaffirms the status quo and yet simultaneously challenges it by valorising individualised retributive justice and the circumvention of the law. Reading superhero comics is about both transgression and reassurance: a game in which moral lines and boundaries are regularly approached, toed and tested, yet which are (almost) always retreated from; what Katz refers to as a 'ritual moral exercise'.[31] The thrill of exposing oneself to transgression is experienced vicariously while the safety and comfort of life within the law is reaffirmed. The formulaic repetition of exposure to these anxieties in comic books, and the subsequent subjection of them to rituals of violent retribution and punishment, renders them (at least temporarily) pleasurable and nonthreatening.[32]

For the reader, the comic world is easily navigable, with visual cues acting as signposts for traversing the comic's moral and political terrain. The

26 Phillips and Strobl (n 5) 24.
27 Phillips and Strobl (n 5) 74.
28 TR Wandtke, *The Meaning of Superhero Comic Books* (MacFarland 2012) 81. Wandtke demonstrates how superhero comics amplify their themes and values through the simplification of them, thus producing simplistic yet powerful notions of crime, victimisation and justice.
29 Phillips and Strobl (n 5) 27.
30 A Young, *The Scene of Violence: Cinema, Crime, Affect* (Routledge 2010) 26.
31 J Katz, 'What Makes Crime "News"?'(1987) 9 *Media, Culture and Society* 47.
32 Phillips and Strobl (n 5) 2.

criminality of the 'bad guys' in superhero comics is established as much by aesthetics as it is by actions. Any lowly street thug is appropriately attired, as is any gangster (pinstripe suit and fedora), while the super villain will undoubtedly be wearing a highly stylised yet utterly impractical costume. This aesthetics of criminality functions as a guide for the reader, whose spectatorial experience of justice is tied to the sensory enjoyment and visual navigation of the representation.[33] These techniques are central to depictions of crime, victimisation and violence in comics. Consider, for example, a comic plot in which a character previously thought to be on the side of the hero (and therefore the reader) reveals their duplicity and emerges as the villain; the character inevitably undertakes a costume change at this juncture, cementing their shift in moral alignment in opposition to the hero. Thus the act of looking is revealed not only as integral to a functional comic narrative, but also as participatory: the realisation of justice depends upon the reader witnessing its violent enactment.[34]

Superheroes and the everyday

Superhero comics, while obviously fantastical, are nonetheless representations of the real world, albeit reimagined as exaggerated, mythologised and nostalgic. This fantasy - the wedding of the mundane with the fantastic - is the central conceit of the superhero genre. It asks, 'What if superheroes existed in the real world, in *our* world?'. Superhero comics thus constitute an encounter between the everyday and the fanciful, the staid and the supernatural. Often mediating this encounter is that most common of superhero tropes - the secret identity - which bridges the gap between normality and fantasy.[35] The plain and everyday quality of a superhero's alter ego, for example, Superman's Clark Kent or Spider-Man's Peter Parker, give credence and tangibility to the fantasy that the superhero - that transcendent, superhuman figure - could be anyone. It could even be *us*.[36] In *Watchmen*, however, this everyday quality is ruthlessly rendered, destabilising the nostalgic and idealised social conceptions that often frame the mundane life of a hero's everyday identity. *Watchmen*'s superheroes, most of whom are retired, are imbued with a concentrated and often bleak ordinariness; for example, Nite Owl II's aging paunch or Sally Jupiter's decline into nostalgic alcoholism.

33 Young (n 2) 84.

34 S McCloud, *Understanding Comics: The Invisible Art* (Harper Perennial 1993) ch 3, 68.

35 T Morris, 'What's Behind the Mask? The Secret of Secret Identities' in M Morris and T Morris (eds), *Superheroes and Philosophy: Truth, Justice and the Socratic Way* (Carus Publishing 2005) 250.

36 M Yockey, 'Retopia: The Dialectics of the Superhero Comic Book' (2012) 3 *Studies in Comics* 350.

Watchmen takes the central animating idea of the superhero genre - 'What if superheroes really existed?' - not simply as a convenient premise with which to explore various fantasies and alternative social realities, but as a question with grave philosophical, existential and socio-cultural consequences. *Watchmen* is a paradigmatic comic text, one that not only altered the superhero genre itself as it continued into the future, but that also cast a revisionist light on the genre's history. It revealed in a critical yet not wholly unkind light the superficiality of the genre's heretofore engagement with its own guiding premise.[37] Thomson describes this unsettling revisionist power as 'retroactive defamiliarisation' - the destabilising of our understanding of everything that came before.[38] *Watchmen*, in offering a simultaneously loyal yet radical realisation of the fantasies that constitute the genre itself, depicting them in stark and discomfiting terms, reorients the genre and renders its tropes suddenly unfamiliar, *uncanny*.[39] For example, the heroes in *Watchmen* are highly unpopular with the public, who are uncomfortable with and intimidated by their anonymity and the impunity with which they operate, demanding instead more institutionalised and formal forms of law enforcement.

Watchmen thus engages the reader in an active and challenging way, not simply deviating from or failing to meet their expectations, but dismantling them through 'hyper-trophic deconstruction': the extreme development of an idea beyond its own limits, resulting in its destruction.[40] In reading *Watchmen*, one simultaneously experiences the expected pleasures associated with the genre - tough, fast-talking and garishly costumed masked vigilantes meting out a stylishly violent justice - while simultaneously witnessing the once-discrete figure of the masked avenger dissembled into its component parts, revealing the fantasy as at best absurdly naïve and at worst downright fascistic. *Watchmen*'s revisionist methodology and uncanny milieu destabilise the spectator's sense of monopolised subjectivity, of the passive, static nature of the text through its loyalty to the tropes of the genre, rather

37 MS Dubose, 'Holding out for a Hero: Reaganism, Comic Book Vigilantes and Captain America' (2007) 40 *Journal of Popular Culture* 916. *Watchmen* was not the first comic to reflexively examine the guiding premise of the superhero genre or to question the monopolised and undemocratic power of superheroes, however it was (and arguably remains) the clearest posing of these ideas within the mainstream body of comics.

38 Thomson (n 1) 103.

39 Thomson (n 1) 104.

40 Thomson (n 1) 106. See also J Baudrillard, *The Vital Illusion* (Columbia University Press 2000).

than the outright rejection of them. The public's opposition to masked heroes in *Watchmen* leads to mass protests and riots, which the superheroes must then attempt to contain the only way they know how: by turning their violence against the very public they ostensibly protect (see Figure 9.1).

While some comics – *Watchmen* included – may be aware of the complexity of the fantasies that they contain, the views and values that superhero comics communicate should not be dismissed simply because of their inclusion in or obsession with the fantastic. Kanno and Norton note that our investment in imagined communities and possible worlds is just as important to the construction of identity as investment in the 'real' world.[41] Superhero comics should thus be understood as contributing to broader cultural understandings of the real world through the themes, images and stories they contain.[42]

The existence of 'heroes'

Watchmen begins with the masked avenger Rorschach, a hard-boiled detective-type vigilante evoking a noir aesthetic (see Figure 9.2).[43] While *Watchmen* does not necessarily have a central protagonist, it is Rorschach who drives the investigatory narrative and his perspective that frames the social world for the reader. An over-developed variant of the traditional vigilante archetype – tough-talking, determined, quick to violence and operating outside the bounds of institutional law – Rorschach traverses the precarious border that separates civility from criminality. Acting according to a rigidly held moral code, Rorschach imposes upon himself an almost divine edict to punish evildoers. Within his fatalistic worldview there is no moral ambiguity and no possibility of reform or rehabilitation, nor any room for hope. For Rorschach justice is purely retributive: the only valid response to the inevitability of continuing evil. Rorschach is a confronting and yet simultaneously pleasurable character for the spectator to watch and accompany. The 'justice' he delivers – which is immediate, informal and anything-but bureaucratic – is the realisation of a fantasy in which the state and its institutions are by-passed in favour of an individualised and cathartic

41 Y Kanno and B Norton, 'Imagined Communities and Educational Possibilities' (2003) 2 *Journal of Language, Identity and Education* 247.

42 Phillips and Strobl (n 5) 19, 67. See also R Ray, *A Certain Tendency of the Hollywood Cinema 1930–1980* (Princeton University Press 1986).

43 Phillips and Strobl (n 5) 21–22. This references the prototypical origins of the comic book superhero in newspaper comic strips that featured plainclothes detectives fighting crime.

Figure 9.1 Nite Owl II and The Comedian attempt to suppress a street riot sparked by anti-superhero sentiment. From: *Watchmen* © DC Comics.

justice. While we may initially imagine Rorschach as a crime-fighting hero, it soon becomes apparent that the reality is very different: at various points in the narrative the spectator witnesses Rorschach dump the mutilated body of a rapist at the front of the police headquarters, burn a hand-cuffed child killer alive and kill a prison inmate by dousing him in boiling cooking fat. While the fantasy of retributive justice may be seductive, it is also threatening: uncontainable and uncontrollable. With Rorschach, the legal and moral boundaries that separate the maintenance of the status quo from the dangerous world of the criminal are obscured. Where often a superhero would stop short of outright murder and thus avoid becoming the very thing against which they fight, Rorschach withholds nothing.[44]

Rorschach's name - along with his eponymous mask: white with shifting blobs of black ink, referencing the famous 'ink-blot test' popularly associated with psychoanalysis - offers a double challenge to the spectator. First, it suggests that this character (and therefore the text and possibly the entire superhero genre) is actually just a meaningless surface upon which the reader projects their own fantasies and desires.[45] Here the act of looking becomes implicative; the spectator is bound to the image (the act of looking imbuing it with meaning) and is thus no longer able to claim distance or detachment from it.[46] Second, Rorschach invites the reader to judge the character for themselves, without the reassuring moral certainty that usually accompanies such narratives to guide them. Attached to this invitation is a warning: that the conclusions the reader arrives at likely reflect more upon themselves than the character or the text more broadly.[47] Rorschach (whose face is a psychic reflection of whoever gazes upon it) casts an accusatory finger back toward the reader, demanding that they take their share of responsibility for what the comic contains. McCloud claims any act committed to paper by the comic artist 'is aided and abetted by a silent accomplice... [a]n equal partner in crime known as the reader' who deliberately participates in any act of violence contained within the text.[48] This means that any indictment of Rorschach must also include the reader within the ambit of judgement.[49] Rorschach functions to disallow the readers' divestment of responsibility: his gaze becomes our gaze, his investigations our main source of knowledge, his renderings of the social world, ours, 'The streets are extended gutters and the gutters are full of blood and when the drains finally scab over, all the vermin will drown'.[50] When looking at Rorschach, readers may not like what they discover gazing back: a hidden facet of themselves.

Rorschach is not the only masked avenger/vigilante to inhabit this world, and while he is one of the more extreme personalities, the others

44 Rorschach is not unique in this respect: there are other masked vigilantes/superheroes who regularly commit murder in their pursuit of 'justice', for example Marvel's *The Punisher*. See Phillips and Strobl (n 5) 116. And, for a discussion on the assessment of 'deathworthiness' in comics heroes' paths to justice, see Chapter 7 in this book.
45 Thomson (n 1) 107.
46 Young (n 2) 86.
47 Morris (n 34) 250.
48 McCloud (n 33) 68.
49 See McCloud (n 33) 94 for an account of how comics create the illusion of time, motion and progress.
50 Moore and Gibbons (n 3) ch 1, 1.

Figure 9.2 Rorschach (pictured here in costume) evokes a noir aesthetic, referencing early detective comics. From: *Watchmen* © DC Comics.

offer little respite. The other 'heroes' - unpowered save for Dr Manhattan - form an unsettling and broadly unlikeable collection of vanities, repressions, mental illnesses, questionable motivations and sectarian sympathies. In one scene for example, Captain Metropolis, a hero active in the 1940s and 1950s openly cites 'black unrest' and 'campus subversion' as problems high on his heroic agenda.[51] The inclusion of such an anachronous and politically fraught statement, while somewhat mitigated by historical contextualisation, highlights *Watchmen*'s unearthing of the political assumptions embedded within heroic figures. By including such historical ignominies - and thus diverging from the nostalgic imaginings of the past common in superhero narratives - *Watchmen* overturns the notion that

51 Moore and Gibbons (n 3) ch 2, 11.

there exists an objective definition of justice as well as the proliferated assumption that superheroes are always on the right side of it.

Watchmen's deconstruction of 'heroism' and the values that we ascribe to it is not delivered via simplistic or one-dimensional renderings.[52] Rather, the unsettling vision of heroism found in *Watchmen* is instead achieved through an excess of detail: their multiple flaws and contradictions become *visible* to the reader, no longer obscured within favourable and uncritical renderings. The masked avengers in *Watchmen* are nuanced beings, inescapably mired in all-too-human complexities, prejudices and their own shallow and self-serving desires. The motivations that drive *Watchmen*'s heroes fall far short of the rarefied air of more traditional imaginings: the petty want for fame, the desire to please an (imagined) parental figure and the repression of one's own homoerotic desire to name a few. Even ostensibly 'noble' motivations are tainted by absolutist worldviews and fascistic sympathies, revealing to the spectator the kind of personality that would seek out the life of a masked vigilante. At the farthest end of the spectrum is The Comedian (a twisted rendition of Captain America): a character whom the reader witnesses attempting to rape a fellow masked avenger, gleefully torching Vietcong soldiers with a flamethrower, and gunning down a Vietnamese teenager pregnant with his own child.[53]

Fantasy's reflection: disillusionment

The lack of faith and conviction (in the figure of the hero, in the governing state, in the fundamental worth of society and humanity itself) that pervades *Watchmen* is the text's most basic subversion of comic norms. *Watchmen* evokes a persistent uncertainty as to whether superheroes *should* pursue their self-imposed obligation for the pursuit of an informal, arbitrary and subjectively defined 'justice'. In fact, it questions whether heroes should exist at all. Absent from the text is the familiar absolute moral authority of the superhero. Instead, as the story progresses, the normally solid and tangible barrier that separates the lawful from the unlawful, the good from the bad, the valorised from the hated, becomes increasingly nebulous.[54] Compounding the moral ambiguity faced by the reader is the looming existential threat of global nuclear holocaust, overshadowing minor instances of crime and rendering any debate around the definition of justice largely moot.

52 Thomson (n 1) 106.
53 In direct contrast to his spiritual ancestor, The Comedian sees the foundations of American society (democracy, liberty, equality, freedom) as irreconcilable with human nature, and so seeks to parody them, embodying this fundamental contradiction of contemporary American society.
54 R Davidson, 'Fighting the Good Fight: Watching *Watchmen*' (2009) 54 *Screen Education* 19.

For the reader, this largely unknown uncertainty increases as the narrative progresses: a growing sense of urgency is exacerbated by the absence of a responsible figure against whom to direct retribution. When Adrian Veidt - a former masked-avenger turned business entrepreneur - merges as the apparent antagonist, it is revealed that his diabolical plot is actually intended to save the world, rather than destroy it. The question arises: of what use is a supervillain when the world is such a thoroughly unjust and cruel place anyway, one that is demonstrably quite capable of destroying itself without the help of a fictional costumed psychopath. Veidt's plan is to trick the warring superpowers into peace by staging an alien invasion; creating a new and terrifying enemy against which the world's superpowers can unite, laying aside their ideological differences. However, to carry off his plan convincingly Veidt intends to destroy half of New York City and three million of its inhabitants. Rorschach, our ostensible 'hero', uncovers Veidt's plot and travels (along with various other heroes) to his Antarctic hideout for a final showdown. Yet the cast of heroes is wholly unable to prevent the culmination of Veidt's plans, which are carried out flawlessly. In the face of their own failure the heroes attempt retribution for the lost lives, but all end up ceding to the 'villain's' consequentialist logic, save for Rorschach. Due to his strict moral code he is unable to admit that in this case the ends may justify the means, and he is murdered out of necessity by Dr Manhattan: another body upon which to base a tenuous and morally questionable world peace.

The ending of *Watchmen* challenges the basic premise of the superhero narrative and of comic spectatorship as well. The world is saved, not from a psychotic villain but from the clutches of international superpowers warring over competing ideologies and political values. Further, the 'hero' that we have accompanied throughout much of the narrative - Rorschach - turns out to be entirely unable to effect any change in outcome: the most he could manage was to bear witness and then die. The reader is here forced to consider two questions, 'What are the moral, ethical and human costs of this apparent "victory"?', and, 'Why have they accompanied this "hero" if he was not the fulcrum upon which the realisation of justice balanced?'. The outcome is, technically, what the reader desires: the restoration of 'order', the aversion of a global catastrophe and the beginning of a new era of 'peace'.[55] Yet none of the heroes (not even

55 Z Bauman, 'Violence in the Age of Uncertainty' in A Crawford (ed), *Crime and Insecurity: The Governance of Crime in Europe* (Willan Publishing 1992) 52. Bauman claims that a 'peaceful social order' is a contradiction in terms; 'peace' and 'order' are not the absence of violence but rather the successful monopolisation of it.

Dr Manhattan) were able to achieve this. Instead it is the 'villain' who, by abandoning the notion of justice itself, is able to avert global nuclear holocaust, albeit at the cost of millions of lives. Thomson claims that those we identify as 'heroes' function to guide a sense of our identity, operating as a mirror that reflects back an idealised self-conception (both individual and communal).[56] *Watchmen* shatters this mirror. The reflection cast by these heroes can in no way be described as idyllic, though of course this is the point. Here looking becomes a fraught undertaking, threatening to reveal to the reader all the uncertainties from which they sought respite, or worse, confronting them with their own fascistic desires and militant sympathies. The aphorism 'be careful what you wish for' comes to mind: the reader, confronted with their fantasy's realisation, finds it is not what they imagined.

Conclusion

In the end, while *Watchmen* does challenge the notion of the active reader and passive image, the text nonetheless invites spectatorship, offering the sublime pleasures of witnessing and participating in violence and the fascistic monopolisation of power over others. Although in this case the text may be aware of its co-opting of the spectator into such problematic ideological spheres, the capacity of a singular text to effect significant change will always be limited. *Watchmen* remains as much a product of its time and the various conventions and contradictions that define the genre as any other superhero text.[57] While it may be stridently critical of that broader generic landscape, the text itself remains embedded inextricably within it, and is therefore unable to exist wholly beyond or outside of its defining features, regardless of how naïve or self-defeating they may be. There is something masochistic about the superhero methodology, as well as displaying symptoms of the hypochondriac. It simultaneously champions the power of the state while undermining its institutional authority; invokes the rhetoric of individual freedom whilst imbuing its most idolised figures with fascistic and totalitarian dogmas and craves the safety of the nostalgic and familiar while constantly subjecting itself to the multiple uncertainties of a liberal social order. The peaceful and just society that superhero narratives long for can, counter-intuitively, only exist through the constant threat of incursions from outsiders. Superhero comics insist on subjecting the society they

56 Thomson (n 1) 100. See also Young (n 30) 11.

57 See A Moore, *Alan Moore: Conversations*, EL Berlatsky (ed) (University Press of Mississippi 2012). Alan Moore has himself been highly sceptical about the extent of *Watchmen*'s effects on the genre and highly critical of the standards of comic authorship in the post-*Watchmen* age.

idolise to the worst, most brutal atrocities conceivable, whilst meticulously checking its structures and systems over for any exploitable weakness or flaw. Yet this is also what makes the genre so seductive and pleasurable for the reader: violence and catastrophe becomes the familiar, and the regular subjection of these constant insecurities to rituals of violence becomes both comforting and indulgent. *Watchmen* thus offers a troubling and reflexive image of what society might actually be like, were our fantasies to come true.[58]

Acknowledgements

I would like to thank Alison Young for both her insightful work as well as her valuable academic guidance. Also Benjamin Riley for his endless patience and impeccable proofreading skills.

Bibliography

Bauman Z, 'Violence in the Age of Uncertainty' in Crawford A (ed), *Crime and Insecurity: the Governance of Crime in Europe* (Willan Publishing 1992).

Baudrillard J, *The Vital Illusion* (Columbia University Press 2000).

Davidson R, 'Fighting the Good Fight: Watching *Watchmen*' (2009) 54 *Screen Education* 19.

Dubose MS, 'Holding Out for a Hero: Reaganism, Comic Book Vigilantes and Captain America' (2007) 40 *Journal of Popular Culture* 916.

Ferrell J, 'Cultural Criminology' (1999) 26 *Annual Review of Sociology* 395.

Hughes JA, '"Who Watches the Watchmen?": Ideology and "Real World" Superheroes' (2006) 39 *Journal of Popular Culture* 546.

Kanno Y and Norton B, 'Imagined Communities and Educational Possibilities' (2003) 2 *Journal of Language, Identity and Education* 247.

Katz J, 'What Makes Crime "News"?' (1987) 9 *Media, Culture and Society* 47.

McCloud S, *Understanding Comics: The Invisible Art* (Harper Perennial 1993).

Moore A, *Alan Moore: Conversations*, Berlatsky EL (ed) (University of Mississippi Press 2012).

Moore A and Gibbons D, *Watchmen* (DC Comics 1987).

Morris T, 'What's Behind the Mask? The Secret of Secret Identities' in Morris M and Morris T (eds), *Superheroes and Philosophy: Truth, Justice and the Socratic Way* (Carus Publishing 2005).

Murray C, 'Propaganda: The Pleasures of Persuasion in Captain America' in Smith MJ and Duncan R (eds), *Critical Approaches to Comics: Theories and Methods* (Routledge 2012).

Phillips ND and Strobl S, *Comic Book Crime: Truth, Justice and the American Way* (New York University Press 2013).

58 Thomson (n 1) 105. For discussion of 'real life' attempts at superheroism, see Chapter 10 in this book.

Ray R, *A Certain Tendency of the Hollywood Cinema 1930–1980* (Princeton University Press 1986).
Skoble AJ, 'Superhero Revisionism in *Watchmen* and *The Dark Knight Returns*' in Morris M and Morris T (eds), *Superheroes and Philosophy: Truth, Justice and the Socratic Way* (Carus Publishing 2004).
Sparks R, 'Dramatic Power: Television, Images of Crime and Law Enforcement' in Sumner C (ed), *Censure, Politics and Criminal Justice* (Open University Press 1990).
Thomson I, 'Deconstructing the Hero' in McLaughlin J (ed), *Comics as Philosophy* (University Press of Mississippi 2005).
Yockey M, 'Retopia: The Dialectics of the Superhero Comic Book' (2012) 3 *Studies in Comics* 349.
Young A, *Imagining Crime: Textual Outlaws and Criminal Conversations* (Sage 1996).
Young A, 'The Scene of the Crime: Is there Such a Thing as "Just Looking"?' in Hayward KJ and Presdee M (eds), *Framing Crime: Cultural Criminology and the Image* (Routledge 2010).
Young A, *The Scene of Violence: Cinema, Crime, Affect* (Routledge 2010).
Wandtke TR, *The Meaning of Superhero Comic Books* (McFarland 2012).
Wynter K, 'Of Depth and Surfaces: Notes on *Watchmen* and Other (Non) reflections on Phenomenological Film Experience' (2009) 77 *CineAction* 68.

Chapter 10

Stepping off the page: 'British Batman' as legal superhero[1]

Nic Groombridge

When Bruce Wayne dons the mask he becomes Batman but he also becomes Bruce Wayne when he removes that mask. He wears the mask of plutocratic respectability that marks him out in one realm but renders him invisible in another. We can all be superheroes and supervillains with the masks we wear. Every day we 'perform' or 'do' gender, 'race', sexuality, age, ability, etc; with much melting/meeting at the intersection. Sometimes we deploy literal masks for superheroism or carnival; or semi-masks in hats or hoodies or, like prestidigitators, misdirect more metaphorically with invisible or naked masks. My mask today is that of the 'academic'.

Some of the concern of scholars of graphic novels to establish the bona fides of their work might be a fear of the 'comic', the low-brow or of just being seen as fanboys and -grrls with degrees. Phillips and Strobl in their acknowledgements note, 'some scholars we knew looked askance at us early-career criminologists focusing on comic books'.[2] Evans and Giddens are more confident, 'comics and graphic novels, as an object of serious academic study, *do not need justification*'.[3] Yet, 'even in the graphic novel admiring community, the superhero genre seems to be regarded as something of a lesser importance. It is the lowbrow of the lowbrow culture, the pulp of the pulp'.[4]

1 The alliterative allure of 'British' should not obscure the different justice system of Scotland, but it too has seen protests by fathers.
2 N Phillips and S Strobl, *Comic Book Crime: Truth, Justice, and the American Way* (New York University Press 2013) 1.
3 JC Evans and T Giddens, 'Introduction' in JC Evans and T Giddens (eds), *Cultural Excavation and Formal Expression in the Graphic Novel* (Inter-Disciplinary Press 2013) x.
4 A Koronowicz, 'Loner, Lover, Hero: Superhero Reads Hemingway' in JC Evans and T Giddens (eds), *Cultural Excavation and Formal Expression in the Graphic Novel* (Inter-Disciplinary Press 2013) 3.

Like Medhurst, 'I'm not sure how qualified I am to write this essay' as I am not a 'fan'.[5] I say this not to distance myself from the material but to seek forbearance from fans with their encyclopaedic knowledge. My intention here is to examine how superheroes burst into my world, the mainstream. My own scant knowledge of superheroes relies on what has become 'mainstream'. That introduces us to the antics of Fathers for Justice (F4J), which are picked up more extensively in the next section. The next question then raised is why Batman? This is followed by a section which addresses the extent to which some of the crimes/anti-social behaviour described can be laid at the door of the comics, before concluding on the need for heroes. The position of women disrupts this discourse. The wives or ex-partners of the protestors are largely silenced.

The camp knight waxes and waynes

My first experience of Batman was at a friend's house who had many DC comics and also the *Dandy* and *Beano*. At my house we had the rather more 'improving' *Eagle*. I remember more about the promise of plenty that the American advertising suggested, but it is Adam West's TV outings as the Caped Crusader that was my first real exposure to Batman as a cultural product. West's occasional returns in *The Simpsons*[6] and *Family Guy* stir a nostalgia I must share with those shows' originators.

I recognise that, as Medhurst says:

> The sixties' TV show remains anathema to the serious Bat-fan precisely because it heaps ridicule on the very notion of a serious Batman. *Batman* the series revealed the man in the cape as a pompous fool, an embodiment of superseded ethics, and a closet queen.[7]

And like Medhurst, Batman and I drifted apart too until Christmas Day 1996 when in the special edition of *Only Fools and Horses* Del Boy and Rodney dress up as Batman and Robin with 'amusing' crime-fighting results. This episode was named in January 2011 as 'Britain's most memorable

5 A Medhurst, 'Batman, Deviance and Camp' in RE Pearson and W Uricchio (eds), *The Many Lives of the Batman: Critical Approaches to a Superhero and His Media* (Routledge 1991) 149.

6 See M Henry, 'Looking for Amanda Hugginkiss: Gay Life on *The Simpsons*' in J Alber (ed), *Leaving Springfield: The Simpsons and the Possibilities of Oppositional Culture* (Wayne State University Press 2004).

7 Medhurst (n 5) 162.

Christmas TV moment' by the *Sun* newspaper.[8] And this was backed up for a global audience at the London Olympics 2012 when the Closing Ceremony featured actors playing David Jason and Nicholas Lyndhurst playing Batman and Robin.

Between these times Batman, and sometimes other superheroes,[9] appeared as 'crusaders' on behalf of campaigning group F4J. Their website[10] still carries the video of member Jason Hatch scaling the walls of Buckingham Palace dressed as Batman in September 2004. All charges relating to his protest were later dropped. Other groups[11] and non-affiliated fathers campaigning for access to their children have also used superhero costume and discourse. The book written by founder of F4J Matt O'Connor, *Fathers 4 Justice: The Inside Story*, has five fancy dress/party store 'superheroes' on the cover.

Perhaps unsurprisingly, whilst Brooker lauds and lists the many Batmen of video game, novel and film, these F4J dads are not mentioned.[12] There seems to be no mention in Hatfield and others nor Durand and Leigh.[13] Perhaps it would be impertinent or un-American to dress as a cultural icon for the purpose of protest - acceptable at *Comic Con* but not on the White House roof? The website of the American branch of F4J has one picture of some protestors in Spider-Man and Superman costumes. Two UK F4J members protested at the Lincoln Memorial on 17 August 2007 as part of an attempt to engage with the US 'chapter'.

It is, perhaps, Miller's, Moore's and Morrison's graphic novels (*The Dark Knight Returns*, *Batman: The Killing Joke* and *Arkham Asylum*), the filmic re-imaginations of Tim Burton and Christopher Nolan, and even video games, that have largely driven Adam West's Batman from the roost. But the actions of desperate fathers, the writers of comedy and stagers of Olympic ceremonies do not follow those narratives, let-alone alternative, 'ret-con'-requiring story arcs. They follow a generic, fancy-dress, costume-store 'British' Batman. The sort who walked into Bradford Police Station,[14] 'The stocky, mystery man was posing as the camp 1960s incarnation of the

8 'Fools and Horses is top of Xmas TV' (*The Sun*, 12 January 2011) www.thesun.co.uk/sol/homepage/news/3255136/Del-Boy-tops-Xmas-TV-moments-poll.html> accessed 24 July 2013.

9 Including the invented-for-purpose 'Captain Conception' and 'Cash Gordon' - and 'Father Christmas'.

10 See www.fathers-4-justice.org/> accessed 7 March 2014.

11 Breakaway group Real Fathers for Justice have an image of someone dressed as Spider-Man on their website: <www.realfathersforjustice.org/> accessed 7 March 2014.

12 W Brooker, *Hunting the Dark Knight: Twenty-First Century Batman* (IB Taurus 2012).

13 C Hatfield, J Heer and K Worcester, *The Superhero Reader* (University Press of Mississippi 2013); KKJ Durand and MK Leigh, *Riddle Me This, Batman! Essays on the Universe of the Dark Knight* (McFarland 2011).

14 It was this event that prompted me to write this chapter.

famous DC Comics character, rather than the dark, black figure familiar to fans of the Tim Burton and Christopher Nolan film versions'.[15] The 'darker' side is illustrated by James Holmes who chose to dress as Batman's nemesis, The Joker, before killing 12 people and wounding 58 others in Aurora, Colorado during a screening of the Batman film *The Dark Knight Rises.*

Clearly, the stories reveal or suggest a variety of reasons to dress, if only partially, as a superhero: from random chance, simple disguise, to misplaced identification. What is clearer is the popularity of superheroes, and of Batman in particular. Particularly popular too with the 'Dad's Army' that is F4J, as Matt O'Connor and many media outlets sometimes style these desperate divorced and divorcing dads. The next section expands on their use of superhero costumes in their campaigns.

Superhero fathers

Neither Crowley nor Flood make mention of superhero stunts nor of the superhero discourse to be found in the popular media and in F4J literature.[16] This might be because they are looking at the wider non-UK 'father's rights' movement and activism. But in a long article, Collier also makes scant mention.[17] He runs through the history of the laws that F4J (and the non-activist Families Need Fathers) complain of and discusses the activism of the wider 'Men's Movement', but the stunts are downplayed as the following quotes show, 'Who are these guys? What does it all mean - the Marvel Comics costumes, the orchestrated gantry stunts, the banners, the Santa outfits, the nooses, the desperate measures?'.[18] And, 'F4J has become most well known for a series of protests involving men

15 'Bradford Batman: "Superhero" Hands Wanted Man Over to Police' (*Evening Standard*, 4 March 2013) <www.standard.co.uk/news/crime/bradford-batman-superhero-hands-wanted-man-over-to-police-8519462.html> accessed 7 March 2014. The arrested man was later charged with handling stolen goods and fraud related offences. 'Batman' may have kept his identity secret from the police but the media were soon on the case. We quickly learn that the 'miscreant' was Daniel Frayne and that Stan Worby was Batman, and that he had the costume to attend a football match (!) the day before. Later we discover that they are friends and that Worby was 'helping' Frayne answer bail and that the pair had been charged a few days later with stealing power tools. They then appear to drop out of the news.

16 J Crowley, 'Taking Custody of Motherhood: Fathers' Rights Activists and Politics of Parenting' (2009) 37 *Women's Studies Quarterly* 223; M Flood, 'Separated Fathers and the "Fathers' Rights" Movement' (2012) 18 *Journal of Family Studies* 235.

17 RS Collier, 'The Fathers' Rights Movement, Law Reform, and the New Politics of Fatherhood: Some Reflections on the UK Experience' (2009) 20 *University of Florida Journal of Law and Public Policy* 65.

18 J Walsh, 'The Caped Crusader' as cited by Collier (n 17) 85.

dressed as comic book characters'.[19] He rightly points to the ongoing legal disputes of individual members and extra-legal direct actions against court staff which undercut their 'fun' 'comic' (?) image. In targeting Buckingham Palace, they aimed at the symbolic fount of the law, but on 21 October 2004 two members dressed as Batman and Robin scaled the front of the Royal Courts of Justice.

Although clearly not a full blown content analysis, a Google image search under 'F4J superheroes' shows a large majority of DC characters, particularly Batman, and from Marvel the occasional Spider-Man and the odd Hulk and some of Disney's Mr Incredible. Having made the DC/Marvel fanboy point, we consider the reason for choosing the costumes later, but first what do the men themselves say? Could they make a DC/Marvel distinction? Do they know Bruce Wayne's parents were killed in front of him?

As we have seen, even where the aims and some of the tactics of the general (but far from homogenous or easily identifiable) 'men's' or specific 'fathers'' movement have been discussed, the superhero elements are often passed over. Jordan appears to be alone in taking this aspect, and the cultural presentation of F4J, seriously, if briefly.[20] She quotes O'Connor in the pride he took in being:

> spoofed by comedy acts ranging from Rowan Atkinson on Comic Relief to Catherine Tate's 'Gingers 4 Justice,' as well as TV adverts for Vodafone and various cartoons. There was Fathers 4 Justice Lego and 'Fathers 4 Justice' the song, written by a punk band called the Molloys.[21]

She carried out one-off, in-depth interviews with nine Real Fathers for Justice (RFFJ). As one respondent told Jordan:

> I know my lad did see me on the telly, . . . he was quite proud of it, quite pleased, he used to tell his friends at school that his dad was Spiderman [sic], he saw the good side of it, and I'm glad I did do it cos even though he's at a young age, he still sort of recognised me, . . . and I was sort of still there.[22]

Much of this can be, and generally is, seen as either special pleading by the men or as part of a wider anti-feminist 'movement' in which 'masculinism'

19 Collier (n 17) 86.

20 A Jordan, '"Dads Aren't Demons. Mums Aren't Madonnas": Constructions of Fatherhood and Masculinities in the (Real) Fathers 4 Justice Campaign' (2009) 31 *Journal of Social Welfare and Family Law* 419.

21 M O'Connor, *Fathers 4 Justice: The Inside Story* (Weidenfeld and Nicolson 2007) 221.

22 Jordan (n 20) 426.

is promoted to counter the ills that the men see as befalling them as a result of feminism. And Blais and Dupuis-Déri mention the superhero protests but also the violence against women and representatives of the law.[23] Batman as backlash? In their discussion of anti-feminism, they mention the rise of the Ku Klux Klan and Nazism as bearing comparison. The significance of costume or uniforms for those organisations is not addressed.

Klan members might hide their faces whilst brandishing their beliefs and Nazis briefly revelled in the dominance of their ideology, marked out by a uniform. Criminals are usually more reticent. Criminologists (and detectives) seek to find the mark behind the mask of the criminal. Lombroso thought he had found this with natal and cultural features like superciliary arches and tattoos. Phillips and Strobl note of the large sample of comics they studied that, 'criminality is often written on the face, or the body, of the villain'.[24] What is behind the F4J's masks?

Why superheroes? Why Batman?

As we have seen, even where the use of superhero costumes is noted in respect of F4J, Del Boy, criminals or vigilantes, there is little discussion. Perhaps it is seen to be either obvious or 'silly'. F4J's own literature and spectacles make much use of the imagery and discourse of 'superheroes'. Yet they never explain. Even Jordan mostly addresses this as the discourse around what constitutes a good father.[25] She identified the discourses of 'nurturing father', 'father as superhero' and 'good enough father' in her interviews with activist fathers. They saw their activism as evidence of their goodness as fathers by enacting the superhero ('doing' superheroism?). She notes O'Connor's claim/slogan that 'every father is a superhero to his child'.[26]

Clearly if you see yourself, want to see yourself, or want your child to see you, as a superhero then you need to be appropriately suited and booted to 'fight' for your rights as a father/man and to gain access to your child. As Jordan suggests, 'dressing up as a child's favourite superhero was viewed as a form of indirect contact and as a message to the child'.[27]

23 M Blais and F Dupuis-Déri, 'Masculinism and the Antifeminist Countermovement' (2012) 11 *Social Movement Studies* 21.

24 Phillips and Strobl (n 2) 220. Although one of the anonymous reviewers points out that villains in Marvel often have no costume. Fennel also makes links between historic cultural practices of retributive scarring and the depiction of comic villains, see J Fennel, 'The Aesthetics of Supervillainy' (2012) 16 *Law Text Culture* 305.

25 Jordan (n 20) 427.

26 Jordan (n 20) 426.

27 Jordan (n 20) 426.

So why not Papa Smurf, then? A children's favourite and, like Santa, nominally a father; yet an internet search reveals only a theft from a convenience store in Australia by three men styled as Smurfs.[28] F4J's first demonstration involved 200 Father Christmases outside the Lord Chancellor's Department in 2002. And F4J are capable of choosing some costumes for their specific appropriateness, for instance as monks, nuns or as a Cardinal (sic) when protesting in 2004 at York Minster, then hosting the Church of England synod.[29] Moreover, despite styling themselves as a 'Dad's Army' they do not appear as those TV characters.[30] Did they like the affectionate term for father combined with the military allusion, whilst failing to see the very mixed and mirth-inducing masculine models the show offered?

Langford's very partial account of the organisation features superhero pictures but no explanation of them or the reasons for their use, but in a paean of praise for one member (Jolly Stanesby) recounts him dressing as Robin for the Royal Courts of Justice episode, in drag as 'Doubtfire Dad' and as the previously mentioned 'Captain Conception', as well as being one of the two who climbed the Lincoln Memorial.[31]

Weltzien sees 'masculinity as masquerade' and makes it clear that his:

> main intention is not so much to distinguish the deceiving mask from any kind of 'real' or unmasked image, but to get hold of an analytical instrument with which to study the moment of change: the dynamic process of masking as it is signified by the variation in clothing.[32]

That is, neither Batman nor Bruce Wayne is 'real' - the significance lies in the process of change from one to the other. He argues that the superhero, 'like his human colleagues, . . . needs two alternative outfits for the construction and performance of masculinity'.[33] As readers we are privileged to see the transformation. Does this work for F4J Batman? Does Jason Hatch or Jolly Stanesby 'need' to dress up? They might move from 'Deadbeat Dad' to 'Super Dad' as they dress up - but we need to hear from the men.

28 'Aus Police Hunt for Papa Smurf' (*Yahoo News NZ*, 9 January 2013) <http://nz.news.yahoo.com/a/-/mp/15789714/aus-police-hunt-for-papa-smurf/> accessed 7 March 2014.

29 'Fathers' Cathedral Protest Ends' (*BBC News*, 12 July 2004) <http://news.bbc.co.uk/1/hi/uk/3884265.stm> accessed 7 March 2014.

30 Although they did use a tank in a march once.

31 N Langford, 'A Short History of Fathers 4 Justice' (*Scribd.com*, 18 February 2013) <www.scribd.com/doc/126039862/Histoire-Father-4-Justice> accessed 7 March 2014.

32 F Weltzien, 'Masque-ulinities: Changing Dress as a Display of Masculinity in the Superhero Genre' (2005) 9 *Fashion Theory: The Journal of Dress, Body and Culture* 229, 229–30.

33 Ibid 232.

Matt O'Connor's book makes extensive mention of superheroes and the cover shows two Batman, two Robin and one Spider-Man yet does not specifically or explicitly address why.[34] Indeed, throughout the book many other costumes are mentioned, including his first, 'I'd had a suit silk-screened with various slogans'.[35] He lists their purchases prior to beginning the campaign, mentioning a number of costumes: Elvis circa 1972, Easter Bunny, monkey, decontamination suits, religious orders, and even Tony Blair masks.[36]

The Elvis costumes were for their second demonstration on Valentine's Day when the Family Courts were to be likened to 'Heartbreak Hotels'. O'Connor mentions purchasing a Purple Phantom costume but it is never mentioned again.[37] Whilst it may not be as recognisable as Batman it might make a better symbol as the Phantom, too, has no super powers but the job (?) is passed from father to son. The purple colour of his costume ties in with their claimed appropriation of it from the Suffragettes.[38]

His idea for 'father as superhero' came from M Night Shyamalan's *Unbreakable* and 'The Men in Tights' from the Mel Brooks film of that name, but only the dispute about who would be Batman rather than Robin between those involved touches on the choice of characters.[39] This broader superheroes campaign started with Spider-Man climbing a crane in London and causing gridlock. Other campaigns involved climbing bridges or gantries on major roads dressed initially as Highwaymen, but people persisted in seeing them as Zorro or the Lone Ranger so they reverted to superheroes.

O'Connor is pretty scathing about the law's and the church's predilection for costume and recognises, indeed often intends, the ludicrousness of the superhero costumes. It might be that they are chosen for their immediate mainstream public recognition and that stems from the films, not necessarily from the comics or graphic novels. Moreover, for the UK public, Batman and Robin come freighted with the pathos of Del Boy and Rodney's fraternal father-and-son act. This might account for the number of costumes available for hire, particularly in Britain.

Whatever O'Connor's original intentions it now seems that Batman is chosen because he has become iconic of F4J. Evidence for this might be seen on Twitter. Thus under the hashtag #fathers4justice we find in mid July 2013 @mattchooholmes tweeting, 'Hope prince Williams has got this

34 O'Connor (n 21).
35 O'Connor (n 21) 29.
36 O'Connor (n 21) 53.
37 O'Connor (n 21) 54.
38 He also expresses admiration for Peter Tatchell and Gandhi.
39 O'Connor (n 21) 51.

batman costume' and @Tim_W_Jones calling out @WhitbreadMartin, 'Still not seen you chained to a building dressed as Batman'. O'Neil suggests Batman has become a meme, and much of the discussion here suggests this may be correct.[40]

One reading of Batman might note his stern paternalism but this is undercut by Del Boy and Rodney who are clearly comic, and – less often noted – operate on the borders of the law: they are scamsters and petty fraudsters. So is a particular English sentiment at work too? Yet Rusch argues that though it is Superman who lays claim to, 'truth, justice and the American Way', it is Batman who is most, 'American' in the way he, 'straddles the line between good and evil'.[41]

Or is it much simpler than these or my reading might suggest. The costumes are cheap and available.[42] As we have seen their commonality and cheapness makes them suitable for disguise or simply to state, 'I am playing at being a superhero'. There is no suggestion that F4J, or any of the other wearers of Batman or other superhero costumes, are 'fans' or have undertaken any textual analysis. Or, indeed, that they will know the significance of fathers in the mythos of many superheroes (eg the murder of Bruce Wayne's parents or the murder of Matt Murdock/Daredevil's father).

Much is made of unmasking in superhero stories and the early criminology claimed to be able to do this to criminals. So the next section examines some specifically, if broadly drawn, criminological themes.

Batman, criminologist

In their contribution to cultural criminology, Phillips and Strobl declaim, 'Holy Criminology, Batman!' and point out that, 'comic books, particularly of the superhero genre, are replete with themes of crime and justice, yet are frequently ignored by criminologists'.[43] Were criminologists to look at these books, they would find, 'that comic books, although diverse most often reflect an ideological orientation that reinforces the dominant notions of retributive justice in American culture'.[44]

Interestingly, criminologists Rafter and Brown make excellent use of movies to explain their discipline but none of those are superhero ones, and

40 D O'Neil, *Batman Unauthorized: Vigilantes, Jokers, and Heroes in Gotham City* (BenBella Books Dallas 2008).

41 KK Rusch, 'Batman in the Real World' as cited by O'Neil (n 40) 192.

42 Attempts to get figures or a list of popularity from an online costume store and the trade association were met with a 'commercial confidence' denial.

43 Phillips and Strobl (n 2) 1.

44 Phillips and Strobl (n 2) 17.

Batman Begins gets only a 'further viewing' recommendation in a chapter on the Chicago School in which *Taxi Driver* is the exemplar.[45] Contributors to *Law Text Culture* introduced by Gómez Romero and Dahlman redress some of these deficiencies.[46] And Sharp pertinently asks, '"Riddle me this . . ?" Would the world need superheroes if the law could actually deliver "justice"?'.[47] Sharp's respondents express a desire for 'justice' which the superhero appears to answer.

Like Cervantes's deluded *Don Quixote*, Dave Lizewski in *Kick Ass* takes up his romantic quest after reading comic books. The mimetic dangers of all media are a commonplace of 'the media' and some psychology but largely derided within cultural studies.[48] The most famous example of the 'media effect' literature is Wertham, who was particularly exercised by the homosexual themes he detected in Batman.[49] Today his fear-mongering is presented as 'one of the first published queer readings of superhero characters'.[50]

Wertham might be better known in criminology for introducing the term 'victimology',[51] but amongst comic book fans he generally enjoys a reputation akin to Lombroso (important, but mostly wrong). Although he was not wrong on the racial stereotyping and advertising of knives and guns.[52] His work as a psychiatrist convinced him that much juvenile crime could be laid at the feet of comics.[53] I speculate, however, in assuming that even Wertham might not ascribe the actions of the dads and the other 'baggy' Batmen described here to reading the comics.

No more heroes

In scene 13 of his *Life of Galileo*, Brecht has his characters say:

45 NH Rafter and M Brown, *Criminology Goes to the Movies: Crime Theory and Popular Culture* (New York University Press 2011).

46 L Gómez Romero and I Dahlman, 'Introduction – Justice Framed: Law in Comics and Graphic Novels' (2012) 16 *Law Text Culture* 3.

47 C Sharp, '"Riddle me this . . ?" Would the World Need Superheroes if the Law Could Actually Deliver "Justice"?' (2012) 16 *Law Text Culture* 353.

48 D Gauntlett, *Media, Gender and Identity: An Introduction* (Routledge 2008).

49 F Wertham, *Seduction of the Innocent* (first published 1954, Rinehart 1972).

50 G Schott, 'From Fan Appropriation to Industry Re-appropriation: The Sexual Identity of Comic Superheroes' (2010) 1 *Journal of Graphic Novels and Comics* 17, abstract.

51 F Wertham, *Show of Violence* (first published 1949, Greenwood 1969).

52 G Kannenberg Jr, 'The Not-So-Untold Story of the Great Comic-Book Scare' (2008) 54 *Chronicle of Higher Education* B19.

53 See, for history and analysis of Wertham's lesser influence in UK and the organised Left's use of his work, M Barker, *A Haunt of Fears: The Strange History of the British Horror Comics Campaign* (Pluto Press 1984).

Andrea: Unhappy the land that has no heroes.
Galileo: Unhappy the land that is in need of heroes.

In this concluding section, there are some thoughts about heroism which question the need for heroes but still the need to understand them.

Dienhart examined couples who shared childcare and uses the term 'hero' three times in her book. The first in a discussion of the 'modern father' who is *not* seen as the 'family expert or hero'.[54] The second and third times are on the tendency to see any man who goes beyond traditional expectations of paternal involvement as a 'hero'.[55] So you do not need a mask or a costume, just a prop – a pram will do. Or, perhaps, a shared interest in a book, even a comic one.

Koronowicz compares superheroes, specifically Batman, to 'Hemingway code heroes' and notes the need for both to do something to be active.[56] The fathers discussed here certainly want to be active in gaining access to their children and, it is suggested by feminists, control over them and their former partners.

Some of Jordan's respondents admired Jason Hatch, the Buckingham Palace Batman,[57] but there was also a feeling he enjoyed the challenge and the media spotlight as much as or more than he loved his children. In dressing as a superhero he, indeed anyone, can become a 'celebrity'. But even Batman can find himself described as a 'grand standing psycho'.[58]

The comic book and graphic novel *oeuvre* is so diverse I would not be surprised if some of the themes mentioned in this chapter have already been tackled implicitly or explicitly in them. As Giddens reminds us:

> one of the overall themes of *Watchmen*. . . works to undermine the historical association of comics with the juvenility of superhero narratives. Hence, *Watchmen* portrays, amongst other things, flabby middle-aged men dealing with the psychological neuroses surrounding actually dressing up in spandex. . .[59]

54 A Dienhart, *Reshaping Fatherhood: The Social Construction of Shared Parenting* (Sage 1998) 8.

55 Ibid 182, 200.

56 Koronowicz (n 4) 3.

57 A Channel 4 documentary showed his exploits, see 'Dad's Army: The Men Who Stormed the Palace' (Channel 4 Television, 11 October 2004).

58 'Batman: Shadow of the Bat, Part 1' (Warner Bros, 13 September 1993). See LA Kort-Butler, 'Justice League? Depictions of Justice in Children's Superhero Cartoons' (2012) 38 *Criminal Justice Review* 50.

59 T Giddens, 'Comics, Law, and Aesthetics: Towards the Use of Graphic Fiction in Legal Studies' (2012) 6 *Law and Humanities* 85, 103 n 83.

The quote continues, '. . . and going out to fight crime'.[60] Perhaps I will write the story in which Bruce Wayne is at Buckingham Palace for a reception when Jason Hatch turns up dressed as Batman and the Queen turns out to have a better knowledge of the canon.

Academic readings of Batman may point out his paternalism. Through the efforts of F4J, Del Boy and the Bradford vigilante might we see that Bruce Wayne dresses up not as a bat but as that foolish old man, your dad? Superhero fans might be upset by the antics of F4J. As a man I am sometimes outraged, but not entirely surprised; and, to paraphrase Medhurst, note that F4J revealed some caped men as pompous fools, the embodiment of superseded ethics, and open sexists.[61]

I too have been distracted by these men's stunts and largely ignored women. There is a clear disparity in the numbers of female superheroes and the gendered and gendering of both male and female superheroes. Sulmicki notes that even where women appear in comics they continue to do so as victim or decoration.[62] Lebel takes Kirsten Dunst's plea to the videogame makers' depiction of her character as the title of her article, 'Tone Down the Boobs, Please!'.[63]

Many of the 'superhero' dads have had the support of second wives/partners but a support group, 'The Purplehearts', get only passing mention by O'Connor.[64] O'Connor quotes an email from a 'single mum' volunteering to be Wonder Woman.[65] Her offer is not taken up, and although the issue is not discussed directly, Chapter 21 is entitled 'Bye Bye, Batman – Hello Wonder Woman' and records the descent of F4J into factions, for which media and Security Service infiltration are mainly blamed.

But what of women protestors and costume? An internet search reveals many campaigning groups of 'Mothers against. . .' and 'Mothers for. . . .' but image searches reveal – and this clearly biased by recent events – most women wearing ordinary clothes or Femen stripping off.[66] It is to be hoped that flabby fathers do not take to sloganising their beer bellies. Islamic dress offers plenty of scope to avoid identification. The Pussy Riot look

60 Ibid.

61 Medhurst (n 5).

62 M Sulmicki, '"And All Right, We Need a Woman": Victimised Heroines and Heroic Victims in Alan Moore's Quasi-Victorian Graphic Novels' in JC Evans and T Giddens (eds), *Cultural Excavation and Formal Expression in the Graphic Novel* (Inter-Disciplinary Press 2013).

63 S Lebel, '"Tone Down the Boobs, Please!": Reading the Special Effect Body in Superhero Movies' (2009) 77 *CineAction* 56.

64 O'Connor (n 21).

65 O'Connor (n 21) 136.

66 See their website <http://femen.org/en> accessed 7 March 2014.

has meme-potential for their supporters. The Suffragettes for whom O'Connor expresses frequent praise dressed in the garb of the day but now some women dress like that to make a point.[67] The five women Greenpeace protestors who climbed the Shard dressed for the job in hand.[68] But stepping back on to the page we find the real life 'hero' Malala accorded her own cartoon strip.[69] It would be tempting to make a gendered distinction, but it is with men we conclude.

Gavaler persuasively argues for ur-text status for Thomas Dixon Jr's 1905 novel *The Clansman* introducing the masked vigilante hero type (Ben Cameron/Grand Dragon), which Superman and Batman follow.[70] And whilst it seems as unlikely that F4J activists know this work or the film based on it (DW Griffiths's *Birth of a Nation* 1915), they clearly see themselves as much under threat from women as the Klan did from black people.

There are further marks of the intertextuality of these matters and the elision of fact and fiction in O'Connor's claim that Will Self admitted gaining some inspiration for the main character both in the *Book of Dave* from him and F4J, and in Scotland Yard's Royal Protection unit commemorating their own embarrassment with a badge showing Batman astride Buckingham Palace and the date 13 September 2004.[71]

Writing for *The Observer* website, Jeffrey A Brown notes that film technology has only now enabled the depiction of superheroes that had only properly been achieved in comics before. His complaint about unflatteringly dressed men was with the actors:

> For the most part, live action superheroes looked like what they were: grown men playing dress-up in unflattering tights. Seeing real people in unitards battling buffoonish supervillains robbed the genre of all the magic and fantasy that could be depicted on an illustrated page.[72]

67 A Topping, 'Olympic Suffragettes Regroup for Women's Rights March on Parliament' (*The Guardian*, 19 August 2012) <www.theguardian.com/uk/2012/aug/19/olympic-suffragettes-rights-march-parliament> accessed 7 March 2014.

68 'Who are the Shard Protest Climbers?' (*ITV News*, 12 July 2013) <www.itv.com/news/update/2013-07-11/who-are-the-shard-protest-climbers/> accessed 7 March 2014.

69 E Dionne, 'A Cartoon Depicts Malala Yousafzai's Courage' (*Clutch*, 11 March 2013) <www.clutchmagonline.com/2013/03/a-cartoon-depicts-malala-yousafzais-courage/> accessed 7 March 2014. Malala was attacked by the Taliban for seeking out and campaigning for girls' education.

70 C Gavaler, 'The Ku Klux Klan and the Birth of the Superhero' (2012) 4 *Journal of Graphic Novels and Comics* 191; T Dixon Jr, *The Clansman: An Historical Romance of the Ku Klux Klan* (first published 1905, NuVision 2005).

71 O'Connor (n 21) 214, 221.

72 JA Brown, 'How Marvel's Superheroes Found the Magic to Make Us All True Believers' (*The Guardian*, 31 August 2013) <www.theguardian.com/film/2013/aug/31/marvel-superheroes-true-believers> accessed 7 March 2014.

No technology looks ready to save many of the men discussed here and Wonder Woman's powers do not seem to include the feminism that might do the trick.[73] In demanding 'justice', they may be demanding 'superhero justice', which Phillips and Strobl note is of the retributive kind.[74] Sadly, for there continues to be faults with the family courts, we may just see 'Fools' (and Horses) when we next see 'Batman' up a building.

We have seen Batman up buildings, on tie pins, at police counters and on UK TV screens as Del Boy and again at the Olympics. Graphic novel and comic book scholars have ignored these emanations, perhaps fearing the ghost of Wertham; and other scholars have seen only the fool on the sill. Both need to be challenged.

Acknowledgements

I would like to thank Thom Giddens for getting me into to this and keeping me to task.

Bibliography

'Aus Police Hunt for Papa Smurf' (*Yahoo News NZ*, 9 January 2013) <http://nz.news.yahoo.com/a/-/mp/15789714/aus-police-hunt-for-papa-smurf/> accessed 7 March 2014.

Barker M, *A Haunt of Fears: The Strange History of the British Horror Comics Campaign* (Pluto Press 1984).

'Batman: Shadow of the Bat, Part 1' (Warner Bros, 13 September 1993).

Blais M, and Dupuis-Déri F, 'Masculinism and the Antifeminist Countermovement' (2012) 11 *Social Movement Studies* 21.

'Bradford Batman: "Superhero" Hands Wanted Man Over to Police' (*Evening Standard*, 4 March 2013) <www.standard.co.uk/news/crime/bradford-batman-superhero-hands-wanted-man-over-to-police-8519462.html> accessed 7 March 2014.

Brooker W, *Hunting the Dark Knight: Twenty-First Century Batman* (IB Taurus 2012).

Brown JA, 'How Marvel's Superheroes Found the Magic to Make Us All True Believers' (*The Guardian*, 31 August 2013) <www.theguardian.com/film/2013/aug/31/marvel-superheroes-true-believers> accessed 7 March 2014.

Cawey S, 'Comics and American Feminism: Wonder Woman' (*The Stockton Postcolonial Studies Project Blog*) <https://blogs.stockton.edu/postcolonialstudies/comics-and-american-feminism-wonder-woman/> accessed 7 March 2014.

73 Although, for arguments about how 'feminist' Wonder Woman is, see S Cawey, 'Comics and American Feminism: Wonder Woman' (*The Stockton Postcolonial Studies Project Blog*) <https://blogs.stockton.edu/postcolonialstudies/comics-and-american-feminism-wonder-woman/> accessed 7 March 2014.

74 Phillips and Strobl (n 2).

Collier RS, 'The Fathers' Rights Movement, Law Reform, and the New Politics of Fatherhood: Some Reflections on the UK Experience' (2009) 20 *University of Florida Journal of Law and Public Policy* 65.

Crowley J, 'Taking Custody of Motherhood: Fathers' Rights Activists and Politics of Parenting' (2009) 37 *Women's Studies Quarterly* 223.

'Dad's Army: The Men Who Stormed the Palace' (Channel 4 Television, 11 October 2004).

Dienhart A, *Reshaping Fatherhood: The Social Construction of Shared Parenting* (Sage 1998) 8.

Dionne E, 'A Cartoon Depicts Malala Yousafzai's Courage' (*Clutch*, 11 March 2013) <www.clutchmagonline.com/2013/03/a-cartoon-depicts-malala-yousafzais-courage/> accessed 7 March 2014.

Dixon Jr T, *The Clansman: An Historical Romance of the Ku Klux Klan* (first published 1905, NuVision 2005).

Durand KKJ and Leigh MK, *Riddle Me This, Batman! Essays on the Universe of the Dark Knight* (McFarland 2011).

Evans JC and Giddens T, 'Introduction' in Evans JC and Giddens T (eds), *Cultural Excavation and Formal Expression in the Graphic Novel* (Inter-Disciplinary Press 2013).

'Fathers' Cathedral Protest Ends' (*BBC News*, 12 July 2004) <http://news.bbc.co.uk/1/hi/uk/3884265.stm> accessed 7 March 2014.

Fennel J, 'The Aesthetics of Supervillainy' (2012) 16 *Law Text Culture* 305.

Flood M, 'Separated Fathers and the "Fathers' Rights" Movement' (2012) 18 *Journal of Family Studies* 235.

'Fools and Horses is top of Xmas TV' (*The Sun*, 12 January 2011) <www.thesun.co.uk/sol/homepage/news/3255136/Del-Boy-tops-Xmas-TV-moments-poll.html> accessed 24 July 2013.

Gauntlett D, *Media, Gender and Identity: An Introduction* (Routledge 2008).

Gavaler C, 'The Ku Klux Klan and the Birth of the Superhero' (2012) 4 *Journal of Graphic Novels and Comics* 191.

Giddens T, 'Comics, Law, and Aesthetics: Towards the Use of Graphic Fiction in Legal Studies' (2012) 6 *Law and Humanities* 85.

Gómez Romero L and Dahlman I, 'Introduction – Justice Framed: Law in Comics and Graphic Novels' (2012) 16 *Law Text Culture* 3.

Hatfield C, Heer J and Worcester K, *The Superhero Reader* (University Press of Mississippi 2013).

Henry M, 'Looking for Amanda Hugginkiss: Gay Life on *The Simpsons*' in Alber J (ed), *Leaving Springfield: The Simpsons and the Possibilities of Oppositional Culture* (Wayne State University Press 2004).

Jordan A, '"Dads Aren't Demons. Mums Aren't Madonnas": Constructions of Fatherhood and Masculinities in the (Real) Fathers 4 Justice Campaign' (2009) 31 *Journal of Social Welfare and Family Law* 419.

Kannenberg Jr G, 'The Not-So-Untold Story of the Great Comic-Book Scare' (2008) 54 *Chronicle of Higher Education* B19.

Koronowicz A, 'Loner, Lover, Hero: Superhero Reads Hemingway' in Evans JC and Giddens T (eds), *Cultural Excavation and Formal Expression in the Graphic Novel* (Inter-Disciplinary Press 2013).

Kort-Butler LA, 'Justice League? Depictions of Justice in Children's Superhero Cartoons' (2012) 38 *Criminal Justice Review* 50.

Langford N, 'A Short History of Fathers 4 Justice' (*Scribd.com*, 18 February 2013) <www.scribd.com/doc/126039862/Histoire-Father-4-Justice> accessed 7 March 2014.

Lebel S, '"Tone Down the Boobs, Please!": Reading the Special Effect Body in Superhero Movies' (2009) 77 *CineAction* 56.

Medhurst A, 'Batman, Deviance and Camp' in Pearson RE and Uricchio W (eds), *The Many Lives of the Batman: Critical Approaches to a Superhero and His Media* (Routledge 1991).

O'Connor M, *Fathers 4 Justice: The Inside Story* (Weidenfeld and Nicolson 2007).

O'Neil D, *Batman Unauthorized: Vigilantes, Jokers, and Heroes in Gotham City* (BenBella Books Dallas 2008).

Phillips N and Strobl S, *Comic Book Crime: Truth, Justice, and the American Way* (New York University Press 2013).

Rafter NH and Brown M, *Criminology Goes to the Movies: Crime Theory and Popular Culture* (New York University Press 2011).

Schott G, 'From Fan Appropriation to Industry Re-appropriation: The Sexual Identity of Comic Superheroes' (2010) 1 *Journal of Graphic Novels and Comics* 17.

Sharp C, '"Riddle me this . . .?" Would the World Need Superheroes if the Law Could Actually Deliver "Justice"?' (2012) 16 *Law Text Culture* 353.

Sulmicki M, '"And All Right, We Need a Woman": Victimised Heroines and Heroic Victims in Alan Moore's Quasi-Victorian Graphic Novels' in Evans JC and Giddens T (eds), *Cultural Excavation and Formal Expression in the Graphic Novel* (Inter-Disciplinary Press 2013).

Topping A, 'Olympic Suffragettes Regroup for Women's Rights March on Parliament' (*The Guardian*, 19 August 2012) <www.theguardian.com/uk/2012/aug/19/olympic-suffragettes-rights-march-parliament> accessed 7 March 2014.

Weltzien F, 'Masque-ulinities: Changing Dress as a Display of Masculinity in the Superhero Genre' (2005) 9 *Fashion Theory: The Journal of Dress, Body and Culture* 229.

Wertham F, *Show of Violence* (first published 1949, Greenwood 1969).

Wertham F, *Seduction of the Innocent* (first published 1954, Rinehart 1972).

'Who are the Shard Protest Climbers?' (*ITV News*, 12 July 2013) <www.itv.com/news/update/2013-07-11/who-are-the-shard-protest-climbers/> accessed 7 March 2014.

Part III

Graphic justice international

Chapter 11

The hero we need, not the one we deserve: vigilantism and the state of exception in *Batman Incorporated*

Chris Comerford

Scholarly research into superhero comic narratives has arguably been neglected, particularly in regard to the latter's use as a lens for social commentary.[1] Accordingly, my interest in writing this chapter in the broadest sense is to enter into a dialogue with others, and provide space in which one can reflect on the value of the superhero comic book as a scholarly resource. Comic book narratives, I believe, offer rich ground for examining the interrelationship between real and fictional worlds, with Batman in particular examining the notions of vigilantism, ethics, and justice. I frame this conversation through discourse with Giorgio Agamben's conceptualisation of the 'state of exception'[2] and an analysis of the *Batman Incorporated* comic book written by Scottish author Grant Morrison and published by DC Comics in three volumes.[3] This analysis not only highlights intersections between graphic literature and the law, but also examines the inherent dangers present in utilising an exceptional state of security contemporaneously. In Morrison's work, Batman presents a more grounded, realistic character in comparison to his supernatural and extra-terrestrial contemporaries, and the *Incorporated* narrative is particularly useful as an analytical lens for ideas regarding the state of exception. This is due to the narrative's recent publication and representation of the post-9/11 United States – and, by extension, its links to the state of exception – through a fictional mode.

1 J Bainbridge, '"This is the Authority. This Planet is Under Our Protection" – An Exegesis of Superheroes' Interrogations of Law' (2007) 3 *Law, Culture and the Humanities* 455, 456.

2 G Agamben, *State of Exception* (first published 2003, K Attell tr, University of Chicago Press 2005).

3 G Morrison, *Batman Incorporated: The Deluxe Edition* (DC Comics 2012); G Morrison, *Batman Incorporated: Demon Star* (DC Comics 2013); G Morrison, *Batman Incorporated: Gotham's Most Wanted* (DC Comics 2013).

'*Necessitas legem non habet*':[4] terrorism and the state of exception

In his 2005 text *State of Exception*,[5] building on political and juridical ideas presented in his 1998 work *Homo Sacer*,[6] Italian philosopher Giorgio Agamben explores the connection between power, necessity and the law relative to the concept of the state of exception, derived from German philosopher Carl Schmitt's seminal text *Dictatorship*.[7] In Agamben's paradigm, the state of exception is an idea that resides on the boundary between law and ethics. It is a state of being, evident in most civilisations dating back to the Roman era and the ideal of *iustitium* (literally, 'standstill' or 'suspension of the law').[8]

Agamben convincingly assesses previous attempts to define the state of exception as limited; averring that the term has been mired in internal contradictions and disjunctions of logic.[9] He further posits that the state of exception 'is a force of law without law';[10] by its nature, the central aporia of the state of exception negates the law itself. The latter exists depending on the 'necessity'. Necessity is not a source of law, nor does it properly suspend the law; it merely releases a particular case from the literal application of the 'norm'[11] for the 'common well-being of men'.[12] This perception is embodied in Agamben's appropriation of the Latin maxim '*necessitas legem non habet* (necessity has no law)'.[13]

The justification for the state of exception is largely represented as an 'emergency' or crisis.[14] It is constructed by those in power as the only means of defending a country or cultural group because of a gap in or absence of law. Agamben argues compellingly that enacting 'law' via the state of exception (eg Barack Obama's order to neutralise the threat of Osama bin Laden) and the prolonged absence of the 'norm',[15] can result in a situation worse than that which necessitated the exception in the first place. After all, an 'emergency' or 'crisis', like 'necessity', is a

4 Agamben (n 2) 1.
5 Agamben (n 2).
6 G Agamben, *Homo Sacer: Sovereign Power and Bare Life* (first published 1995, D Heller-Roazen tr, Stanford University Press 1998).
7 C Schmitt, *Dictatorship* (first published 1921, M Hielzl and G Ward tr, Polity Press 2013).
8 Agamben (n 2) 41.
9 Agamben (n 2) 1–2.
10 Agamben (n 2) 39.
11 Agamben (n 2) 25.
12 Agamben (n 2).
13 Agamben (n 2) 24.
14 Agamben (n 2) 21.
15 Agamben (n 2) 23.

subjective, not objective, phenomenon.[16] Autocracy, Agamben postulates, is a real threat to democracy if full executive powers are not returned in a timely manner to the usual mechanisms of a democratic government.[17] However, it must be noted that democracies employ the state of exception frequently. This is exemplified historically not just by totalitarian regimes such as Hitler's Germany,[18] but also by democratic ones, such as the Weimar Republic.[19]

The tragedy of al-Qaeda's 2001 terrorist[20] attack on the World Trade Center irrevocably affected the world. This momentous event escalated the War on Terror to a 'global civil war'[21] and created the 'necessity' for a state of exception. In effect, the state of exception denotes a situational emergency where usual faculties of law and judicial process are suspended and superseded by the emergency itself. In this scenario, a central figure or organisational entity determines the exceptional status of the state (when a state of exception can be declared), usually during crises such as war, and as such suspends proper legal processes to exclusively wield authority. This conception has its origins in the Roman notion of *auctoritas*.[22] In effect, the declarant of a state of exception becomes an arbiter of power largely devoid of official legal strictures. In this context, an organisational entity or central figure determines the exceptional status of the state. Agamben declares that the state of exception 'constitutes rather a kenomatic state, an emptiness of law'.[23]

Agamben's *State of Exception* persuasively analyses historical events from Roman to contemporary epochs, from totalitarian regimes, dictatorships, and terrorist organisations to democracies in his erudite examination of the state of exception as a paradigm in and of itself. A discussion by Agamben of former US President George W Bush's USA Patriot Act[24] exemplifies democratic instances of the state of exception in response to 9/11. In particular, the discussion notes how these acts can be classified as state-sanctioned vigilantism, in which citizens in a democracy can be deprived of their citizenship and human rights, through the example of captured Taliban agents in Afghanistan 'not [enjoying] the status of POWs as defined by the Geneva Convention'.[25]

16 Agamben (n 2) 31.
17 Agamben (n 2) 20.
18 Agamben (n 2) 2.
19 Agamben (n 2) 15.
20 'Foreign Terrorist Organisations' (*US Department of State*) <www.state.gov/j/ct/rls/other/des/123085.htm> accessed 18 June 2014.
21 Agamben (n 2) 2.
22 Agamben (n 2) 74–88.
23 Agamben (n 2) 6.
24 Agamben (n 2) 3.
25 Agamben (n 2).

Advocating American strength in the face of adversity and declaring a War on Terror[26] was the beginning of a chain of security-driven events initiated by Bush in 2001 that eventually lead to the 2011 death of 9/11's chief architect, Osama bin Laden, during President Barack Obama's Operation Neptune Spear.[27] Although hailed by Obama himself[28] and others[29] as an affirmative action taken for the purposes of security, the killing of bin Laden - discussed later in this chapter - raised questions regarding its legality and ethics.[30] The killing also highlighted ways in which the contemporary United States could be seen as existing, to a degree, within its own state of exception.

'Batman is everywhere. And if he didn't exist, well . . . I guess we'd just have to invent him':[31] vigilantism and *Batman Incorporated*

It is within the real world context of the state of exception that we find the fictional text *Batman Incorporated* and contemplate the character of Batman as an agent who enacts the state of exception. Batman is an anti-heroic vigilante and superhero whose narrative 'highlights the inadequacies of the present [real world] system in the same way a test case might highlight the inadequacies of law.'[32]

During the 13 years since 9/11, comic book superheroes have gained greater popularity and worldwide exposure, primarily through motion pictures but also graphic literature. Arguably, one reason for the rise in

26 'President Declares "Freedom at War with Fear"' (*George W Bush White House Archives*, 20 September 2001) <http://georgewbush-whitehouse.archives.gov/news/releases/2001/09/print/20010920-8.html> accessed 20 March 2014.

27 M Phillips, 'Osama Bin Laden Dead' (*The White House Blog*, 2 May 2011) <www.whitehouse.gov/blog/2011/05/02/osama-bin-laden-dead> accessed 14 June 2013.

28 Ibid.

29 'Celebrating the Death of Osama bin Laden' (*Time Magazine*, 2 May 2011) <www.time.com/time/photogallery/0,29307,2068860,00.html> accessed 18 July 2013; O Bowcott, 'Osama bin Laden: US Responds to Questions about Killing's Legality' (*The Guardian*, 4 May 2011) <www.theguardian.com/world/2011/may/03/osama-bin-laden-killing-legality> accessed 18 March 2014; KH Govern, 'Operation Neptune Spear: Was Killing Bin Laden a Legitimate Objective?' in C Finkelstein, J David Ohlin and A Altman (eds), *Targeted Killings: Law and Morality in an Asymmetrical World* (Oxford University Press 2012) 348; D Wallace, 'Operation Neptune's [sic] Spear: The Lawful Killing of Osama Bin Laden' (2012) 45 *Israel Law Review* 367.

30 DA Green, 'Law, Justice and the Death of Osama bin Laden' (*New Statesman*, 2 May 2011) <www.newstatesman.com/blogs/david-allen-green/2011/05/bin-laden-osama> accessed 14 June 2013; R Lambert, 'What if Bin Laden had Stood Trial?' (*The Guardian*, 3 May 2011) <www.newstatesman.com/blogs/david-allen-green/2011/05/bin-laden-osama> accessed 14 June 2013.

31 Morrison, *Deluxe Edition* (n 3) 118.

32 Bainbridge (n 1) 462.

popularity of superheroes is the reciprocal relationship between fictitious and real worlds.[33] Fictional superheroes in the real global world of 'civil war'[34] facilitate a conversation between contemporaneous real world events vis à vis crime (domestic and international), justice, vigilantism and ethics. This is a reciprocal relationship; life mirrors art and art mirrors life.

Such a position is supported by academic Jason Bainbridge's premise that 'consideration of the superhero becomes a consideration of the relationship between law and justice - another way of thinking discursively about the law'.[35] The latter enables conversation with real world ideas through a fictional mode; the debut of *Iron Man*, for example, sees the character's arms trading backstory and violent origin both influenced and galvanised respectively by Middle Eastern extremists,[36] whilst *Captain America: The Winter Soldier* confronts contemporary corruption in US politics.[37] Where Batman is concerned, Christopher Nolan's *Dark Knight* trilogy[38] interrogates and reflects contemporary issues such as the Global Financial Crisis, the threat of domestic terrorism, and societal anxieties that have manifested since 9/11.

Several narratives released since Batman's 1939 creation[39] draw attention to lawless aspects of the character's practice,[40] as well as scholarship examining the role of Batman as a representation of vigilantism,[41] prominent popular culture figurehead,[42] and significantly as an enactor of a state of exception.[43] The value of a particular exploration of real world vigilantism - and, by extension, its relation to implementing and maintaining an exceptional state - in a popular culture text such as Batman is that the popularity and wide circulation of the text suggests that the comic both articulates contemporary concerns about this practice and identifies the ways in which it has been reconciled in the popular imagination.

The narrative of *Batman Incorporated* follows the formation of an eponymous global peacekeeping effort under the leadership of the Dark

33 G Morrison, *Supergods: Our World in the Age of the Superhero* (Jonathan Cape 2011).
34 Agamben (n 2) 3.
35 Bainbridge (n 1) 457.
36 J Favreau (dir), *Iron Man* (Paramount Pictures 2008).
37 A Russo and J Russo (dirs), *Captain America: The Winter Soldier* (Walt Disney Studios Motion Pictures 2014).
38 C Nolan (dir), *Batman Begins* (Warner Bros 2005); C Nolan (dir), *The Dark Knight* (Warner Bros 2008); C Nolan (dir), *The Dark Knight Rises* (Warner Bros 2012).
39 B Kane and B Finger, *Detective Comics #27* (Detective Comics, Inc 1939).
40 See eg, E Brubaker and G Rucka, *Gotham Central: In the Line of Duty* (DC Comics 2011); G Johns, *Batman: Earth One* (DC Comics 2012).
41 Morrison (n 33).
42 W Brooker, *Hunting the Dark Knight: Twenty-First Century Batman* (IB Tauris 2012).
43 T McGowan, 'The Exceptional Darkness of *The Dark Knight*' (2009) 51 *Jump Cut: A Review of Contemporary Media* <www.ejumpcut.org/archive/jc51.2009/darkKnightKant/text.html> accessed 11 June 2014.

Knight (hereafter referred to as 'Incorporated' or the 'Incorporated initiative'). Its purpose is to combat crime in almost every country worldwide by soliciting members from its international contributors, including Japan,[44] France,[45] China[46] and Australia.[47] All international agents fall under the aegis of Batman himself, operating centrally out of Gotham City.

The Incorporated initiative's chief antagonist is a terrorist network named Leviathan. The network utilises brainwashing, suicide bombers, child soldiers and religiously-informed symbolism to exert violence ostensibly against Incorporated and the world at large, preaching a campaign of anarchy and the overthrowing of the social order.[48] Their leader, Talia al Ghul, is of Middle Eastern descent.[49]

The war between Incorporated and Leviathan escalates and triggers a destructive battle in Gotham that kills Batman's son[50] and destroys most of Wayne Tower.[51] Subsequently, though Batman defeats Leviathan, Incorporated is officially outlawed and ostracised from both Gotham and the world at large, with police enforcing strict measures to halt Batman's crime-fighting efforts.[52] Incorporated enters liquidation, and the narrative concludes with Batman resuming his vigilante protection of Gotham alone.[53] Despite Incorporated's failure, the potential exists for Batman to revive the initiative in the future.[54]

The discourse in the current chapter, on *Batman Incorporated*'s narrative, is situated within the concept of the state of exception. It proposes that Batman enacts his own state of exception through vigilantism. Despite its problematic nature, vigilantism is not necessarily immoral or unethical. Indeed, it may be construed as a legitimate response to a vacuum in lawful agency, one that has perhaps more ethics than real-world scenarios, including those constructed by Barack Obama's Operation Neptune Spear.

The body of literature on vigilantism offers a plethora of definitions and interpretations. The antecedent of the term 'vigilante' is from the Spanish word *vigilante* meaning 'watchman, or guardian'.[55] Some assert that this positive connotation has shifted to a more sinister contemporary

44 Morrison, *Deluxe Edition* (n 3) 20.
45 Morrison, *Deluxe Edition* (n 3) 125.
46 Morrison, *Deluxe Edition* (n 3) 128.
47 Morrison, *Deluxe Edition* (n 3) 129.
48 Morrison, *Demon Star* (n 3) 77.
49 Morrison, *Demon Star* (n 3) 55.
50 Morrison, *Gotham's Most Wanted* (n 3) 50.
51 Morrison, *Gotham's Most Wanted* (n 3) 113.
52 Morrison, *Gotham's Most Wanted* (n 3) 80.
53 Morrison, *Gotham's Most Wanted* (n 3) 138.
54 Morrison, *Gotham's Most Wanted* (n 3) 204.
55 B Newby, 'Watchful Guardian or Dark Knight? The Vigilante as a Social Actor' (*International Foundation for Protection Officers*, July 2012) <www.ifpo.org/wp-content/uploads/2013/08/Newby_Vigilante.pdf> accessed 19 June 2014, 1.

definition representing the transition from 'a heroic, selfless person' to 'a darker, more dangerous character'.[56] Brian Newby, in his study of the multifaceted nature of real world vigilantism historically and contemporaneously, proposes that one reason people are drawn to vigilantism is its capacity as an answer to 'a cause that they do not see being addressed through institutional channels'.[57] Vigilantes (both real and fictional) believe the 'current social structure to be ineffective in resolving a specific social problem'[58] that has been neglected; 'not in a lack of recognition of the problem, but in a lack of action against it'.[59] Jared Keller, in his informative study of vigilantism particularly in comic books, records the 'popular conception of vigilantism is of individual citizens "taking the law into their own hands" where conventional law enforcement is perceived to be absent or ineffective'.[60] Keller confesses he has been 'an avid reader and collector of comic books' and this fascination is the 'creative basis for examining vigilantism as a historical, political, and social occurrence'.[61] He further defines the comic book 'vigilante' through a historical lens as:

> [A] costumed adventurer who exhibits the characteristics of an anti-hero, or 'a good guy who does bad things for the right reasons.' In typical dichotomy between good and evil that characterizes the classic superhero stories of the 1940s and 1950s, the costumed vigilante lies somewhere in between the two, using violent methods and constantly forced to escape pursuit from regular law enforcement.[62]

Batman has been interpreted as the original anti-hero of the superhero genre 'employing illegal and morally dubious tactics (like torture and intrusive surveillance), instilling fear in his enemies, and displaying a strong willingness to work outside the law to capture criminals'.[63] The character has even been likened to 'a terrorist who fights criminals'[64] and who enacts a state of exception reflective of real world situations:

> Because of its non-contractual and public nature, vigilantism necessarily appeals to a different breed of sovereignty rooted in its reaction to crisis. Vigilantism ... consists of violent acts that stand 'outside of

56 Ibid 2.
57 Ibid.
58 Ibid 4.
59 Ibid.
60 J Keller, '*Pax Vigilanticus*: Vigilantism, Order, and Law in the Nineteenth Century American West' (*Wesleyan University*, April 2009) <wesscholar.wesleyan.edu/cgi/viewcontent.cgi?article=1241&context=etd_hon_theses> accessed 20 June 2014, 3.
61 Ibid.
62 Ibid 3–4.
63 Ibid 4.
64 Ibid.

> the formal boundaries of an established socio-political order which, however, are intended by the violators to defend that order from some form of subversion.' In this sense, the nature of vigilante sovereignty closely resembles the paradigm of government stemming from the idea of a state of exception ... as basis for 'emergency powers' in constitutional governments.[65]

In contrast, academics Scott Vollum and Cary D Adkinson represent Batman in a more positive light suggesting that this vigilante label originates from Batman '[fighting] for justice on his own terms and in the context of what he considers to be just'[66] without the impediments of the law.

At an early age, Bruce Wayne witnessed Joe Chill murder his parents. As an adult, Wayne responded by dedicating his life to leading a campaign against crime no matter the personal or public cost.[67] Wayne styled himself as the Batman, a figure solely concerned with answering the criminal element of Gotham City. This answer appears in the form of physical violence and psychological tactics to combat the city's antagonists without any form of official legal process. In this reading, Batman is positioned more heroically: the unwilling victim of a lawless murder, transformed and imbued with agency. Batman is arguably driven by ethical precepts. He is bound by a non-lethal code and at times co-operates with Gotham City's Police Department, the latter often occurring within a paradox of simultaneously condoning and condemning the Batman's vigilantism.[68]

Readers that legitimise Batman's vigilante status represent him as a self-proclaimed ethical defender of innocents who utilises violence judiciously and justly, one who uses 'fear on those who prey upon the fearful'.[69] In the fictional world of Gotham, no sanctioned power validates Batman's campaign; his existence answers the lawlessness and ineffectual and corrupt police enforcement.[70] In the character's mind, legal strictures are secondary to the moral imperatives, 'Batman refuses to accept the official definition of law and takes it upon himself to become an arbiter of justice, deriving the sense of law from within himself'.[71]

Batman's self-appointed guardianship is articulated in the informative work of Cassandra Sharp. Sharp characterises a vigilante as one who,

65 Ibid 153, citing HJ Rosenbaum and PC Sedberg, 'Vigilantism: An Analysis of Establishment Violence'.
66 S Vollum and CD Adkinson, 'The Portrayal of Crime and Justice in the Comic Book Superhero Mythos' (2003) 10 *Journal of Criminal Justice and Popular Culture* 96, 101.
67 F Miller, *Batman: Year One* (DC Comics 1988); Morrison, *Deluxe Edition* (n 3) 125.
68 Brubaker and Rucka (n 40).
69 Nolan, *Batman Begins* (n 38).
70 See eg, Miller (n 67).
71 Vollum and Adkinson (n 66) 102.

'autocratically assumes responsibility for societal power and authority on the basis that not only do circumstances warrant such exceptional action, but that popular sovereignty demands it'.[72] The notions of 'popular sovereignty' and vigilante justice in democracies including the United States are interrelated.[73] Underpinning popular sovereignty is the belief that 'the people' are the legitimate basis of government and thus, 'the people possess the right to reform, alter, or abolish their government at any time'.[74] Some interpretations go further and advocate that American vigilantism is enshrined in the US Constitution, cited explicitly in the Declaration of Independence.[75] These views work towards legitimating Batman's vigilantism as well as popular conceptions of vigilantism itself.

For Batman, it is a moral imperative to engage in social action, to enact 'popular sovereignty' and to assume responsibility in extraordinary circumstances to serve justice and Gotham's beleaguered citizenry who out of 'necessity' desire his presence at a time of crisis rooted in an absence of effective law. This paralegal guardianship gives readers an experience of 'justice' achieved at the expense of the legal and judicial constraints that the real world justice system enforces.

'An endless circle that feeds upon itself':[76] Batman, aporia and exceptional justice

Necessity acts as the platform for Batman's moral imperative; he is *needed*, because he believes the law has failed. This failure is at least implicitly confirmed by the law itself; Police Commissioner James Gordon, one of Gotham's few effective law enforcers, becomes a member of Incorporated, wearing a Bat-symbol badge and asking if his membership, 'makes [him] Batman, too'.[77] This suggests a measure of the law within Gotham has acknowledged its lack of efficacy and ceded to Batman's necessitous campaign. Indeed, Todd McGowan analyses that necessitous aspect and Batman's explicit connection to Agamben's work,[78] the state of exception through Christopher Nolan's *The Dark Knight* film,[79] and the use of Batman as 'a figure of exception'[80] and the issues inherent to that aspect.

72 C Sharp, '"Riddle Me This . . ?" Would the World Need Superheroes if the Law Could Actually Deliver "Justice"?' (2012) 16 *Law Text Culture* 353, 360.
73 CG Fritz, 'Popular Sovereignty, Vigilantism and the Constitutional Right of Revolution' (1994) 63 *Pacific Historical Review* 39.
74 Ibid 39.
75 Keller (n 60) 158.
76 Morrison, *Deluxe Edition* (n 3) 225.
77 Morrison, *Deluxe Edition* (n 3) 119.
78 McGowan (n 43).
79 Nolan, *The Dark Knight* (n 38).
80 T McGowan, *The Fictional Christopher Nolan* (University of Texas Press 2012) 126.

Batman embodies a fundamental aporia - an endless contradiction between law, existing to be upheld but still failing at achieving justice, and necessity superseding the law in order to achieve justice - by using Incorporated to enact a global state of exception. Batman exemplifies the state of exception by acting as a central entity exerting supreme power that supersedes legality. McGowan, through application of Agamben's paradigm to *The Dark Knight*,[81] offers that the state of exception enables one to 'realise the justice that ordinary law is incapable of realising'.[82]

Batman's moral code advocates non-lethal tactics and an ardent refusal to kill in order to maintain an affirmative status quo; this, at least, is a semi-adherence to some form of juridical upholding, rather than pure self-obsessed goal attainment. A central tenet of Batman's *modus operandi* is the restoration of order, despite the character's own refusal of complete adherence to such order; much like the ouroboros theme and imagery that permeates the comic book narrative,[83] Incorporated's aporia presents its own endless contradictory paradigm.

Batman breaks the law, by self-admission, to protect it; this exemplifies the state of exception's topological form relying on 'being-outside, and yet belonging'[84] to the structure of the law, with the figure declaring the exception being 'logically defined in his being by the exception' itself.[85] Batman's international network answerable only to him[86] and explicit declaration of 'war' with Leviathan[87] can be seen as an exertion of sovereignty, creating an entity acting with autonomy[88] primarily concerned with 'security of the nation and its citizens'.[89] In this manner, Incorporated almost becomes its own nation-state, a figure exclusively declaring a global state of exception that self-legitimises a campaign against terrorism.

Despite a lack of legal legitimisation of Incorporated's actions, Batman perceives this autocracy as wholly beneficial; eliminating Leviathan will bring a measure of peace in the fictional world much the same way the campaign against al-Qaeda and the killing of Osama bin Laden works towards real-world peace.[90]

On 1 May 2011, US President Barack Obama authorised Operation Neptune Spear, a military incursion which resulted in the death of Osama bin

81 Nolan, *The Dark Knight* (n 38).
82 McGowan (n 43).
83 Morrison, *Deluxe Edition* (n 3) 73, 79, 225.
84 Agamben (n 2) 35.
85 Agamben (n 2) 35.
86 Morrison, *Deluxe Edition* (n 3) 121.
87 Morrison, *Deluxe Edition* (n 3) 125.
88 R Jackson, *Sovereignty* (Polity Press 2007).
89 Ibid 136.
90 Phillips (n 27).

Laden. The operation saw a team of US Navy SEALs crossing international borders into the city of Abbottabad, Pakistan. The team conducted a raid on bin Laden's high-security compound, located by US intelligence, killing the leader of al-Qaeda under cover of darkness. Obama declared that bin Laden's death was a positive step and 'the most significant achievement to date in [the United States'] effort to defeat al-Qaeda'.[91]

Reaction to the killing of bin Laden outside the White House was polarised; one school of thought argued the killing was rationalised and necessary given the danger bin Laden posed to the rest of the world,[92] especially in light of the myriad issues a criminal trial would present to both the public and the prosecutors.[93] Kevin H Govern opined bin Laden's death was warranted and, 'in theory', no further amendments to current international jurisdiction laws would be necessary to execute similar tactical terrorist neutralising operations in future.[94] Conversely, *New Statesman* legal correspondent David Allen Green believed the operation could 'perhaps [be] an unlawful one',[95] while researcher and academic Robert Lambert noted the killing, amongst other elements, was a loss of 'moral authority'[96] in the ongoing War on Terror. The blurred legal and ethical boundaries stemming from defining in which manner bin Laden was intercepted and killed by the United States - that is, whether the killing was part of a legally-defined 'armed conflict' or as an assassination in its own right[97] - make it difficult to reach a determination regarding unlawful behaviour.

Irrespective of Operation Neptune Spear's definitive legitimacy, Obama's order opened his administration up to claims that he had acted illegally; in effect, as a vigilante '[fighting] for justice on his own terms and in the context of what he considers to be just'.[98]

Consider for a moment surface parallels between the actions taken by the Obama administration and the fictional Incorporated initiative.

91 Phillips (n 27).
92 D Searcey, 'Killing Was Legal Under US and International Law, Many Experts Say' (*The Wall Street Journal*, 6 May 2011) <http://online.wsj.com/news/articles/SB10001424052748704810504576305470980463628> accessed 18 March 2014; Wallace (n 29).
93 JS Chanen 'If I Represented Bin Laden . . .' (*ABA Journal*, 1 September 2007) <www.abajournal.com/magazine/article/if_i_represented_bin_laden/> accessed 20 March 2014.
94 Govern (n 29) 348.
95 Green (n 30).
96 Lambert (n 30).
97 M Allen, 'Osama bin Laden Raid Yields Trove of Computer Data' (*Politico*, 2 May 2011) <www.politico.com/news/stories/0511/54151.html> accessed 24 March 2014; M Apuzzo and A Goldman, 'Bin Laden was Unarmed when SEALs Stormed Room' (*The Salt Lake Tribune*, 3 May 2011) <www.sltrib.com/sltrib/world/51742983-68/bin-laden-seals-compound.html.csp?page=1> accessed 2 April 2014; Govern (n 29); APV Rogers and D McGoldrick, 'Assassination and Targeted Killing - The Killing of Osama bin Laden' (2011) 60 *International and Comparative Law Quarterly* 778.
98 Vollum and Adkinson (n 66) 101.

A Western figure executes an order or initiative as an autocratic decision (in terms of the order taking place with explicit assistance of other entities). An argument is made for the order being in and of itself without legal legitimacy. The order supersedes all other concerns, legal, juridical and moral, for a self-admitted affirmative act by its executor (in several ways, representing a kind of contemporaneous *iustitium*).[99] This order, once executed, draws the ire of many and opens questions as to the nature of its legality and, oppositionally, whether its architect is not a cure worse than the symptom.

Aspects of academic Jason Bainbridge's body of work involve using superhero texts to interrogate real world law. Because of their unique position, Bainbridge believes superheroes are able to '[put] into question whether the law itself can be proactive',[100] rather than its realistic reactionary nature towards criminal acts, through an idea of 'premodern law'[101] legitimising superhero justice that ignores legality 'through [a] "direct line" to the truth and lack of accountability'.[102] While this does not legitimise the real world consequences, if such characters did exist it goes towards legitimising them within the fictional narrative and presents a springboard for beginning the comparison between the fact and the fantasy. The latter is emphasised by Bainbridge's statement that 'a consideration of the superhero becomes a consideration of the relationship between law and justice',[103] with belief that such narratives are uniquely positioned to do so.

Superhero texts and Batman texts in particular rely on 'the human ability to create forms that are larger than humanity itself' and that allow us to relate to the form's actions, 'to struggle with and repossess [them] as [our] own agency'.[104] Batman's realism in comparison to other superheroes makes the character a popular and more effective analytical lens for contemporary issues. Researcher Liam Burke notes, '[He's] an average guy . . . wealthy [and] intelligent, at the peak of human fitness, but an average guy nonetheless'.[105] Batman's fictional texts aid an understanding of contemporary acts and events through a paradigm based on but

99 See Agamben (n 2) 41.
100 Bainbridge (n 1) 465.
101 Bainbridge (n 1) 457.
102 Bainbridge (n 1) 457–58.
103 Bainbridge (n 1) 457.
104 S Carney, 'The Function of the Superhero at the Present Time' (2005) 6 *Iowa Journal of Cultural Studies* 100.
105 A Davies, 'Why Comic Book Superhero Batman is Still Popular after 75 Years' (*ABC Radio National*, 20 June 2014) <www.abc.net.au/radionational/programs/drive/why-batman-is-still-so-popular-after-75-years/5535986> accessed 20 June 2014.

not entirely adherent to laws and strictures of reality; Burke cites Batman's use as a 'social barometer'[106] and that superhero comics can be 'an instantaneous reaction to what's happening in the culture ... they sort of respond symptomatically to the culture'.[107]

The *Batman Incorporated* narrative acts as both a symptom and interrogation of real world law and practices whilst mirroring elements of both encountered in history. The text is situated within a post-9/11 attitude through content, images and linguistic context; the narrative deals with a global extremist network in Leviathan (explicitly referred to as a 'terrorist organisation')[108] similar to the Obama administration combating al-Qaeda. Both networks launch worldwide attacks, utilising succinct nomenclatures evoking a symbolic apropos: Leviathan as a reference to Thomas Hobbes's work regarding the state of nature and war against all[109] (emphasised through the fictional Leviathan's campaign of anarchy against the established social order);[110] al-Qaeda as 'the Base' or 'the Foundation'[111] from which to initiate a global campaign. Batman's army of robotic Batmen (named with the portmanteau 'ro-bats') built to enter high-danger zones for combat[112] target crime in a similar fashion to the United States' real world use of drone strikes.[113] Several images bear similarities to hallmarks of the War on Terror, particularly a series of panels depicting the destruction of Wayne Tower[114] as a parallel to the fall of the World Trade Center.

One of the biggest points of comparison is the sovereign executors of power: the fictional Batman Incorporated, and the real world Obama administration. Headed by and answerable to a Western – specifically, American – figure of authority, overseen from the United States and executing worldwide

106 Ibid.
107 Ibid.
108 Morrison, *Gotham's Most Wanted* (n 3) 64.
109 T Hobbes, *Leviathan* (first published 1651, Everyman's Library 1965).
110 Morrison, *Demon Star* (n 3) 77.
111 G Foden, 'What is the Origin of the Name al-Qaida?' (*The Guardian*, 24 August 2002) <www.theguardian.com/books/2002/aug/24/alqaida.sciencefictionfantasyandhorror> accessed 16 June 2014.
112 Morrison, *Deluxe Edition* (n 3) 205.
113 For a further exploration of the use of drone strikes in relation to comic books, see Chapter 12 in this book. See also, K DeYoung, 'Judge Backs Obama Administration on Secrecy of Targeted Killings of Terrorism Suspects' (*The Washington Post*, 3 January 2013) <www.washingtonpost.com/world/national-security/2013/01/02/83799c18-5515-11e2-8b9e-dd8773594efc_story.html?hpid=z3> accessed 7 June 2013; C Savage, 'Pentagon Says US Citizens with Terrorism Ties can be Targeted in Strikes' (*The New York Times*, 22 February 2012) <http://atwar.blogs.nytimes.com/2012/02/22/pentagon-says-u-s-citizens-with-terrorism-ties-can-be-targeted-in-strikes/?ref=world> accessed 7 June 2013.
114 Morrison, *Gotham's Most Wanted* (n 3) 113.

activities motivated and justified as necessary and for the sake of justice; existing, for all intents and purposes, within their own self-defined states of exception. Both entities and their respective sovereignties would fall under what Stephen Krasner terms an 'organised hypocrisy',[115] their perceived lawless actions 'legitimated . . . [by] the need to preserve international stability'.[116] Implicitly, both figures of authority believe the world deserves a firmer, autocratic hand for the sake of security rather than a more lawful, potentially less swiftly effective approach.

Interrogations of justice and real world events by superhero texts are referred to by Bainbridge as texts '[that present] an alternative or corollary to modernity'[117] through utilising a fictional 'world founded on irrationality'.[118] This allows the texts to engage in 'a process of estrangement by which to highlight the inadequacies'[119] perceived in the real world by conversing with them through a fictional mode. *Batman Incorporated*, as a symptom of contemporary events that converses with and interrogates them, offers an alternative interpretation of the affirmative guardianship that both Batman and Obama identify with. As the enactor of a state of exception, a 'figure of necessity'[120] existing within 'a zone in which application [of the norm] is suspended',[121] Batman, by all accounts, 'has no limits'.[122] Devoid of boundary, Incorporated offers a dark alternative: what if Batman, and not Leviathan, is interpreted as the force of terror?

The *Batman Incorporated* narrative questions Batman's form of affirmative protection; Leviathan views Batman as an impediment towards their newer world order free of contemporary Western yoke. Batman sees himself and the Incorporated initiative as a necessary 'force of law without law',[123] believing the world is ill-equipped to deal with the nature of Leviathan's threat. To reinforce an oppositional viewpoint, Batman even refers to fashioning Incorporated into 'a terror made of shadows and flapping wings'[124] as an ominous, indistinct presence without legal oversight.

Incorporated effectively declares a state of exception by self-appointing itself as an enforcer against Leviathan outside juridical boundaries; in effect, Incorporated adopts a state of being 'devoid of law'[125]

115 SJ Krasner, 'Abiding Sovereignty' (2001) 22 *International Political Science Review* 229, 242.
116 Ibid.
117 Bainbridge (n 1) 462.
118 Bainbridge (n 1) 42.
119 Bainbridge (n 1) 42.
120 Agamben (n 2) 28.
121 Agamben (n 2) 31.
122 Nolan, *The Dark Knight* (n 38).
123 Nolan, *The Dark Knight* (n 38) 39.
124 Morrison, *Deluxe Edition* (n 3) 130.
125 Morrison, *Deluxe Edition* (n 3) 50.

within 'a zone of anomie in which all legal determinations . . . are deactivated',[126] with such determinations solely executed by Incorporated's own sovereignty and oversight. The absolutist policies with which Incorporated brazenly pursues Leviathan internationally implicitly defy the individual laws of national sovereignties for the purpose of sustaining Incorporated's own sovereign authority, with the justification that these acts are undertaken with the intent of achieving justice and security.

Taking Incorporated as existing under a state of exception that, at the very least, self-legitimises its campaign, problems arise. Agamben notes that a state of exception implies the production of 'a situation in which the emergency becomes the rule, and the very distinction between peace and war (and between foreign and civil war) becomes impossible'.[127] This posits a question: if Incorporated had not been liquidated, and had instead merely defeated Leviathan, how long would Batman's necessitous edict have lasted? How long could that state of *exception* exist for, even if the primary catalyst of the exception were removed?

Conclusion

Superhero comic books offer expediency towards justice[128] of which the real world is either deficient or devoid. By representing greater efficacy in comparison to real world justice, the texts '[consider] the relationship between law and justice'[129] by presenting and interrogating a world much like ours but 'founded on irrationality'.[130]

Narratives like *Batman Incorporated* evidence the interaction between fictional and real world paradigms. Though the narrative refrains from drawing a definitive conclusion as to the efficacy, usefulness, morality or deservedness of exceptional tactics to attain justice, it does offer a pyrrhic outlook regarding its implementation of a state of exception, leading to problems greater than the symptom. Terrorism may have been thwarted by Incorporated, but the damage to Batman, the Incorporated initiative and the world is tremendous in comparison to the gains brought by Leviathan's downfall.

The *Batman Incorporated* text upholds Bainbridge's notion that superhero narratives 'highlight the inadequacies in the present system in the same way a test case might highlight the inadequacies in the law'.[131] Consider, then, *Batman Incorporated* as a test case that highlights the ineffectiveness of exceptional security; a state of exception might offer a figure

126 Morrison, *Deluxe Edition* (n 3) 50.
127 Agamben (n 2) 22.
128 Bainbridge (n 1) 458.
129 Bainbridge (n 1) 457.
130 Bainbridge (n 1) 462.
131 Bainbridge (n 1) 462.

of absolute authority, capable of circumventing the impediment of the law to achieve 'true justice' with the belief that such a state deserves autocratic governance. However, if the end result is a state devoid of law capable of protecting the law, the exception raises questions regarding the symptom of necessity that could prove more troublesome than the opposition it answers. This coincides with Agamben's appropriated maxim: *Necessitas habet non legem* (necessity has no law).[132]

Superhero comic books occupy a unique position in their ability to reflect and converse with the epoch in which they're published. As an examination of the interrelationship between real and fictional worlds, *Batman Incorporated*'s representation of the state of exception interrogates applications of justice through grounding in contemporaneous events, averring a world where the justice we need may not be what we deserve.

Acknowledgements

Thanks to Lonie, Dianne, David, Anne and Thom for their feedback and invaluable assistance in writing this chapter.

Bibliography

Agamben G, *Homo Sacer: Sovereign Power and Bare Life* (first published 1995, D Heller-Roazen tr, Stanford University Press 1998).

Agamben G, *State of Exception* (first published 2003, K Attell tr, University of Chicago Press 2005).

Allen M, 'Osama bin Laden Raid Yields Trove of Computer Data' (*Politico*, 2 May 2011) <www.politico.com/news/stories/0511/54151.html> accessed 24 March 2014.

Apuzzo M and Goldman A, 'Bin Laden was Unarmed when SEALs Stormed Room' (*The Salt Lake Tribune*, 3 May 2011) <www.sltrib.com/sltrib/world/51742983-68/bin-laden-seals-compound.html.csp?page=1> accessed 2 April 2014.

Bainbridge J, '"This is the Authority. This Planet is Under Our Protection" – An Exegesis of Superheroes' Interrogations of Law' (2007) 3 *Law, Culture and the Humanities* 455.

Bowcott O, 'Osama bin Laden: US Responds to Questions about Killing's Legality' (*The Guardian*, 4 May 2011) <www.theguardian.com/world/2011/may/03/osama-bin-laden-killing-legality> accessed 2 April 2014.

Brooker W, *Hunting the Dark Knight: Twenty-First Century Batman* (IB Tauris 2012).

132 Agamben (n 2) 1.

Brubaker E and Rucka G, *Gotham Central: In the Line of Duty* (DC Comics 2011).

Carney S, 'The Function of the Superhero at the Present Time' (2005) 6 *Iowa Cultural Studies Journal* 100.

'Celebrating the Death of Osama bin Laden' (*Time Magazine*, 2 May 2011) <www.time.com/time/photogallery/0,29307,2068860,00.html> accessed 18 July 2013.

Chanen JS, 'If I Represented Bin Laden . . .' (*ABA Journal*, 1 September 2007) <www.abajournal.com/magazine/article/if_i_represented_bin_laden/> accessed 20 March 2014.

Davies A, 'Why Comic Book Superhero Batman is Still Popular After 75 Years' (*ABC Radio National*, 20 June 2014) <www.abc.net.au/radionational/programs/drive/why-batman-is-still-so-popular-after-75-years/5535986> accessed 20 June 2014.

DeYoung K, 'Judge backs Obama Administration on Secrecy of Targeted Killings of Terrorism Suspects' (*The Washington Post*, 3 January 2013) <www.washingtonpost.com/world/national-security/2013/01/02/83799c18-5515-11e2-8b9e-dd8773594efc_story.html?hpid=z3> accessed 7 June 2013.

Favreau J (dir), *Iron Man* (Paramount Pictures 2008).

Foden G, 'What is the Origin of the Name al-Qaida?' (*The Guardian*, 24 August 2002) <www.theguardian.com/books/2002/aug/24/alqaida.sciencefictionfantasyandhorror> accessed 16 June 2014.

'Foreign Terrorist Organizations' (*US Department of State*) <www.state.gov/j/ct/rls/other/des/123085.htm> accessed 18 June 2014.

Fritz CG, 'Popular Sovereignty, Vigilantism and the Constitutional Right of Revolution' (1994) 63 *Pacific Historical Review* 39.

Govern KH, 'Operation Neptune Spear: Was Killing Bin Laden a Legitimate Objective?' in Finkelstein C, Ohlin JD and Altman A (eds), *Targeted Killings: Law and Morality in an Asymmetrical World* (Oxford University Press 2012).

Green DA, 'Law, Justice and the Death of Osama bin Laden' (*New Statesman*, 2 May 2011) <www.newstatesman.com/blogs/david-allen-green/2011/05/bin-laden-osama> accessed 14 June 2013.

Hobbes T, *Leviathan* (first published 1651, Everyman's Library 1965).

Jackson R, *Sovereignty* (Polity Press 2007).

Johns G, *Batman: Earth One* (DC Comics 2012).

Kane B and Finger B, *Detective Comics #27* (Detective Comics, Inc 1939).

Keller J, '*Pax Vigilanticus*: Vigilantism, Order, and Law in the Nineteenth Century American West' (*Wesleyan University*, April 2009) <wesscholar.wesleyan.edu/cgi/viewcontent.cgi?article=1241&context=etd_hon_theses> accessed 20 June 2014.

Krasner S J, 'Abiding Sovereignty' (2001) 22 *International Political Science Review* 229.

Lambert R, 'What if Bin Laden had Stood Trial?' (*The Guardian*, 3 May 2011) <www.newstatesman.com/blogs/david-allen-green/2011/05/bin-laden-osama> accessed 14 June 2013.

McGowan, T, 'The Exceptional Darkness of *The Dark Knight*' (2009) 51 *Jump Cut: A Review of Contemporary Media* <www.ejumpcut.org/archive/jc51.2009/darkKnightKant/text.html> accessed 11 June 2014.

McGowan, T, *The Fictional Christopher Nolan* (University of Texas Press 2012).

Miller F, *Batman: Year One* (DC Comics 1988).

Morrison G, *Supergods: Our World in the Age of the Superhero* (Jonathan Cape 2011).

Morrison G, *Batman Incorporated: The Deluxe Edition* (DC Comics 2012).

Morrison G, *Batman Incorporated: Demon Star* (DC Comics 2013).

Morrison G, *Batman Incorporated: Gotham's Most Wanted* (DC Comics 2013).

Newby B, 'Watchful Guardian or Dark Knight? The Vigilante as a Social Actor' (*International Foundation for Protection Officers*, July 2012) <www.ifpo.org/wp-content/uploads/2013/08/Newby_Vigilante.pdf> accessed 19 June 2014.

Nolan C (dir), *Batman Begins* (Warner Bros 2005).

Nolan C (dir), *The Dark Knight* (Warner Bros 2008).

Nolan C (dir), *The Dark Knight Rises* (Warner Bros 2012).

Phillips M, 'Osama Bin Laden Dead' (*The White House Blog*, 2 May 2011) <www.whitehouse.gov/blog/2011/05/02/osama-bin-laden-dead> accessed 14 June 2013.

'President Declares "Freedom at War with Fear"' (*George W Bush White House Archives*, 20 September 2001) <http://georgewbush-whitehouse.archives.gov/news/releases/2001/09/print/20010920-8.html> accessed 20 March 2014.

Rogers APV and McGoldrick D, 'Assassination and Targeted Killing – The Killing of Osama bin Laden' (2011) 60 *International and Comparative Law Quarterly* 778.

Russo A and Russo J (dirs), *Captain America: The Winter Soldier* (Walt Disney Studios Motion Pictures 2014).

Savage C, 'Pentagon Says US Citizens with Terrorism Ties can be Targeted in Strikes' (*The New York Times*, 22 February 2012) <http://atwar.blogs.nytimes.com/2012/02/22/pentagon-says-u-s-citizens-with-terrorism-ties-can-be-targeted-in-strikes/?ref=world> accessed 7 June 2013.

Schmitt C, *Dictatorship* (first published 1921, Michael Hielzl and Graham Ward tr, Polity Press 2013).

Searcey D, 'Killing Was Legal Under US and International Law, Many Experts Say' (*The Wall Street Journal*, 6 May 2011) <http://online.wsj.com/news/articles/SB10001424052748704810504576305470980463628> accessed 18 March 2014.

Sharp C, '"Riddle Me This . . .?" Would the World Need Superheroes if the Law Could Actually Deliver "Justice"?' (2012) 16 *Law Text Culture* 353.

Vollum S and Adkinson CD, 'The Portrayal of Crime and Justice in the Comic Book Superhero Mythos' (2003) 10 *Journal of Criminal Justice and Popular Culture* 96.

Wallace D, 'Operation Neptune's [sic] Spear: The Lawful Killing of Osama Bin Laden' (2012) 45 *Israel Law Review* 367.

Chapter 12

Judge, jury and executioner: *Judge Dredd*, Jacques Derrida, drones

Chris Lloyd

Introduction

The context for this chapter is set by the meeting of an unlikely trio: Nigella Lawson, *Judge Dredd* and Jacques Derrida. The trio met in Lawson's 1995 article in *The Times*, 'Is This Trivia Really Worth Studying?', in which she penned belittling critiques against both the academic study of popular culture in the mid-1990s and the association of French intellectuals with such a practice.[1] Regarding the former, referring specifically to a grant funding a study of the audiences of the 1995 film *Judge Dredd*[2] she quipped, '[t]hese days it simply isn't intellectually respectable to have an interest in any form of culture that isn't popular'.[3] Lawson then deduced that 'most people who turn their critical faculties towards mass entertainment just wouldn't be up to anything else. They lack the references, they lack the reading, they lack the information'.[4] She then insulted such studies for their 'excessive claims of self-styled culture analysts – those who have . . . read some Barthes but not many books, and think that by regurgitating what some French intellectual wrote a couple of decades back counts for originality'.[5] Her article then concluded with an *ad hominem* attack against the French theorist Jacques Derrida, premised on a guest

1 N Lawson, 'Is this Trivia Really Worth Studying?' *The Times* (London, 4 July 1995) 15.

2 M Barker and K Brooks, *Knowing Audiences: Judge Dredd, its Friends, Fans and Foes* (University of Luton Press 1998) 2: 'The proposal accepted by the ESRC [Economic and Social Research Council] was for an 18-month study of the audiences of the film version of *Judge Dredd*, paying particular attention to the ways in which different groups might "negotiate the meanings of the film"'.

3 Lawson (n 1).

4 Lawson (n 1).

5 Lawson (n 1).

lecture he had given at the University of Oxford[6] and her step-father's, that is AJ Ayer's, comment afterwards, '*Mais monsieur, vous vous foutez de nous!*'.[7]

This chapter opens with reference to Lawson's article because it recalls a crude and uncritical stance long since denounced; such brash sneers at popular culture studies (here particularly against the *Judge Dredd* comics) and banal *ad hominem* attacks against 'French intellectuals' (here particularly against Derrida) no longer have *locus standi*. Rather, comics have long since been recognised as rich sources for academic engagement[8] and Derrida himself has retorted against *ad hominem* attacks stating that they occur because 'the[ir] authors haven't read a single line of my work'.[9] Yet when the academic study of law is combined with these two reputable areas it only finds favour with the latter and not the former. Indeed when legal studies are transposed onto the medium of comics, the ghost of Lawson's mockery returns. For 'comics still remain drastically under-researched in the context of interdisciplinary legal studies'[10] and are 'conspicuously neglected in legal scholarship'.[11]

In contributing to this book, this chapter seeks to further the study of comics and law by commenting upon the controversy surrounding the Obama Administration's drone programme via a reading of the *Judge Dredd* comics, in particular the 1978 John Wagner story 'The Day the Law Died'.[12] This reading will be framed via Jacques Rancière's 'politics of aesthetics' in order to illustrate the *Judge Dredd* comics as exemplars of 'critical

6 Lawson (n 1). See C Malabou and J Derrida, *Counterpath: Traveling with Jacques Derrida* (David Wills tr, Stanford University Press 2004) 292 for details of Derrida's 1979 visit to the University of Oxford.

7 Lawson (n 1). For details of the 'Oxbridge' critique of Derrida, see J Derrida, '*Honoris Causa:* <<This is *Also* Extremely Funny>>' in E Weber (ed), *Points . . . Interviews, 1974–1994* (M Hobson and C Johnson trs, Stanford University Press 1995).

8 See eg, D Kunzle, *The Early Comic Strip: Narrative Strips and Picture Stories in the European Broadsheet from c 1450 to 1825* (University of California Press 1973); M Barker, *Comics: Ideology, Power and the Critics* (Manchester University Press 1989); D Carrier, *The Aesthetics of Comics* (Pennsylvania State University Press 2000); and J Gardner, *Projections: Comics and the History of Twenty-First Century Storytelling* (Stanford University Press 2012).

9 M d'Ancona, 'Urbane Derrida Answers Critics' *The Times* (London, 13 June 1992) 3.

10 T Giddens, 'Comics, Law, and Aesthetics: Towards the Use of Graphic Fiction in Legal Studies' (2012) 6 *Law and Humanities* 85, 87.

11 L Gómez Romero and I Dahlman, 'Justice Framed: Law in Comics and Graphic Novels' (2012) 16 *Law Text Culture* 3, 4. However cf C Lloyd, '"Sakaarson the World Breaker": Violence and *Différance* in the Political and Legal Theory of Marvel's Sovereign' (2012) 16 *Law Text Culture* 119.

12 J Wagner, 'The Day the Law Died' in J Wagner and others, *Judge Dredd: The Complete Case Files 02* (Rebellion 2006).

art' that satirise issues of law, policing and state violence.[13] This framework will be intertwined with Derrida's deconstructive thoughts concerning the '*voyou*',[14] alongside Walter Benjamin's analysis of 'the "great" criminal',[15] in order to critically read the Administration's drone programme within international law.[16] The chapter begins, first, by examining the Administration's drone programme, before then re-reading the programme through the aesthetics of *Judge Dredd*.

Drones and Dredd

In 2013, the Obama Administration's drone programme (originally exposed by *The New York Times* in 2009[17]), and the CIA's practice of targeted killings, became fully known to the public. Weekly 'Terror Tuesday' meetings saw the Administration wield astonishing executive powers of state violence.[18] As detailed by *The Guardian*'s Glenn Greenwald, '[t]he president's underlings compile their proposed lists of who should be executed, and the president . . . then chooses from "baseball cards" and decrees in total secret who should die'.[19] Such meetings sealed the fates of four American

13 See generally Jacques Rancière's works: J Rancière, *The Politics of Aesthetics: The Distribution of the Sensible*, G Rockhill (ed) (G Rockhill tr, Bloomsbury Publishing 2006) 45–61; J Rancière, *Aesthetics and its Discontents* (S Corcoran tr, Polity 2009) 45–60; and J Rancière, *Dissensus: On Politics and Aesthetics*, S Corcoran (ed) (S Corcoran tr, Bloomsbury 2013) 134–51. Note that Rancière states that his 'politics of aesthetics' 'operates at a complete remove' from Walter Benjamin's 'aestheticization of politics': *Discontents* 25. See W Benjamin, 'The Work of Art in the Age of Mechanical Reproduction' in H Arendt (ed), *Illuminations* (Harry Zorn tr, Pimlico 1999) 234: 'The logical result of Fascism is the introduction of aesthetics into political life'.

14 J Derrida, *Rogues: Two Essays on Reason* (P Brault and M Naas trs, Stanford University Press 2005) 63–70.

15 W Benjamin, 'Critique of Violence' in M Bullock and MW Jennings (eds), *Walter Benjamin: Selected Writings Volume 1, 1913–1926* (E Jephcott tr, Belknap Press 2004) 239, 241.

16 For examples of critical (Derridean) accounts of international law, see A Orford, 'The Destiny of International Law' (2004) 17 *Leiden Journal of International Law* 441, 453–68; A Orford, 'Critical Intimacies' in P Goodrich, F Hoffman, M Rosenfeld and C Vismann (eds), *Derrida and Legal Philosophy* (Palgrave Macmillan 2008) 116–20.

17 D Kilcullen and A McDonald, 'Death from Above, Outrage Down Below' (*New York Times*, 16 May 2009) <www.nytimes.com/2009/05/17/opinion/17exum.html> accessed 21 July 2014.

18 J Becker and S Shane, 'Secret "Kill List" Proves a Test of Obama's Principles and Will' (*New York Times*, 29 May 2012) <www.nytimes.com/2012/05/29/world/obamas-leadership-in-war-on-al-qaeda.html> accessed 21 July 2014.

19 G Greenwald, 'Chilling Legal Memo from Obama DOJ Justifies Assassination of US Citizens' (*The Guardian*, 5 February 2013) <www.theguardian.com/commentisfree/2013/feb/05/obama-kill-list-doj-memo> accessed 21 July 2014.

citizens without charge or trial.[20] February 2013 saw *NBC News* publish a leaked 2011 Department of Justice memo legally authorising these targeted assassinations.[21] Simultaneously, the ultimate question was asked of the Administration's drone programme: was it legal for an American citizen to be executed, on US soil, without charge or trial? John Brennan, Director of the CIA, refused to answer this question but the Attorney General Eric Holder stated that in 'extraordinary circumstances' it 'would be necessary and appropriate under the Constitution and applicable laws of the United States for the President to authorize the military to use lethal force within the territory of the United States'.[22]

Holder's reply fuelled the accusation that the Obama Administration was acting as 'judge, jury and executioner'[23] because its targeted assassinations were beyond judicial oversight or accountability (and were perhaps even legally questionable[24]). Yet in May 2013, President Obama defended the legality of the actions undertaken, 'America's actions are legal... Under domestic law, and international law, the United States *is at war* with al Qaeda, the Taliban, and their associated forces'.[25] Obama then decried the

20 C Savage and P Baker, 'Obama, in a Shift, to Limit Targets of Drone Strikes' (*New York Times*, 22 May 2013) <www.nytimes.com/2013/05/23/us/us-acknowledges-killing-4-americans-in-drone-strikes.html> accessed 21 July 2014.

21 DOJ, 'Lawfulness of a Lethal Operation Directed against a US Citizen Who is a Senior Operational Leader of Al-Qa'ida or An Associate Force' (Department of Justice White Paper, 8 November 2011) <http://msnbcmedia.msn.com/i/msnbc/sections/news/020413_DOJ_White_Paper.pdf> accessed 21 July 2014.

22 N Lennard, 'Yes, the President Can Kill Americans on US Soil' (*Salon*, 5 March 2013) <www.salon.com/2013/03/05/yes_the_president_can_kill_americans_on_u_s_soil/> accessed 21 July 2014.

23 E McClam, '"Judge, Jury and Executioner": Legal Experts Fear Implications of White House Drone Memo' (*NBC News*, 5 February 2013) <http://usnews.nbcnews.com/_news/2013/02/05/16855539-judge-jury-and-executioner-legal-experts-fear-implications-of-white-house-drone-memo> accessed 21 July 2014. Naureen Shah of Columbia Law School and the ACLU is to be credited with the phrase 'judge, jury and executioner': 'We should be concerned when the White House is acting as judge, jury and executioner... And there's no one outside of the White House who has real oversight over that process': ibid.

24 UNCHR, 'Report of the Special Rapporteur on the Promotion and Protection of Human Rights and Fundamental Freedoms while Countering Terrorism' (2013) UN Doc A/86/389. At paras 57, 59, 64, 71 and 79, Ben Emmerson QC posits that there is 'no clear international consensus' on numerous points of law relating to the Administration's drone programme. See also UNCHR, 'Report of the Special Rapporteur on Extrajudicial, Summary or Arbitrary Executions' (2013) UN Doc A/68/382 at paras 85–94 for similar concerns expressed by Professor Christof Heyns regarding questions of 'self-defence' under Article 51 of the UN Charter.

25 Obama B, 'The Future of our Fight against Terrorism' (prepared Presidential remarks, 23 May 2013) <www.whitehouse.gov/the-press-office/2013/05/23/remarks-president-barack-obama> accessed 21 July 2014, emphasis added. For a critique of Obama's move to the state of exception necessitated by this 'war on terror' – *qua* extra-legal vigilante – see Chapter 11 in this book.

use of drones on 'US soil', believing it would be '[un]constitutional for the government to target and kill any US citizen – with a drone, or a shotgun – without due process'.[26]

In questioning the legality of the Administration's programme we recall that since the terror attacks of 9/11, significant developments in international law (namely UN Security Council Resolutions 1368[27] and 1373[28]) have been interpreted to 'permit such a notion'.[29] Accordingly, the programme can be 'reinterpret[ed]' as a legal use of force within international law.[30] Nevertheless the Administration's programme is revelatory because its high water-mark discloses the practice of state-sanctioned executions, against American citizens on US soil, beyond judicial review, within a geo-political climate where 'the world becomes the battlefield'.[31] This practice has been identified as a 'global policing function to counter potential threats'[32] resulting from 'the catch-all invocation of the "security forces"'.[33] As the French theorist Grégoire Chamayou explains, the Administration's drone programme illustrates a '[c]ynegetic power [which] is exercised over prey, living beings that escape and flee'[34] and as such '[t]he drone is the emblem of contemporary cynegetic war'.[35] Chamayou's use of the term 'cynegetic' highlights the drone programme's focus on 'the chase', or 'the hunt', of the enemy *qua* prey: 'cynegetic power is essentially predatory'.[36]

When Chamayou's analysis of the Administration's all-pervasive policing regime is brought to bear alongside its actions as 'judge, jury and executioner', one finds its drone programme lends itself to an interpretation through the satirical 'critical art' of *Judge Dredd*.

26 Ibid. See also Presidential Policy Guidelines, 'US Policy Standards and Procedures for the Use of Force in Counterterrorism Operations Outside the United States and Areas of Active Hostilities' <www.whitehouse.gov/sites/default/files/uploads/2013.05.23_fact_sheet_on_ppg.pdf> accessed 21 July 2014.
27 UNSC Res 1368 (20 December 2001) UN Doc S/RES/1386.
28 UNSC Res 1373 (28 September 2001) UN Doc S/RES/1373.
29 UNCHR, 'Arbitrary Executions' (n 24) para 88.
30 G Chamayou, 'The Manhunt Doctrine' (tr S Lillis, 2011) 169 *Radical Philosophy* 2, 3:

> If the practice of targeted assassination stretches back into the ancient history of state violence, what is new is the fact that it is no longer confined to clandestine activity, but instead is made legitimate by the states that carry it out. This strategy involves the reinterpretation of the principles of international law, even if it means emptying them of their meaning, in order to authorise arbitrary executions soberly called 'targeted killings'.

31 Ibid.
32 UNCHR, 'Arbitrary Executions' (n 24) para 103.
33 D Gregory, 'Drone Geographies' (2014) 183 *Radical Philosophy* 7, 12. Here Gregory illustrates drone warfare blurs '[t]he traditional distinction between military and police operations'.
34 G Chamayou, *Manhunts: A Philosophical History* (S Rendall tr, Princeton University Press 2012) 15.
35 Chamayou (n 30) 4.
36 Chamayou (n 34) 16.

Judge Dredd began in 1977 in the British *2000AD* comics series and starred Judge Dredd as the incarnation par excellence of a futuristic dystopia's judicial system.[37] 'Dredd himself is machine-like: judge, jury and executioner all in one. Humourless, living only for '"the Law", he is a grim, merciless enforcer of all laws'.[38] In a crime-plagued futuristic world, Dredd epitomises a character of 'sardonic politics',[39] exercising an 'automaton and dogmatic approach to law enforcement'.[40] Accordingly the *Judge Dredd* comics are not 'posthistorical',[41] as they reflect 'their original Thatcherite and Reaganite context of production'.[42] And in doing so, they also contain an embedded and distinct political context, as co-creator John Wagner explained in 2002:

> [W]ith Thatcher on the rise there was a right-wing current in British politics which helped inspire Judge Dredd. He seemed to capture the mood of the age - he was a hero and a villain. That villainous aspect to Dredd's character - and the Draconian law of Mega-City One - really caught the readers' imagination. Occasionally we'd get letters from children who seemed to be agreeing with his hard-right stance, so we made the strip more political to bring out the fact that we didn't agree with Dredd. We introduced a democratic movement in Mega-City One as a counterpoint.[43]

Accordingly, *Judge Dredd* is readily identifiable as a satirical critique to fascist authoritarian political ideologies, as per Wagner's express remarks.[44] And yet as much as the comics could nevertheless be read through an alternate interpretation positing Dredd as a hero-figure of law and order,[45] specific reference to the story 'The Day the Law Died' will show how

37 R Sabin, *Comics, Comix and Graphic Novels: A History of Comic Art* (Phaidon 1996) 134–38.

38 Barker and Brooks (n 2) 200.

39 Barker and Brooks (n 2) 201.

40 S Greenfield and G Osborn, 'Film, Law and the Delivery of Justice: The Case of Judge Dredd and the Disappearing Courtroom' (1999) 6 *Journal of Criminal Justice and Popular Culture* 35, 40.

41 D Carrier (n 8) 107–23.

42 M Barker and K Brooks, 'Waiting for Dredd' (1995) 5(8) *Sight and Sound* 16, 19.

43 From Wagner's BBC News 'Real Time' series interview: J Wagner, 'I Invented Judge Dredd' (*BBC News*, 28 February 2002) <http://news.bbc.co.uk/1/hi/uk/1820832.stm> accessed 21 July 2014.

44 This point is also expressed in B Ireland, 'Errand into the Wilderness: *The Cursed Earth* as Apocalyptic Road Narrative' (2009) 43 *Journal of American Studies* 497, 505. Quoting from CM Jarman and P Acton, *Judge Dredd: The Mega-History* (Lennard Publishing 1995) 17.

45 Ireland (n 44) 531. However, even putting aside the intended satire, Dredd's blurring of the state functions of legislature, executive and judiciary arguably constitute a useful case-study in the teaching of Constitutional Law: see Chapter 4 in this book.

the comics' intent is moreover 'to hold Dredd's fascist tendencies up to ridicule', akin to Wagner's explanation.[46]

Following this reading, the comics' 'satirical element'[47] aligns them with what Rancière calls 'critical art'; that is, art which 'sets out to build awareness of the mechanisms of domination to turn the spectator into a conscious agent of world transformation'.[48] Explained further, 'critical art' attempts the above transformation via a three stage process in which 'a strangeness' is produced in order to then engender an awareness of the reasons underlying that strangeness, to then mobilise the viewer based upon the awareness of the strangeness at hand.[49] Hence when this process is mapped onto *Judge Dredd*, the strangeness revealed in the comics is that of an uncanny authoritarian regime of social control, underpinned by a fascist ideology, enabling the reader to 's[ee] in Dredd a dire warning of things to come'.[50]

This three-stage process resides in *Judge Dredd* because the comics hyperbolise an account of a 'possible future as authoritarian' where judges (such as Dredd) are deliberately portrayed as 'terrifying symbols of oppression and fear' in order to unsettle the reader.[51] They patrol the streets of Mega-City One, home to 800 million people, enforcing the law as both police officers and judicial figures. As evidenced from the comics, in this 'fascist city state in which democracy has been consigned to the history books as a failed political experiment',[52] even questioning the authoritarian regime leads to death, 'Dredd actually represents an antidemocratic, illiberal police state, in which dissent is ruthlessly crushed'.[53] The story 'A Letter to Judge Dredd' tells of an inquisitive boy who questions the high crime rate in Mega-City One despite the Judges' having 'extreme powers', and asks why 'a citizen is almost as likely to be killed by a Judge as by a criminal?', as well as why '[those] things called juries' are outlawed?[54] The boy's questions go unanswered as he is brutally killed at the hands of the system supposed to protect him. Indeed, as the boy had previously cautioned Dredd, 'your kind of law is so final'.[55]

Judge Dredd's 'critical art' can thus critique the Administration's drone programme because the comics vividly illustrate 'the common world of

46 Ireland (n 44) 534.

47 Barker and Brooks (n 2) 203.

48 Rancière, *Discontents* (n 13) 45.

49 Rancière, *Dissensus* (n 13) 142.

50 Ireland (n 44) 516.

51 Barker and Brooks (n 2) 228. In the classic J Wagner and C MacNeil, *Judge Dredd: America* (Rebellion 2008), pro-democratic movements are labelled as terrorism and fatally eradicated.

52 Ireland (n 44) 502.

53 Ireland (n 44) 531.

54 J Wagner, 'A Letter to Judge Dredd' in J Wagner and others, *Judge Dredd: The Complete Case Files 13* (Rebellion 2009).

55 Ibid.

which the work is a product'.[56] That is, the '*dispositif* of the critical work' comments on the world which produces the comics and then 'contribute[s] to changing the cartography of the sensible and the thinkable' within that world.[57] Specifically, the comics' satirical account of a dystopian police-state patrolled by judges highlights and exposes to critique the parallel '*cynegetic burlesque*'[58] attached to the police-state drone programme. For both social programmes exude the same 'danger to the protection of life'[59] caused by the same all-pervasive policing known to 'lower social barriers in society against the deployment of lethal force'.[60] Consequently for both Dredd and Obama, 'accuser, prosecutor, judge, jury, and executioner are all consolidated in this one man'.[61] As such, the comics house an inherent critique of the unchecked and yet legitimate police power wielded by both the judges and the Administration.

But beyond this simplistic account of the 'critical art' in *Judge Dredd* lies a more nuanced critique, which can be read in the story 'The Day the Law Died', and explained by reference to the work of Derrida and Benjamin.

Derrida and the day the law died

The 1978 story 'The Day the Law Died' sees Judge Dredd being framed for multiple homicides under the tyrannical regime of Chief Judge Cal (Emperor Caligula transposed).[62] In order to escape the corrupt judicial sentence imposed upon him – 'twenty years penal servitude on the colony of Titan'[63] – and to prove his innocence, Dredd leads a rebellion against Cal's regime. Dredd declares to the people of Mega-City One, 'Citizens, you all know my views on law and order. But today I take a drastic step. Today I challenge the authority of the Hall of Justice' (see Figure 12.1).[64]

Dredd's act of resistance is, in part, responsible for the story's significance. For Dredd is shown, quite unfathomably, resisting the very system he would usually uphold as the irrefutable source of truth and justice[65]

56 Rancière, *Politics of Aesthetics* (n 13) 80.
57 Rancière, *Dissensus* (n 13) 143.
58 Chamayou (n 30) 5. See also Chamayou (n 34) 73, where '*cynegetic burlesque*' is explained as the contrast between the 'baseness of the means employed [in both the drone programme and the authoritarian rule in *Judge Dredd*] and the grandeur of the style with which they are adorned'.
59 UNCHR, 'Arbitrary Executions' (n 24) para 103.
60 UNCHR, 'Arbitrary Executions' (n 24) para 17.
61 Greenwald (n 19).
62 Wagner (n 12).
63 Wagner (n 12).
64 Wagner (n 12).
65 J Wagner, 'Tale of the Dead Man' in J Wagner and others, *Judge Dredd: The Complete Case Files 14* (Rebellion 2009): 'He [Dredd] stands for the Iron Rule of Law, for the certainty of retribution, for the maintenance of good order'.

Figure 12.1 From J Wagner, 'The Day the Law Died' in J Wagner and others, *Judge Dredd: The Complete Case Files 02* (Rebellion 2006). Judge Dredd® is a registered trademark © Rebellion A/S, all rights reserved. Used with permission.

(despite the fact that this very system is portrayed satirically as a dystopian authoritarian future, with 'distrust of authority in general and state power in specific'[66]). Dredd's resistance against the judicial system is wholly uncharacteristic of his character and yet he is forced to resist, as a

66 P Suderman, '"Judge Dredd": A Liberal Creation with Accidental Appeal to Conservatives' (*Washington Times*, 19 September 2012) <www.washingtontimes.com/news/2012/sep/19/judge-dredd-liberal-creation-appeal-conservatives/> accessed 21 July 2014.

last-resort, in the name of the very law (nevertheless authoritarian) which he endorses, 'We're fighting for law and order – not against it!'.[67]

Consequently, Dredd's unfathomable resistance against the *truly* tyrannical regime intensifies the 'critical art' of the comics because it induces both a sublime 'strangeness' (an 'aesthetic clash') and an awareness able to 'mobilize bodies through the presentation of [the] strangeness'.[68] Said differently, what this specific *Judge Dredd* story illustrates is a rupture in the standard satirical reading of the comics, which then dissociates 'what is seen and what is thought'.[69] For what is revealed throughout the story's arc is that even if Dredd himself loyally adheres to an authoritarian police-state regime, in order to serve as a satirical critique to such a regime, there are then some regimes which *even Judge Dredd cannot abide by.* And as is made clear, Cal's regime is one such regime. For Cal is an insane tyrant who equates mere violence with law, 'I will make the laws – and you will obey them. Any who dare to oppose me will be eliminated!'.[70]

In resisting Cal's enforcement of omnipresent violence-*qua*-law over the citizens of Mega-City One, Dredd distinctly mirrors Benjamin's '"great" criminal',[71] who exerts a 'violence [which] confronts the law with the threat of declaring a new law'.[72] In doing so, Dredd enters into the 'dialectical oscillation between the violence that posits law and the violence that preserves it',[73] wielding his own law-positing violence. Here, once again, Dredd exudes the 'strangeness' of 'critical art' because in acting as 'the "great" criminal' he stands against unilateral violence, and therefore 'fascinates because he defies the state, that is, the institution that, in representing the law, secures and maintains for itself a monopoly on violence'.[74] Here we find Dredd challenging Cal, asserting, 'Judge Cal, you're under arrest! You are surrounded. There's no escape'.[75] And it is in challenging Cal's monopoly on violence that Dredd then triggers a crazed reaction

67 Wagner (n 12).
68 Rancière, *Dissensus* (n 13) 143.
69 Rancière, *Dissensus* (n 13).
70 Wagner (n 12). See also the comment of another judge, 'That tyrant Cal is making a mockery of the law!'.
71 Benjamin (n 15) 239.
72 Benjamin (n 15) 241. On this point of violence which threatens the posited law, see Giorgio Agamben's account of Carl Schmitt's reading of Benjamin's 'Critique of Violence': G Agamben, *State of Exception* (K Attell tr, University of Chicago Press 2005) 52–64.
73 G Agamben, *Homo Sacer: Sovereign Power and Bare Life* (D Heller-Roazen tr, Stanford University Press 1998) 63.
74 Derrida (n 14) 68. See also, J Derrida, 'Autoimmunity: Real and Symbolic Suicides' in G Borradori (ed), *Philosophy in a Time of Terror: Dialogues with Jürgen Habermas and Jacques Derrida* (P Brault and M Naas trs, University of Chicago Press 2003) 102.
75 Wagner (n 12).

from the insane tyrant. For Cal attempts to quell the rebellion by declaring, 'Citizens of Mega-City One, I sentence you to . . . DEATH!'[76] (see Figure 12.2).

Figure 12.2 From J Wagner, 'The Day the Law Died' in J Wagner and others, *Judge Dredd: The Complete Case Files 02* (Rebellion 2006). Judge Dredd® is a registered trademark © Rebellion A/S, all rights reserved. Used with permission.

76 Wagner (n 12).

This death sentence, imposed on 800 million people without charge or trial, then further intensifies the 'critical art' in the story because it acutely satirises the executive violence found at the high water-mark of the Obama Administration's drone programme; it presents an unadulterated image of 'artistic shock'[77] regarding the impact which unfettered executive actions deliver, notwithstanding their seemingly legal basis. For, recalling from Greenwald's article on the Administration's drone programme, '[t]he most extremist power any political leader can assert is the power to target his own citizens for execution without any charges or due process'.[78] Here the Administration personifies what Derrida has previously identified as the '*voyou*', 'the rouge', of the international community:[79]

> [T]hose states that are able or are in a state to denounce or accuse some 'rogue state' of violating the law, of failing to live up to the law, of being guilty of some perversion or deviation, those states that claim to uphold international law and that take the initiative of war, of police or peacekeeping operations because they have the force to do so, these states, namely, the United States and its allied states in these actions, are themselves, as sovereign, the first rogue states.[80]

Derrida's critique of the *voyou* (originally voiced in the aftermath of 9/11) was aimed at previous US Administrations, and their ideologies and foreign policies.[81] Nevertheless the critique doubtless still applies at the time of writing. Of particular importance in Derrida's critique is the blur between military operations ('war') and policing tactics ('police or peacekeeping operations') both of which are backed by lawful executive power ('the force to do so').[82] For we note that it is through this hybrid violence that the Administration exercises its fatal power, as Benjamin had previously warned, because it is through a specific government faction that the most repression and violence occurs, that 'institution of the modern state: the police'.[83] Through the police, and indeed with 'global policing',[84] violence is simultaneously everywhere and nowhere:

> [T]he 'law' of the police really marks the point at which the state, whether from impotence or because of the immanent connections

77 Rancière, *Dissensus* (n 13) 143.
78 Greenwald (n 19).
79 Derrida (n 14) 64–70.
80 Derrida (n 14) 102.
81 Derrida (n 14) 95–103.
82 Derrida (n 14) 102.
83 Benjamin (n 15) 242.
84 UNCHR, 'Arbitrary Executions' (n 24) para 103.

> within any legal system, can no longer guarantee through the legal system the empirical ends that it desires at any price to attain. Therefore, the police intervene 'for security reasons' in countless cases where no clear legal situation exists, when they are not merely, without the slightest relation to legal ends, accompanying the citizen as a brutal encumbrance through a life regulated by ordinances, or simply supervising him. Unlike law, which acknowledges in the 'decision' determined by place and time a metaphysical category that gives it a claim to critical evaluation, a consideration of the police institution encounters nothing essential at all. Its power is formless, like its nowhere-tangible, all-pervasive, ghostly presence in the life of civilised states.[85]

Benjamin's words echo powerfully today, some 90 years after they were originally penned. But they also echoed powerfully when the first *Judge Dredd* story was published in 1977.[86] For at that time, during the ascent of Thatcherite and Reaganite policies of state control, *Judge Dredd* satirically portrayed the police as an institution which 'combine[d] the roles of law-maker, policeman, jury, jailer and (frequently) executioner',[87] to the point that death sentences were readily being dealt to 'perps' in the name of justice. The comics were therefore warning of, and critiquing, the very same rampant authoritarian police violence which Benjamin had written of in 1921. Accordingly the very fabric of their aesthetic is one which, in the name of 'critical art', has always 'negotiate[d] between the tension which pushes art towards "life" as well as that which, conversely, sets aesthetic sensorality apart from the other forms of sensory experience'.[88] Said differently, the comics have always embodied legal and political critiques (as expressed by Wagner above)[89] because they have engaged in 'the reconfiguration of worlds of experience based on which police consensus or political dissensus are defined'.[90]

85 Benjamin (n 15) 243. See also J Derrida, 'Force of Law: The "Mystical Foundation of Authority"' in G Anidjar (ed), *Acts of Religion* (M Quaintance tr, Routledge 2002) 277 for Derrida's reflections on Benjamin's account of the police: 'the police invent the law, publish ordinances, and intervene whenever the legal situation is unclear to guarantee safety – which is to say, these days, nearly all the time'.
86 P Mills and J Wagner, 'Judge Whitey' in J Wagner and others, *Judge Dredd: The Complete Case Files 01* (Rebellion 2005). 'Judge Whitey' was the first *Judge Dredd* story published 5 March 1977.
87 M Barker, 'Taking the Extreme Case: Understanding a Fascist Fan of Judge Dredd' in D Cartmell and others (eds), *Trash Aesthetics: Popular Culture and its Audience* (Pluto Press 1997) 15.
88 Rancière, *Discontents* (n 13) 46.
89 Wagner (n 43).
90 Rancière, *Politics of Aesthetics* (n 13) 60.

And yet here, in the story 'The Day the Law Died', *Judge Dredd* can be seen to offer a heightened critique of the Administration's drone programme. For not only does it extend the critique of authoritarian social order by inverting Dredd's own rigid adherence to the law into resistance against it as the '"great" criminal', but it also pours scorn on a state acting as a *voyou* through its sheer executive actions of targeted assassinations, where those actions exhibit the horrific proliferation, and oppressive *telos*, of the 'all-pervasive' police-state Benjamin warned of. Hence this particular story in the comics vividly (*visually*)[91] engages with the cumulative elements of oppressive policing and unfettered violence which reside in the Obama Administration's drone programme and its 'birds of prey and angels of death': '"Predator, Global Hawk", "Reaper"'.[92]

However, it is noted that Rancière's theorisations of 'critical art' acknowledge the concept's limitations. For as much as it aims to 'produce a new perception of the world' and to 'create a commitment to its transformation',[93] it is limited by a 'vicious circle' which impinges on it.[94] Consequently, although it is tasked to 'produce forms of political awareness and mobilization',[95] the practice may nevertheless produce art which does not illustrate 'political energies of refusal'.[96] And yet, Rancière quickly dispels the notion that this paradox cancels the potentiality of 'critical art' ('the critical work is not annulled by this contradiction'[97]) because this form can always still challenge '"our" assigned places in a given state of things'.[98]

Conclusion

Recalling Lawson's article, we note her specific criticism against academics claiming they had 'boldly go[ne] where no one ha[d] before' by studying

91 Note here the importance of 'the image' in contemporary discussions of 'the pictorial turn' regarding post-9/11 global politics. See WJT Mitchell, 'Cloning Terror: The War of Images 2001–04' in D Costello and D Willsdon (eds), *The Life and Death of Images: Ethics and Aesthetics* (Cornell University Press 2008); WJT Mitchell, *Cloning Terror: The War of Images, 9/11 to the Present* (University of Chicago Press 2011).
92 Chamayou (n 30) 4.
93 Rancière, *Dissensus* (n 13) 142.
94 Rancière, *Discontents* (n 13) 46.
95 Rancière, *Dissensus* (n 13) 143.
96 Rancière, *Discontents* (n 13) 46. See also, at 45–46:

> Insofar as it asks viewers to discover the signs of Capital behind everyday objects and behaviours, critical art risks being inscribed in the perpetuity of a world in which the transformation of things into signs is redoubled by the very excess of interpretative signs which brings things to lose their capacity of resistance.

And see M Lazzarato, 'Art, Work and Politics in Disciplinary Societies and Societies of Security' in É Alliez and P Osborne (eds), *Spheres of Action: Art and Politics* (A Toscano tr, Tate Publishing 2013) 88, 90.
97 Rancière, *Dissensus* (n 13) 143.
98 Rancière, *Dissensus* (n 13) 143.

popular culture.[99] However, this chapter has sought to contribute to an area of interdisciplinary legal scholarship which, as aforementioned, is notably under-represented.

In doing so it has argued how the 'critical art' inherent in the *Judge Dredd* comics can comment upon the Obama Administration's drone programme. For the programme arguably induces its own parallel account of the comics' distinctive 'claustrophobic, teeming, urban nightmare, where all citizens are potential perpetrators, where the line between guilt and innocence is determined only by the Judges, and where [the Administration] *judges* without mercy'.[100] Indeed, such a commentary was intended by the comics, as their 'critical art' aimed to satirically 'transpose us to "America" to play out the futuristic drama of the complete realisation of Thatcherite law and order politics, on a global scale'.[101] As such, the high water-mark of the Administration's programme is uncanny next to Judge Cal's city-wide decree of execution, his 'death sentence', in 'The Day the Law Died', 'THE WHOLE CITY IS SENTENCED TO DEATH!'.[102] Through this warped match, the horror of a legalised cynegetic war is revealed. And it is precisely such a ruthlessly extreme act of power, executed by a sovereign, which Derrida claimed must face the penetrating critique of deconstruction, for he claimed that 'never has any philosophy *as such* contested the legitimacy of the death penalty'.[103] This chapter now closes by recalling Derrida's framework for examining this violent exercise of sovereignty because, for him, the death penalty always takes place through a totalitarian hybrid action, where the judge, the jury and the executioner, are one:

> But this accusation, this charge . . . by a state power, as sovereign . . . like all sovereignty, is marked by the right of life and death over the citizen, by the power of deciding, laying down the law, judging, and *executing* the order at the same time as the condemned one.[104]

Acknowledgements

The author would like to thank Thom Giddens for his vision and guidance on this project, Matt Smith at *Rebellion* for his copyright permissions, the two anonymous reviewers of this chapter, and all those who assisted in the development of this work.

99 Lawson (n 1).
100 Barker and Brooks (n 42) 17.
101 Barker and Brooks (n 42) 19.
102 Wagner (n 12).
103 J Derrida, 'Death Penalties' in J Derrida and E Roudinesco (eds), *For What Tomorrow . . .: A Dialogue* (J Fort tr, Stanford University Press 2004) 146.
104 J Derrida, *The Death Penalty: Volume 1*, G Bennington, M Crépon and T Dutoit (eds) (P Kamuf tr, University of Chicago Press 2014) 5.

Bibliography

Agamben G, *Homo Sacer: Sovereign Power and Bare Life* (D Heller-Roazen tr, Stanford University Press 1998).

Agamben G, *State of Exception* (K Attell tr, University of Chicago Press 2005).

Barker M, *Comics: Ideology, Power and the Critics* (Manchester University Press 1989).

Barker M, 'Taking the Extreme Case: Understanding a Fascist Fan of Judge Dredd' in Cartmell D and others (eds), *Trash Aesthetics: Popular Culture and its Audience* (Pluto Press 1997).

Barker M and Brooks K, 'Waiting for Dredd' (1995) 5(8) *Sight and Sound* 16.

Barker M and Brooks K, *Knowing Audiences: Judge Dredd, its Friends, Fans and Foes* (University of Luton Press 1998).

Becker J and Shane S, 'Secret "Kill List" Proves a Test of Obama's Principles and Will' (*New York Times*, 29 May 2012) <www.nytimes.com/2012/05/29/world/obamas-leadership-in-war-on-al-qaeda.html> accessed 21 July 2014.

Benjamin W, 'The Work of Art in the Age of Mechanical Reproduction' in Arendt H (ed), *Illuminations* (Harry Zorn tr, Pimlico 1999).

Benjamin W, 'Critique of Violence' in Bullock M and Jennings MW (eds), *Walter Benjamin: Selected Writings Volume 1, 1913–1926* (E Jephcott tr, Belknap Press 2004).

Carrier D, *The Aesthetics of Comics* (Pennsylvania State University Press 2000).

Chamayou G, 'The Manhunt Doctrine' (tr S Lillis) (2011) 169 *Radical Philosophy* 2.

Chamayou G, *Manhunts: A Philosophical History* (S Rendall tr, Princeton University Press 2012).

d'Ancona M, 'Urbane Derrida Answers Critics' *The Times* (London, 13 June 1992) 3.

Derrida J, '*Honoris Causa*: <<This is *Also* Extremely Funny>>' in Weber E (ed), *Points... Interviews, 1974–1994* (M Hobson and C Johnson trs, Stanford University Press 1995).

Derrida J, 'Force of Law: The "Mystical Foundation of Authority"' in Anidjar G (ed), *Acts of Religion* (M Quaintance tr, Routledge 2002).

Derrida J, 'Autoimmunity: Real and Symbolic Suicides' in Borradori G (ed), *Philosophy in a Time of Terror: Dialogues with Jürgen Habermas and Jacques Derrida* (P Brault and M Naas trs, University of Chicago Press 2003).

Derrida J, 'Death Penalties' in Derrida J and Roudinesco E (eds), *For What Tomorrow...: A Dialogue* (J Fort tr, Stanford University Press 2004).

Derrida J, *Rogues: Two Essays on Reason* (P Brault and M Naas trs, Stanford University Press 2005).

Chamayou G, *The Death Penalty: Volume 1*, Bennington, G Crépon M and Dutoit T (eds) (P Kamuf tr, University of Chicago Press 2014).

Department of Justice, 'Lawfulness of a Lethal Operation Directed against a US Citizen Who is a Senior Operational Leader of Al-Qa'ida or An Associate Force' (Department of Justice White Paper, 8 November 2011): <http://msnbcmedia.msn.com/i/msnbc/sections/news/020413_DOJ_White_Paper.pdf> accessed 21 July 2014.

Gardner J, *Projections: Comics and the History of Twenty-First Century Storytelling* (Stanford University Press 2012).

Giddens T, 'Comics, Law, and Aesthetics: Towards the Use of Graphic Fiction in Legal Studies' (2012) 6 *Law and Humanities* 85.
Gómez Romero L and Dahlman I, 'Justice Framed: Law in Comics and Graphic Novels' (2012) 16 *Law Text Culture* 3.
Greenfield S and Osborn G, 'Film, Law and the Delivery of Justice: The Case of Judge Dredd and the Disappearing Courtroom' (1999) 6 *Journal of Criminal Justice and Popular Culture* 35.
Greenwald G, 'Chilling Legal Memo from Obama DOJ Justifies Assassination of US Citizens' (*The Guardian*, 5 February 2013) <www.theguardian.com/commentisfree/2013/feb/05/obama-kill-list-doj-memo> accessed 21 July 2014.
Gregory D, 'Drone Geographies' (2014) 183 *Radical Philosophy* 7.
Ireland B, 'Errand into the Wilderness: *The Cursed Earth* as Apocalyptic Road Narrative' (2009) 43 *Journal of American Studies* 497.
Jarman C and Acton P, *Judge Dredd: The Mega-History* (Lennard Publishing 1995).
Kilcullen D and McDonald A, 'Death from Above, Outrage Down Below' (*New York Times*, 16 May 2009) <www.nytimes.com/2009/05/17/opinion/17exum.html> accessed 21 July 2014.
Kunzle D, *The Early Comic Strip: Narrative Strips and Picture Stories in the European Broadsheet from c 1450 to 1825* (University of California Press 1973).
Lawson N, 'Is this Trivia Really Worth Studying?' *The Times* (London, 4 July 1995) 15.
Lazzarato M, 'Art, Work and Politics in Disciplinary Societies and Societies of Security' in Alliez É and Osborne P (eds), *Spheres of Action: Art and Politics* (A Toscano tr, Tate Publishing 2013).
Lennard N, 'Yes, the President Can Kill Americans on US Soil' (*Salon*, 5 March 2013) <www.salon.com/2013/03/05/yes_the_president_can_kill_americans_on_u_s_soil/> accessed 21 July 2014.
Lloyd C, '"Sakaarson the World Breaker": Violence and *Différance* in the Political and Legal Theory of Marvel's Sovereign' (2012) 16 *Law Text Culture* 119.
Malabou C and Derrida J, *Counterpath: Traveling with Jacques Derrida* (David Wills tr, Stanford University Press 2004).
McClam E, '"Judge, Jury and Executioner": Legal Experts Fear Implications of White House Drone Memo' (*NBC News*, 5 February 2013) <http://usnews.nbcnews.com/_news/2013/02/05/16855539-judge-jury-and-executioner-legal-experts-fear-implications-of-white-house-drone-memo> accessed 21 July 2014.
Mills P and Wagner J, 'Judge Whitey' in Wagner J and others, *Judge Dredd: The Complete Case Files 01* (Rebellion 2005).
Mitchell WJT, 'Cloning Terror: The War of Images 2001–04' in Costello D and Willsdon D (eds), *The Life and Death of Images: Ethics and Aesthetics* (Cornell University Press 2008).
Mitchell WJT, *Cloning Terror: The War of Images, 9/11 to the Present* (University of Chicago Press 2011).
Obama B, 'The Future of our Fight against Terrorism' (prepared Presidential remarks, 23 May 2013) <www.whitehouse.gov/the-press-office/2013/05/23/remarks-president-barack-obama> accessed 21 July 2014.

Orford A, 'The Destiny of International Law' (2004) 17 *Leiden Journal of International Law* 441.
Orford A, 'Critical Intimacies' in Goodrich P, Hoffman F, Rosenfeld M and Vismann C (eds), *Derrida and Legal Philosophy* (Palgrave Macmillan 2008).
Presidential Policy Guidelines, 'US Policy Standards and Procedures for the Use of Force in Counterterrorism Operations Outside the United States and Areas of Active Hostilities' <www.whitehouse.gov/sites/default/files/uploads/2013.05.23_fact_sheet_on_ppg.pdf> accessed 21 July 2014.
Rancière J, *The Politics of Aesthetics: The Distribution of the Sensible*, Rockhill G (ed) (G Rockhill tr, Bloomsbury Publishing 2006).
Rancière J, *Aesthetics and Its Discontents* (S Corcoran tr, Polity 2009).
Rancière J, *Dissensus: On Politics and Aesthetics*, Corcoran S (ed) (S Corcoran tr, Bloomsbury 2013).
Sabin R, *Comics, Comix and Graphic Novels: A History of Comic Art* (Phaidon 1996).
Savage C and Baker P, 'Obama, in a Shift, to Limit Targets of Drone Strikes' (*New York Times*, 22 May 2013) <www.nytimes.com/2013/05/23/us/us-acknowledges-killing-4-americans-in-drone-strikes.html> accessed 21 July 2014.
Suderman P, '"Judge Dredd": A Liberal Creation with Accidental Appeal to Conservatives' (*Washington Times*, 19 September 2012) <www.washingtontimes.com/news/2012/sep/19/judge-dredd-liberal-creation-appeal-conservatives/> accessed 21 July 2014.
UNCHR, 'Report of the Special Rapporteur on Extrajudicial, Summary or Arbitrary Executions' (2013) UN Doc A/68/382.
UNCHR, 'Report of the Special Rapporteur on the Promotion and Protection of Human Rights and Fundamental Freedoms while Countering Terrorism' (2013) UN Doc A/86/389.
UNSC Res 1373 (28 September 2001) UN Doc S/RES/1373.
UNSC Res 1368 (20 December 2001) UN Doc S/RES/1386.
Wagner J, 'I Invented Judge Dredd' (*BBC News*, 28 February 2002) <http://news.bbc.co.uk/1/hi/uk/1820832.stm> accessed 21 July 2014.
Wagner J, 'The Day the Law Died' in Wagner J and others, *Judge Dredd: The Complete Case Files 02* (Rebellion 2006).
Wagner J, 'A Letter to Judge Dredd' in Wagner J and others, *Judge Dredd: The Complete Case Files 13* (Rebellion 2009).
Wagner J, 'Tale of the Dead Man' in Wagner J and others, *Judge Dredd: The Complete Case Files 14* (Rebellion 2009).
Wagner J and MacNeil C, *Judge Dredd: America* (Rebellion 2008).

Chapter 13

Crimes against (super) humanity: graphic forms of justice and governance

Chris Boge

Introduction

In this chapter, I focus on graphic and verbal constructions of the concepts of justice and governance in two mainstream comics series, published by DC: Ross's *Justice*[1] and Jurgens's *Justice League International*.[2] If it is true that comics hold a special appeal for scholars working in the field of law and the humanities - as they remind the reader, who is also something akin to a viewer/watcher, of the manifold (and sometimes diametrically opposed) ways of perceiving, constructing and knowing (social) reality, thereby overtly or implicitly challenging a predominantly logo-centric approach to and positivistic understanding of law - it must also be true that this appeal to more than one of the reader's senses and (cognitive) faculties can be misused. Put simply, comics can serve as carriers of ideology, and it is my impression that the superhero genre - which, historically, is distinctly American - is ideally suited for the task. When superhero comic books are well-crafted, aesthetically pleasing, and appealing to moral intuitions without offering metafictional commentary, means of self-deconstruction or self-reflexivity this becomes especially problematic, as I intend to show. I further believe that it is impossible to understand how superhero narratives construct the notions of justice and governance without learning more about American history first. A full explanation of this fact, which I cannot give here, entails my conviction that the United States is the only nation in the world that, through aggressive foreign/neo-colonial policies and sophisticated marketing of cultural exports, on the whole has succeeded

1 A Ross, J Krueger and D Braithwaite, *Justice* (DC Comics 2011).

2 D Jurgens, A Lopresti and M Ryan, *Justice League International Volume I: The Signal Masters* (DC Comics 2012); D Jurgens, A Lopresti and M Ryan, *Justice League International Volume II: Breakdown* (DC Comics 2012).

in being perceived as *not* being the white postcolonial settler society that it clearly is.[3]

Sometimes, the *dramatis personae* of the superhero genre allude to pre-Columbian histories, as is signified by the character of OMAC in *Justice League International Volume II: Breakdown*, who strikingly resembles a monstrous, daft and driven Iroquois who wants nothing more than to assimilate into civilisation. Mostly, though, the genre is populated by characters based on figures from Old World mythology (mainly Roman and Greek, see eg Wonder Woman) but adapted to the needs of a capitalist society manifestly destined to blaze a trail of Westward expansion through landscapes purged of alterity. To understand how the American superhero genre visualises and verbalises justice and governance, such notions must be read and viewed, I believe, through a postcolonial lens. As I have argued elsewhere, extra-legal forms of governance like vigilantism went hand in hand with the white settlement of the American continent, as did pre-modern modes of thought equating justice with revenge, reckoning and retaliation[4] – forms of justice and governance which play a predominant role in the two graphic fictions discussed below.

Justice is a case in point. Other than Ross's and Waid's earlier and more self-reflexive *Kingdom Come* that seemed – rather than sought – to balance legal authority as embodied by human institutions against the rule of self-appointed (superhuman) guardians of law and order, *Justice*, like so many superhero stories, iterates the myth of American exceptionalism, which is integral to the work's aesthetics. Ross's hyper-realism endows the characters with an otherworldly sheen: hyper-masculine and hyper-feminine, they are enveloped in soft light, like airbrush paintings or photoshopped pictures of gods and goddesses too sexy to be true. Gender politics apart, otherworldly authority and power become palpable in these images. As the appendix to *Kingdom Come* informs the reader, Ross frequently uses photographic references to depict (super)human bodies and postures; more often than not, the finished painted artworks are reminiscent of personality cult in totalitarian societies – national(ist) heroes purportedly fostering the common good of mankind.[5] To put it in

3 One of the few notable exceptions to discuss North America in light of postcolonial theory is B Ashcroft, H Tiffin and G Griffiths, *The Empire Writes Back: Theory and Practice in Post-Colonial Literatures* (Routledge 1989).

4 See eg, C Boge, 'Visualizing Histories and Stories: Revisionary Graphic Novels of the 1980s and 1990s' in A Barberi and others (eds), *Medienimpulse 2012–2013* (New Academic Press 2014); C Boge, 'Suspending Democracy: Vigilante Justice and the Rule of Law in Christopher Nolan's Dark Knight Trilogy' in M Aristodemou, F Macmillan and P Tuitt (eds), *Crime Fiction and the Law* (Birkbeck Law Press 2015).

5 M Waid and A Ross, *Kingdom Come* (DC Comics 2008) 222ff.

a nutshell, global governance amounts to little more than US economic, cultural and political dominance in the cultural products discussed in this chapter which thereby help foster and maintain American supremacy in the extra-textual world. (As you can gather from this phrase, I am not an adherent of early Derridean post-structuralism.) Ironically, the fending off of totalitarian threats by heroes that appear to embody democratic ideals is central to Ross's image/text construction. Through its illusion of depth, which contrasts with the more cartoon-like depiction of space in Jurgens's *Justice League International*, Ross's *Justice* invites the reader to suspend disbelief and step into a three-dimensional (other)world. Yet, this might also be the work's undoing. Lack of abstraction may well be counterproductive here: whereas it is easy for the average comics reader to identify with CM Schulz's *Peanuts*, the hypostatised figures in Ross function as a distancing device between the human and the superhuman. In contrast, Jurgens's *Justice League International* gives us a superhero team that, at first sight anyway, claims to be a product of international institutional forces, and the artwork strikes a finer balance between realism and abstraction.

Justice, arguably one of the most frequently used and least understood ethico-legal concepts, figures prominently in the titles of both works considered in this chapter. To the critical reader, this opens up a range of questions such as, 'Do humans, regardless of their country of origin, have an intuitive grasp of justice?', as Michael Walzer claims, and if so, 'Do the DC series play into the hands of our preverbal understanding of the term?'.[6] As they progress, both visual-verbal narratives become diffuse, depicting different forms of justice without making the distinctions between them sufficiently clear to the reader. Whether this is done on purpose, I leave to the reader of this chapter to speculate along with me. If the ensuing discussion at times appears complex that is how it should be: if we are to take seriously the implications of the interdisciplinary endeavour that is law and the humanities, or law and culture, there is no escaping the fact that one must try and fathom the depths if one wishes to surface with a clearer view. However, for several reasons, one of them being the word count imposed on contributors to edited collections, I can offer only suggestions and an outline in what follows. It makes sense, therefore, to see this chapter as part of an ongoing research project in which this author tries to make sense of the ideological implications of superhero comics and films within and beyond the confines of the study of law and culture.

6 M Walzer, *Thick and Thin: Moral Argument at Home and Abroad* (University of Notre Dame Press 1994) 1–2.

From retributive to social and environmental justice: Alex Ross's *Justice*

If the rumours on the internet are true, Hollywood's latest (2013) take on the *Man of Steel* may constitute a prelude to Superman's on-screen joining of the Justice League of America (JLA), a superhero group that, according to Wonder Woman in Alex Ross's *Justice*, 'seeks more than the good of America - but of all peoples and all nations'.[7] To achieve this goal, the group monitors domestic and international criminal activities from a satellite that in effect constitutes a global surveillance system. It is not difficult to see in the days of the Edward Snowden affair that this set up implies problematic conclusions: that a means-ends calculation balancing privacy against global security is a suspicious quagmire.

'Who decided we needed to be saved? Who decided to roll out the red carpet for the saviors?', Superman's eternal antagonist, earthling Lex Luthor, demands to know at the beginning of the hyper-realistic *Justice* series.[8] When Luthor begins to doubt the legitimacy of the self-appointed guardians of law and order, four narrow vertical panels illustrate the necessity of this extra-legal form of governance by depicting a burning object that could be a comet or plane. It is later revealed to be a rocket bomb, traversing night to day as it flies over high-rise buildings in South-east Asia, the Middle East, and London, where we see the iconic clock tower of the Houses of Parliament as a signifier of Western democratic constitutionalism under threat. Eventually, the bomb detonates in what looks like the typical central business district of a North American city. The transformation from darkness to light seems to trace a progressivist narrative of Western enlightenment, endangered by forces of unreason emanating from the East. At the end of this nightmare vision, which shows individual members of the JLA powerless to prevent the concerted terrorist attack[9] on the globe and incapable of protecting the lives of innocent civilians, Lex Luthor's captions read, 'We all fall down. Ashes. Ashes. And so it ends. The never-ending battle is over. There's no one left to demand justice'.[10] But how do we define justice and what forms of justice are introduced by Ross?

Justice reflects on ethical dilemmas resulting from the thought experiment that superhumans not only exist but intend to govern the lives of

7 Ross, Krueger and Braithwaite (n 1) 105.
8 Ross, Krueger and Braithwaite (n 1) 7.
9 The plots of these narratives unfold against the backdrop of a distinct American ideology fuelled by a sense of trauma and loss that is clearly reminiscent of the terror attacks of 9/11. The Joker blows up high-rise buildings on Independence Day; Luthor refers to his 'cohorts' as 'known criminals and super-powered terrorists': Ross, Krueger and Braithwaite (n 1) 303, 97.
10 Ross, Krueger and Braithwaite (n 1) 17–18.

ordinary mortals. According to Luthor's interior monologue, they insist on being trusted and adored by 'the Earth's men' who have come to regret having given their world 'to the aliens and to the robots and to the myths that demanded with their presence that we believe in them'.[11] As the story unfolds, it becomes apparent that surveillance and control are instrumental to an arbitrary use of power supporting a conception of justice that is based on forms of retribution coupled with an excess of emotional involvement on the part of the judge and jury. Teleported to the farthest reaches of existence by his enemies and trapped in the life-sustaining confines of his ring, Hal Jordan, both a member of the JLA and the galaxy-wide operating Green Lantern peace corps, dreams of setting up a totalitarian system of governance that offers controllability and predictability. Not long thereafter he is reminded by the voice of reason in the form of the Phantom Stranger that, if his 'idea of justice' equates with revenge, he will only find himself trapped in a world of his own design 'where everything and everyone has to resemble [him]'.[12]

While this is just a fantasy, criminal mastermind Brainiac is about to put this idea into practice: out of hatred for anything organic, he creates microscopic mechanical worms fused to people's nerve endings, modifying humans into controllable 'organic machinery'.[13] He plans to use armies of identical robotic copies of himself to supplant the social fabric of human existence.[14] Not only does this dystopia substitute infinite replicability[15] for human rights and the values of personal autonomy, it renders questionable the meaningfulness of criteria such as choice/intent and responsibility established in international criminal justice and practical ethics to determine offenders' individual and collective guilt. Choice – as an expression of the power to make your own decisions – and responsibility are key mantras of the American superhero genre that seem firmly grounded in (the level of) the individual. In a purely deterministic world such as the one set up by Brainiac, choice and responsibility become meaningless, as

11 Ross, Krueger and Braithwaite (n 1) 7.

12 Ross, Krueger and Braithwaite (n 1) 235. The evocation of totalitarian societies, centred around the figure of a charismatic ruler, which Jordan fantasises about and Brainiac tries to create, sketches a model of cultural uniformity and conformity that is at odds with America's political mantra of multiculturalism as the celebration of diversity and difference. This is hardly accidental; see the discussion of the myth of American exceptionalism in the conclusion of this chapter. Interestingly, Ross's story also implies that wiping clean the slate of history, a move usually regarded as distinctive of totalitarian regimes, can be liberalising when the open ending offers the prospect of a fresh start in a world devoid of weapons of mass destruction.

13 Ross, Krueger and Braithwaite (n 1) 257.

14 Ross, Krueger and Braithwaite (n 1) 176, 194–96.

15 For a philosophical discussion on mechanical selfhood, including the problem of replicability, see Chapter 6 in this book.

does the ethico-legal attempt at evaluating criminal behaviour. In Kantian deontology, however, the concepts overlap in a unique way: according to the mandate of practical reason, I only want what duty commands me to want. My freedom to reason and deliberate 'forces' me to acknowledge the fact that opting to do what I need to do is the best choice I can make. Yet as Nussbaum and Sen's capabilities approach points out, one major problem often overlooked in deontological thinking is that *ought* implies *can*: you have the duty to do something if, and only if, you are capable of doing it or if there is a realistic chance that you will succeed in fulfilling your duty.[16] Even if we buy into deontological premises without bothering to ask by or towards whom we are supposed to have duties, we may wonder whether *can* equally implies *ought*. That is to say, are you obliged to act in a certain way just because you are capable of it? Furthermore, what if you are uniquely equipped for the task, as superheroes appear to be? Do your duties increase exponentially with your power, as Uncle Ben claims in *Spider-Man* ('with great power comes great responsibility')? Furthermore, if the league of superheroes constitutes the highest level of authority on Earth, governing the lives of lesser beings like an elitist oligarchy or an unelected miniature world government,[17] its legitimacy must be self-grounded. Or must it? What is the relation between those extremely powerful superhuman beings and the lesser humans? If the former were not elected by the latter, does one group have duties towards another, and, if so, why and how? Moreover, how do we define this 'good of all peoples and all nations' that Wonder Woman speaks of as an attainable goal, how is it distributed across time and space, and how is it related to international and intergenerational forms of justice - criminal, social, economic, ecological?

Few of these questions are answered convincingly by Ross, yet *Justice* takes pains to convey to the reader the idea that the JLA adhere to a set

16 MC Nussbaum, 'Capabilities as Fundamental Entitlements: Sen and Social Justice' in T Brooks (ed), *The Global Justice Reader* (Blackwell 2008). Actually, this is not Nussbaum's but my rephrasing of deontological lines of thinking. Nussbaum is a neo-Aristotelian virtue ethicist who, thinking about entitlements rather than correlative duties, points out that (ibid 603): the language of capabilities has one further advantage over the language of rights: it is not strongly linked to one particular cultural and historical tradition, as the language of rights is believed to be ... When we speak simply of what people are actually able to do and to be, we do not even give the appearance of privileging a Western idea. Ideas of activity and ability are everywhere, and there is no culture in which people do not ask themselves what they are able to do and what opportunities they have for functioning.

17 C Lu, "World Government" in EN Zalta (ed), *The Stanford Encyclopedia of Philosophy* (2012) <http://plato.stanford.edu/archives/fall2012/entries/world-government/> accessed 3 November 2013.

of moral principles that is incompatible with the notion of revenge. Their sense of justice, ultimately, is referred to as reckoning:

> **Aquaman:** This is not a conspiracy. Not just against us, and not just against humanity. Brainiac is behind this. He's behind it all. Anything living, anything organic is his enemy. He told me this before he cut into me. This is him against everything that breathes. He's a machine. Only a machine. And maybe that's for the best. Because I'm going to kill him.
>
> **Superman (in captions, commenting):** These were not words of vengeance, or hatred. Arthur wanted a reckoning. He knew that this was a fight to save our enemies as much as it was to save his son.[18]

Used in stock melodramatic phrases such as *the day of reckoning*, the word alludes to the notion of retributive justice by signifying 'events regarded as retribution of earlier behaviour'.[19] In 'legal-philosophical discourse', retribution commonly 'refers to deserved sanctions' rather than simply 'severe punishment': 'a conception of punishment is retributive to the extent that the penalty should be based on the blameworthiness of the conduct'.[20] This is the theory of desert, and, to ensure that the reader condemns the conduct of Brainiac and sympathises instead with the protagonists who seek 'just' retribution, Brainiac's malice is anchored on different levels: he openly despises humanity; he not only deceives and harms his enemies (which is to be expected) but also brainwashes, instrumentalises and modifies those who trust him;[21] he cuts into the brains of the 'goodies'; he abducts and manipulates (non-combatant) civilians (friends and families of the superheroes, both human and superhuman); he experiments on children; his control and use of atomic weaponry threatens to annihilate the world. Brainiac thus commits crimes against both humanity and superhumanity.

As Alston and Goodman explain, the concept of crimes against humanity 'developed the earlier international law . . . Crimes against humanity were directed primarily to planned conduct, to systematic conduct'.[22] There can be no doubt about the determination with which Brainiac pursues his

18 Ross, Krueger and Braithwaite (n 1) 240–41.

19 As defined in the *New Penguin English Dictionary*.

20 A von Hirsch, 'Retribution' in P Cane and J Conaghan (eds), *The New Oxford Companion to Law* (Oxford University Press 2008) 1020.

21 The other supervillains, who form the Injustice League as the JLA's dark other, are constructed as (duped) victims of someone else's scheme. Their conduct must be assessed differently from that of Brainiac, and the JLA is shown as perceptive in its ability to differentiate between the deeds of the various 'baddies' and administer different kinds of punishment.

22 P Alston and R Goodman, *International Human Rights* (Oxford University Press 2013) 123.

goal. His acts are 'committed as part of a widespread or systematic attack directed against' civilians,[23] and for a long time in Ross there is talk of a conspiracy, though Aquaman's analysis of Brainiac's criminal intent ('Anything living, anything organic is his enemy. . . . This is him against everything that breathes') indicates that this is also a case of environmental, or ecological, justice. Social and environmental justice, criminal law and medical ethics intertwine when the supervillains create oases in desert regions, cure chronic diseases and disabilities, and offer the prospect of a carefree life for the underprivileged in artificial living spaces. As far as Brainiac is concerned, this is a sham and a mere prelude to modifying humans into machines.[24] Whereas the other supervillains are exposed as dupes, Brainiac intentionally commits 'inhumane acts . . . causing . . . serious injury to body or to mental or physical health'.[25] For a long stretch of time, however, it seems that the supervillains truly have turned into mankind's benefactors, and if it was not for the revealing twist that re-establishes the status quo and the clear-cut dichotomy of goodies versus baddies, the *can implies ought* complication would need to be rephrased: rather than merely thwarting criminal activities over and over again, should the superheroes not have fostered the common good of mankind in a similar vein? Should ecological sustainability not be one of their long-term goals?

Environmental justice is key to environmental ethics, a sub-discipline of philosophy that faces a number of problems on epistemological, meta-ethical and normative grounds; in fact, key tenets of environmental science are somewhat counterintuitive. When Wonder Woman tries to remind Poison Ivy of the 'fact' that she forgets 'how much the plant life of earth needs us', meaning superheroes and supervillains alike, because 'there's a balance',[26] this suggests the importance of ecological homeostasis, or equilibrium. However, as Kristin Shrader-Frechette points out, it is far from clear whether it exists, or if it is vital to the emergence and survival of ecosystems. The balance of nature may be no more than a quaint metaphor or a 'vague and incoherent' ecological concept as there is 'no precise, confirmed sense in which one can claim that natural ecosystems proceed towards homeostasis, stability, or some balance'.[27] Other bones of contention in environmental ethics involve human rights law and concern 'questions of distributive justice and the fact that people have rights to equal protection and rights to control the risks that others impose on them'.[28]

23 Article 7(1) of the Rome Statute of the International Criminal Court 1998.
24 If there is even a difference between the two, see Chapter 6 in this book.
25 Article 7(1)(k) of the Rome Statute of the International Criminal Court 1998.
26 Ross, Krueger and Braithwaite (n 1) 173.
27 K Shrader-Frechette, 'Environmental Ethics' in H LaFollette (ed), *The Oxford Handbook of Practical Ethics* (Oxford University Press 2003) 205–6.
28 Ibid 202.

Lex Luthor claims to be building 'new cities for a new humanity. For a people who feel they have a right to a better life'.[29]

The just distribution of resources is not merely a spatial but also a temporal issue, which brings us back to Wonder Woman's *dictum* about the pursuit of the common good. Are we to be held responsible for the welfare of future generations? Those who have children of their own will instinctively reply in the positive, but they can be accused of biological selfishness. In the early 1970s, Martin Golding argued that:

> [I]n order for present people to have obligations to future ones, they must be members of the same moral community or else have a shared conception of the human good. But present and future people cannot be members of the same moral community . . . because such membership presupposes reciprocity, and future people cannot reciprocate present people for their sacrifices. Moreover, because the precise nature of the good that present and future persons might share is unclear . . . responsibilities to future persons are minimal.[30]

Reciprocity is key to almost any definition of justice. The concept may thus be informed by an *aesthetic* appreciation of symmetry which is not necessarily arrived at through introspection yet seems to be prevalent in different societies. As David Johnston points out:

> A sensibility for reciprocity in relations among human beings is integral to [their]. . . sense [of justice]. It is commonplace for people who have received significant benefits from others to feel that they ought to requite those benefits in some fashion, if they are able to do so. Perhaps even more strikingly, people will often go to great lengths to retaliate against others who have inflicted harm, if they are able to do so. It is not unusual for people to retaliate against perpetrators of harm even if they are not the victims and the act of retaliation is costly to themselves. . . . [B]oth monocultural and cross-cultural studies of behaviour related to fairness have found that people generally are motivated by considerations of reciprocity and are willing to make personal sacrifices in order to satisfy the demands of reciprocity.[31]

It is in this sense of an intuitive appreciation of *justice as reciprocity* that reckoning as a sum total of a person's actions – actions that you disapprove

29 Ross, Krueger and Braithwaite (n 1) 152.
30 As quoted in Shrader-Frechette (n 27) 195–96.
31 D Johnston, *A Brief History of Justice* (Wiley-Blackwell 2011) 224–26.

of – and the redressing of imbalance becomes plausible for the reader. Yet, the dividing line between the notions of revenge, retribution, reckoning, and justice is not drawn accurately in the superhero genre, nor has this been the case in the history of the terms:

> In Homeric Greece, 'revenge' and 'justice' were more or less equivalent, but Plato's Socrates taught that 'the return of evil for evil' is always unjust . . . Modern social philosophy generally rejects the very idea of revenge as irrational and always unjustified. But among those philosophers who still defend the idea of retribution (as opposed to deterrence and rehabilitation), the line between revenge and retribution is not obvious . . . In fact, revenge is sometimes justified and often deliberative, and it is a much debated question to what extent revenge should be part of the purpose of punishment in the criminal law. Nor should revenge be viewed as simply a raw, unreasonable emotion. Revenge is a dish, says one ancient proverb, which is 'best served cold'.[32]

The term reckoning, moreover, suggests reciprocation of harm. The principle is enshrined in the old testamentary *lex talionis* ('an eye for an eye' in its literal execution), which appears to be a crude forerunner to contemporary forms of jurisdiction. The latter seek to translate a crime (eg rape) into a different 'currency' (eg solitary confinement of the perpetrator instead of raping him back) in which the punishment is supposed to be commensurate with the form of transgression of the law in question, and therefore considered 'just'. The superheroes in Ross are modern in this respect: they do not cut into Brainiac's brain or abduct any of his children or friends in return for his deeds. (It is not specified in *Justice* whether they *could* have punished him in accordance with the *lex talionis*, that is, whether he has an organic brain or friends and relatives at all.) Leaving the planet to atomic annihilation, Brainiac shrinks himself and his spaceship to get away unnoticed but is caught and 'incarcerated' by the JLA. 'Still frozen in his ship', he is now on display in the 'Kandorian museum' in Superman's Fortress of Solitude in the Arctic polar wastes.[33] As the DC supervillain was initially established by his stealing and miniaturising Kandor, the capital city of Superman's home planet, Krypton, this seems a just punishment, requiting like with like.

32 RC Solomon, 'Revenge' in T Honderich (ed), *The Oxford Companion to Philosophy* (Oxford University Press 1995) 772.
33 Ross, Krueger and Braithwaite (n 1) 369.

Justice League International and the myth of American exceptionalism

'We do not live in a just world', writes Thomas Nagel:

> This may be the least controversial claim one could make in political theory. But it is much less clear what, if anything, justice on a world scale might mean, or what the hope for justice should lead us to want in the domain of international or global institutions, and in the policies of states that are in a position to affect the world order.[34]

One nation-state constantly affecting and upsetting the world order is the United States, and it is crucial to note that the superhero genre is a distinctly American phenomenon, which, in its more mainstream forms, is often used for propaganda purposes. Not surprisingly, therefore, ethical concepts and issues related to international law and politics are refracted through a prism of nationalist ideology in both Ross and Jurgens. In his article on 'The Problem of Global Justice', Nagel continues to ponder:

> pressing practical questions that we now face about the legitimate path forward in the governance of the world. These are, inevitably, questions about institutions, many of which do not yet exist . . . What creates the link between justice and sovereignty is something common to a wide range of conceptions of justice: they all depend on the coordinated conduct of large numbers of people, which cannot be achieved without law backed up by a monopoly of force.[35]

One non-existent institution outlining a 'legitimate path forward in the governance of the world' and asserting a monopoly of force is shown in Dan Jurgens's *Justice League International*. In contrast to the members of the JLA, who seem to feel compelled to form an alliance of 'compatriots' against the forces of evil (referred to as 'cohorts') by their inherent sense of justice, *Justice League International* legitimises the actions of another superhero team by depicting them as being selected and held accountable by the fictitious UN Global Security Group.

In the first volume, the team defends the globe from being depleted of natural resources by an intergalactic miner who starts extracting broken down 'portions of the planet' from subterranean sites in Peru, Russia, Canada, and Africa.[36] From the start, the rhetoric is militant and smacks of

34 T Nagel, 'The Problem of Global Justice' in T Brooks (ed), *The Global Justice Reader* (Blackwell 2008) 416.

35 Ibid 416–17.

36 Jurgens, Lopresti and Ryan, *Signal Masters* (n 2).

the need to make urgent decisions during a crisis. The first speech bubble in the volume is uttered by Andre Briggs, a suited black man and 'Head of UN Intelligence', who can be seen standing in front of a projected vertical array of more than 20 superheroes, 'Confidence in every level of authority is at an all-time low', Briggs claims:

> Every government, and, by extension, every law enforcement agency and security force, is woefully underfunded and lacking resources. We believe it's time for the United Nations to assemble its own team, representing select nations, uniquely equipped to overcome those issues.[37]

The 'we' Briggs refers to is an American we. The same claim is repeated on the next page, when Briggs can be seen standing in front of three video screens showing the leaders of the UN Global Security Group, which has the 'honor of making the final decision' as to which superheroes shall be on the team.[38]

In the real world of readers and writers, the three nations making up the fictitious Security Group - namely, China, Russia and the UK - are select members of the UN Security Council, consisting of 15 member states, five of which are permanent (China, France, the Russian Federation, the UK and the United States). One can only speculate as to why France has been left out in Jurgens; the United States is represented as making the proposal and constantly reiterating the need for a new international executive force. Thus, we have in effect only four member states in the comic book and are faced with the possibility of a stalemate in voting that could never happen in real life. In Jurgens, Anglo-American ties are covertly set against the former Red scare and Yellow Peril while the United States is displayed as passive and having no say in the matter at all. The impression is that America is selflessly trying to help without reaping any benefits.

As the cover of volume one indicates, though, it is for the American superheroes to lead and for the representatives of other nations to follow: Booster Gold, Green Lantern, Guy Gardner and JLA veteran Batman are being followed by their team-mates from Brazil, Zambezi, Norway, Russia, China and the UK. Discussing the probability of the voting outcome with his assistant, Briggs states, 'We're at a volatile crossroads, and they know the old ways aren't working'. It is an *us* versus *them* dichotomy, a case of *othering*: the United States is established as more foresighted and alert than other nations; the land of the free and the home of the brave is

37 Ibid.
38 Ibid.

uniquely equipped to bring about change in global politics.[39] This is hardly surprising, for the myth of American exceptionalism is a persistent one that is only recently beginning to be dispelled. It can be traced back to an unsavoury mix of religious zealousness and territorial expansionism in the early white settler colony.[40] Closely connected to the myth of America as 'a city on a hill' and 'a beacon of liberty and democracy' inspiring other nations is the idea of America's democratic mission, the idea that the world requires America 'to release it into freedom'.[41]

This sense of ultra-nationalism and missionary zeal is not questioned in Jurgens. The enduring myth of American 'specialness' 'does not rest on one particular creation story or narrative derived from a specific series of events . . . [but] is more akin to a cluster of stories that provides buttresses for pseudo-analytical judgements about American national identity.'[42] Arguably, the cluster of American superhero stories helps to foster, refashion and maintain the myth at home and abroad. In Volume I of *Justice League International*, the prospective members of the newly formed Justice League International (JLI) assemble at the Hall of Justice. Rather than resembling an international institution like the International Court of Justice in The Hague, the JLI Hall of Justice is reminiscent of the Lincoln Memorial in Washington DC, a familiar architectural emblem of American democratic constitutionalism.[43]

Volume I ends with a terrorist attack on the UN, and Volume II is dispersed with traumatic imagery of dead, hospitalised and crippled humans and superhumans (Briggs and his assistant are killed in the attack, as is

39 'Don't worry', a beautiful Indian girl Somita, with a tikka on her forehead and dressed in classical garb, writes to her parents with a fountain pen held by her new hand prosthesis in Ross's *Justice*, 'it wasn't a trick. The man who governs this city was a criminal once. But it's not like you said': Ross, Krueger and Braithwaite (n 1) 278. She was born into a station of life there can be no escape from within the rigid social stratification of the traditional Indian caste system, so Somita runs away from home to live the American Dream. Hers too is a rhetoric of (the freedom of) choice that is uniquely granted by Western ideology and that starkly contrasts with notions of destiny/fate/determinism. 'Don't I deserve this, Father? To be here? If I were as happy as you said I was, why would I choose this place?': ibid.

40 H Zinn, 'The Myth of American Exceptionalism' (MIT World Lecture Series on Myths about America, 2005) <http://videolectures.net/mitworld_zinn_mae/> accessed 10 November 2013.

41 Ibid; P Smith, *Time No Longer: Americans After the American Century* (Yale University Press 2013).

42 I Tyrrell, 'What is American Exceptionalism?' (*Ian Tyrrell*) <http://iantyrrell.wordpress.com/papers-and-comments/> accessed 17 January 2014.

43 We later learn that the 'remnants of the Hall of Justice', featuring a toppled spherical column that signifies the globe, lie in 'Washington, DC'.

Russian superhero Gavril Ivanovich). Returning home from Paris, where 'a coordinated attack by Rogue Firestorms nearly destroyed one of the world's most famous landmarks', the Chinese August General in Iron narrates while the JLI fly over and land by the Statue of Liberty, 'We are tired, hungry and exhausted. We have suffered casualties . . . America is still in grave danger and the prospect of failure looms over us all. Unacceptable for the Justice League International'.[44]

The priorities are clear: even for the Chinese ally, America comes first. The Statue of Liberty, in whose shadow the heroes find shelter like the 'wretched refuse' invited to step on to American shores (cf E Lazarus's 1883 sonnet 'The New Colossus' plaque on the statue), was a gift from France, and has the same (co-)designer as the Parisian landmark, Alexandre-Gustave Eiffel. Despite all the threats, the principle of America as a safe haven for all - at least all who are 'good' - still holds. Ties to old world Europe are being reiterated but in a superficial, allusive, and even condescending way.

Conclusion

Compared to radical, 'revisionary' works such as Alan Moore's *Watchmen* and Frank Miller's *Batman: The Dark Knight Returns*, the amount of self-reflexivity is rather limited in Ross and virtually non-existent in Jurgens.[45] Yet it is worth analysing these series for much of what is not overtly said or shown. Similar to Snyder's *Man of Steel*, who, like real-life icon Frank Sinatra declares he needs to do everything his way, Booster Gold and his team are eventually outlawed in Volume II of *Justice League International*. This comes as no major surprise. Whether working alone or in a team, superheroes are always constructed as 'self-governing entities' that are not accountable to lesser beings whose laws simply do not apply to them. These (global) vigilante figures make up their own rules of (world) policing that are legitimated by the existence of vague threats and an unsubstantiated claim to moral superiority which entitles them to determine the best course for the world and,

44 Jurgens, Lopresti and Ryan, *Breakdown* (n 2).

45 In Ross, we find a certain amount of meta-fictionality, eg when E Nigma asks philosophical questions such as, 'Why is there crime? Where do we go when we die? Why is there suffering in the world?', or when Batman ponders the function of Arkham Asylum as 'not to secure the psychological health of the patients, but for the safety around it. No one even wants to admit the possibility of ills for which there are no cures': Ross, Krueger and Braithwaite (n 1) 58, 61. Yet in Miller's work such observations are subtler, and therefore more radical. In *Batman: The Dark Knight Returns*, Arkham is not designated as a 'Home for the Criminally Sick' but is depicted as a 'Home for the Emotionally Troubled' - a definition that, on a 'bad day' anyway, could apply to almost anyone, including the reader. See F Miller, *Batman: The Dark Knight Returns* (DC Comics 2002) 15.

using necessity as a justification, make use of superior firepower. Just like America.[46]

In light of the ethico-legal and political concepts discussed in this chapter, the graphic forms of justice and governance displayed by Ross and Jurgens appear ambiguous. If the image conveyed to the reader is that of a nation selflessly helping other nations without reaping any benefits, the demand that reciprocity inform any given conception of justice remains unfulfilled. Costs and benefits are distributed unequally among different political players. In these constructions, the selfless helper exhibits a 'natural' sense of 'responsibility' and 'fairness', a moral intuition that wrongs and power imbalances need to be redressed. As it lies within the helper's responsibility to attempt to re-establish 'balance' (*yes we can* implying *yes we ought*), it seems inevitable that he or she will come under attack while trying to free decent, powerless others from oppression, provide shelter, etc.[47] Highlighting the malice of the attacker and the moral rectitude of the defender, this will be seen as doubly unjust by the reader ('He was only trying to help!'). Consequently, DC has devised a League of Injustice in which the deeds and character traits of the baddies converge: culpability no longer rests in the attribution of cognitive and volitional capacities at the time of perpetrating a crime. Similar to attesting manifest madness in criminal law, culpability is structurally inscribed in the criminal (master)mind, as part of the personality structure of the most uncontrollable superheroes.[48] Can they be brought to their senses, or are we talking about categorical differences rather than gradual ones? In the less self-reflexive examples of the genre, the other does not simply act unlawfully but becomes an evil other that cannot be reasoned with and seems beyond redemption. How can they be brought to justice? America, in these tales, does not seek retribution. Instead, the evil other is banished to outer space, detained, or, as a 'last resort', killed.[49] This is commonly done in ways that construct American superheroes as having a superior moral outlook on life, acting like an impartial judge and jury in the interest of the 'common

46 See also Chapter 10 in this book, on vigilantism, the United States and the state of exception.

47 The discussion on ecological homeostasis suggested that the existence of a pre-stabilised harmony may be no more than a fiction.

48 See A Loughnan, *Manifest Madness: Mental Incapacity in Criminal Law* (Oxford University Press 2012).

49 In Jurgens, Lopresti and Ryan, *Signal Masters* (n 2), Galactus is fended off and doomed to roam the galaxy in search of easier prey. For detention, here coupled with the prospect of rehabilitation, see the 'gulag . . . built to imprison the deadliest and most uncontrollable of the superhuman' in Waid and Ross (n 5) 113. Superman kills his enemy in Snyder's film *Man of Steel* (2013) when the latter symbolically threatens to destroy the democratic constitution (he cuts the Greco-Roman pillars in a building sheltering ordinary humans with laser beams emanating from his eyes). On superheroes' determinations of 'deathworthiness', see also Chapter 7 in this book.

good'. The reading of Jurgens moreover suggests that characters are used as metonymies for nation-states. Yet, it appears doubtful whether this is a successful answer to the challenge of state versus individual agency/ responsibility. That is to say, it is doubtful that individuals can represent anything beyond themselves, that a single characteristic and will to act (intent) can emerge from the heterogeneous mass of people(s), ethnicities, customs, mores, territorial boundaries, etc, loosely grouped under the heading of the nation-state. After all, even the most radical totalitarian regimes have failed to maintain the fiction of efficient single-minded governance.

Bibliography

Alston P and Goodman R, *International Human Rights* (Oxford University Press 2013).

Ashcroft B, Tiffin H and Griffiths G, *The Empire Writes Back: Theory and Practice in Post-Colonial Literatures* (Routledge 1989).

Boge C, 'Suspending Democracy: Vigilante Justice and the Rule of Law in Christopher Nolan's Dark Knight Trilogy' in Aristodemou M, Macmillan F and Tuitt P (eds), *Crime Fiction and the Law* (Birkbeck Law Press 2015).

Boge C, 'Visualizing Histories and Stories: Revisionary Graphic Novels of the 1980s and 1990s' in Barberi A and others (eds), *Medienimpulse 2012–2013* (New Academic Press 2014).

Johnston D, *A Brief History of Justice* (Wiley-Blackwell 2011).

Jurgens D, Lopresti A and Ryan M, *Justice League International Volume I: The Signal Masters* (DC Comics 2012).

Jurgens D, Lopresti A and Ryan M, *Justice League International Volume II: Breakdown* (DC Comics 2012).

Loughnan A, *Manifest Madness: Mental Incapacity in Criminal Law* (Oxford University Press 2012).

Lu C, 'World Government' in Zalta EN (ed), *The Stanford Encyclopedia of Philosophy* (2012) <http://plato.stanford.edu/archives/fall2012/entries/world-government/> accessed 3 November 2013.

Miller F, *Batman: The Dark Knight Returns* (DC Comics 2002).

Nagel T, 'The Problem of Global Justice' in Brooks T (ed), *The Global Justice Reader* (Blackwell 2008).

Nussbaum MC, 'Capabilities as Fundamental Entitlements: Sen and Social Justice' in Brooks T (ed), *The Global Justice Reader* (Blackwell 2008).

Ross A, Krueger J and Braithwaite D, *Justice* (DC Comics 2011).

Shrader-Frechette K, 'Environmental Ethics' in LaFollette H (ed), *The Oxford Handbook of Practical Ethics* (Oxford University Press 2003).

Smith P, *Time No Longer: Americans after the American Century* (Yale University Press 2013).

Solomon RC, 'Revenge' in T Honderich (ed), *The Oxford Companion to Philosophy* (Oxford University Press 1995).

Tyrrell I, 'What is American Exceptionalism?' (*Ian Tyrrell*) <http://iantyrrell.wordpress.com/papers-and-comments/> accessed 17 January 2014.

von Hirsch A, 'Retribution' in P Cane and J Conaghan (eds), *The New Oxford Companion to Law* (Oxford University Press 2008).

Waid M and Ross A, *Kingdom Come* (DC Comics 2008).

Walzer M, *Thick and Thin: Moral Argument at Home and Abroad* (University of Notre Dame Press 1994).

Zinn H, 'The Myth of American Exceptionalism' (MIT World Lecture Series on Myths about America, 2005) <http://videolectures.net/mitworld_zinn_mae/> accessed 10 November 2013.

Chapter 14

Graphic reporting: human rights violations through the lens of graphic novels

Jérémie Gilbert and David Keane

Introduction

There is a growing interest in the world of graphic novels from a legal viewpoint, but the interconnection between law and graphic novels has not yet been fully assessed in the area of human rights law.[1] In addition, there is an emergent body of authors who are seeking to use graphic novels to advance what can be broadly understood as human rights awareness-raising, through the depiction or reporting of wide-scale atrocities or rights denial. This raises questions as to the status and potential of a nascent connection between human rights and graphic novels, especially from the perspective of human rights law which is at present largely driven by reports from international organisations not receptive to graphic novels as a means of communication and reporting. From the viewpoint of the graphic novel sphere, there is a question as to whether there is a need to recognise an emergent body of work that could be termed the 'human rights graphic novel'. Furthermore, the direct engagement by graphic authors with human rights violations leads to potential for greater reciprocity between these graphic reporters and the international system designed to monitor rights protection, and prevent and punish perpetrators.

This chapter explores, first, the concept of graphic reporting, seeking to understand the nature of depicting human rights questions in graphic novel form, as well as identifying texts that fit within the graphic reporting discourse. Second, it asks what the added value is, arguing that graphic reporting constitutes a distinct contribution to the reporting of human

1 The term 'human rights' has many connotations but the term 'human rights law' is more readily delineated. It refers to the collection of international treaties and standards overseen by the UN, drawing its authority from the 1945 Charter of the United Nations, and articulated first as a global standard in the 1948 Universal Declaration of Human Rights. The contemporary contours of 'human rights law' are expressed in the mandate of the Office of the High Commissioner for Human Rights, available at <www.ohchr.org> accessed 15 April 2014.

rights violations that provides particular context and character not achieved by other forms. Third, it identifies the belief that the medium is not sufficiently serious to engage with instances of rights violations or wide-scale atrocities, looking at the expression of this viewpoint and the countering arguments. Lastly, it seeks to delineate the future of graphic reporting, pointing to the potential for graphic novels to make a marked contribution to the human rights discourse, as well as the broader effects of providing effective detail on situations of human rights violations.

Overall, if this collection is intended for law to meet comics, the present chapter is intended for human rights to meet graphic novels. It asks whether the work of certain pioneering authors can be built upon to understand a space in which the reporting of human rights violations in graphic form can be better understood and recognised, within the international human rights, as well as the graphic novel, spheres.

What is graphic reporting?

The figure of the reporter has featured strongly in graphic novels. A number of prominent characters employ the guise of a reporter to advance the plot or focus the story, as well as explain key elements such as why the central character has the ability and time to travel extensively and conduct investigations. In this regard, Tintin is one of the best-recognised character-reporters, while Superman worked for the *Daily Planet*, and Spider-Man was a photographer at the *Daily Bugle*. These fictional representations see reporting primarily as a background occupation, used for the purpose of setting the scenes and the characters and allowing them the necessary freedom to interact across the storylines. In addition, their experiences are entirely fictional and removed from any association with human rights violations, real or imagined, and are absent any requisite call for change or action inherent in reporting on actual abuses.

A more recent generation of graphic novelists has cast aside the fictional representation of reporting, to place such investigations to the fore. These have started to undertake reporting, notably on war situations but also on wider human rights violations, by using graphic novels as a main source of reporting. They take a point-of-view approach to eschew the characterisation of the reporter and place the experience of the novelist as central, documenting the experiences of war or other atrocities in a representation of human rights violations as lived in graphic form. Joe Sacco's works are immediately identifiable but he is not an isolated example, arguably being representative of a new generation of graphic authors (the word 'novelists' may not be correct given its association with fiction, but is the prevailing descriptor) who are using graphic novels to report on real situations and chart serious human rights abuses. In this context, these authors do not invent or create a character that will do the reporting, but are themselves reporting on a real situation, often placing themselves within the narrative as the reporter in question.

Sacco has drafted a manifesto to capture what these graphic authors are doing, arguing it is not correct to divorce journalism and graphic novels, and implicitly demanding that graphic accounts be taken seriously as a source. The title of his work, which draws together a number of different scenarios of factual atrocities, experiences, injustice and violations, and compiles them in one volume, is *Journalism* – a deliberate choice of nomenclature. In a succinct overview of where he sees his work, he compares the graphic author with the journalist, and draws out the similarities and differences:

> The journalist's standard obligations – to report accurately, to get quotes right, and to check claims – still pertain. A writer can breezily describe a convoy of UN vehicles as 'a convoy of UN vehicles' and move on to the rest of the story. A comics journalist must draw a convoy of vehicles, and that raises a lot of questions. So, what do these vehicles look like? What do the uniforms of the UN personnel look like? What does the road look like? And what about the surrounding hills?[2]

The use of the phrase 'comics journalist' is not attributed, and it is not certain if Sacco in fact coined this phrase; he is in any case widely attributed as a pioneer of comics journalism, as recognised in the handful of commentaries on this emerging field.[3] Sacco's works *Palestine*,[4] and *Safe Area Gorazde*,[5] are seen as seminal texts in comics journalism, with *The Comics Journal* calling him 'virtually a one-man comics genre: the cartoonist-journalist'.[6] Indeed, Sacco was formally trained in journalism.[7] The number of graphic novels that are reporting on real situations is growing; some journalists have even used the term 'conflict-based, nonfiction comic reporting'.[8] Yet

2 Preface to J Sacco, *Journalism* (Metropolitan Books 2012).
3 See eg, Nalvic, 'A Quick Guide to Comics Journalism' (*Nalvic's Reviews*, 12 June 2012) <http://nalvicreviews.wordpress.com/2012/06/12/a-quick-guide-to-comic-journalism/> accessed 15 April 2014.
4 J Sacco, *Palestine* (Jonathan Cape 2003).
5 J Sacco, *Safe Area Gorazde* (Jonathan Cape 2007).
6 G Groth, 'Joe Sacco on *Footnotes in Gaza*' (2011) 301 *The Comics Journal* <www.tcj.com/tcj-301-joe-sacco-on-footnotes-in-gaza/> accessed 15 April 2014.
7 D Crumm, 'Sacco Nails down Comic Credentials in Journalism' (*Read the Spirit*) <www.readthespirit.com/explore/joe-sacco-nails-down-comic-credentials-in-journalism/> accessed 15 April 2014.
8 A Holpuch, 'Joseph Kony Graphic Novel Illustrates Personal Stories of Violent Campaign' (*The Guardian*, 15 March 2013) <www.theguardian.com/books/2013/mar/15/joseph-kony-graphic-novel-violent> accessed 15 April 2014.

Sacco himself has noted that his more recent work is stepping back from conflict to cover broader situations of human rights violations, evident in his depiction of the Dalits of India and their experience of trenchant caste discrimination.[9] In this regard, perhaps Sacco is not really a journalist in that the focus of his work is not necessarily topical or current, and may lack a 'hook'; but rather a human rights reporter in graphic form.

In 2000, Emmanuel Guibert published *The Photographer*, which was labelled by the New York Times as 'part photojournalism and part graphic memoir'.[10] *The Photographer* was received as a novel way of describing in detail the impact of war on the daily lives of the civilian population, and as such provided a new platform to undertake reporting: not quite a documentary, nor a film, nor a novel, but a detailed graphic depiction of the situation. Guibert's work is an illustration of this new generation of authors using the graphic novel form to provide a detailed and differing account on human rights abuses. A further example is the work of Guy Delisle in a series of graphic novels about his travels with strong human rights themes.[11] All these graphic novels contain a high level of reporting on the human rights situation in the countries covered in the books. The number of graphic novels that are reporting on real life situations, but more particularly on real life human rights abuses, is growing, as clearly graphic novels are becoming a distinct medium to report on atrocities and abuses.

These authors are following the same rules of reporting as foreign correspondents sent to conflict situations by media outlets, or documentary film-makers intent on providing greater background and commentary on situations of violence and conflict. The aims are manifold but share a desire to raise awareness on situations of human rights violations. The new approach is the medium, which instead of writing or documentary film, is using graphic representation of the atrocities. These authors are not labelled as journalists, or human rights reporters, but share many of their functions, and have adopted a similar ethos. In his introduction to *Safe Area Gorazde*, Christopher Hitchens distinguishes Sacco from 'the hacks', the journalists gathered in the disfigured Holiday Inn in Sarajevo, describing instead 'the oblique figure at the edge of the scene' with the eye and the ear to record and outlive the

9 J Sacco, 'Kushinagar: A Comics Journalist Chronicles the Struggles of UP Dalits' (*The Caravan*, 1 January 2012) <www.caravanmagazine.in/reporting-and-essays/kushinagar> accessed 15 April 2014.

10 C Hedges, 'What War Looks Like' (*New York Times*, 24 May 2009) <www.nytimes.com/2009/05/24/books/review/Hedges-t.html?_r=2&> accessed 15 April 2014.

11 G Delisle, *Shenzhen* (Drawn and Quarterly 2000); G Delisle, *Pyongyang* (Drawn and Quarterly 2003); G Delisle, *Burma Chronicles* (Drawn and Quarterly 2007); and G Delisle, *Jerusalem* (Drawn and Quarterly 2011).

carnage, and perhaps contribute to rebuilding the community.[12] The distinction is effusively made. Similarly, the journalistic approach is extended in the sense that broader situations of human rights violations not necessarily linked to conflict are entering the consciousness of graphic authors.

Traditionally, graphic or comics authors used to have a small space, and in the best cases a few pages in newspapers or magazines, to illustrate the 'serious' report undertaken by the journalist. The illustration was there only as an aid or accompaniment to the main text. This has changed, notably with the emergence of 'proper' news outlets that are providing a space for graphic reporting to be expressed, not as an added illustration but as the main vehicle to carry the information. For example, in France the news magazine *La Revue 21* was created with the particular aim of using graphic novels as a medium of reporting.[13] The result is a periodical graphic account of human rights abuses taking place across the globe, presumably the first such publication. This has led to the recent publication of *Grand Reporters: 20 Histoires Vraies*, a collective work that includes authors such as Sacco, Guibert, Ferrandez, Tronchet and Stassens, under the rubric of reporting on 'real life stories' with a backdrop of political or military events or everyday hardship, and its perpetrators and victims.[14] Although more prominent in the Francophone world, where graphic novels are considered the 'ninth art' form, there is evidence of a small take-up of this approach in the Anglophone world as well.[15]

As well as reporting directly on human rights issues, graphic novels may also raise or generate human rights issues. For example, the theme of racial discrimination offers a vein of inquiry. *Tintin in the Congo* was recently the subject of failed legal proceedings in a Belgian court, with consequent commentary emerging around the limits of hate speech legislation.[16] Michael Farr writes in his notes on the Tintin series, 'if *Tintin in the Congo* gives a wildly inaccurate picture of Africa, it does at least illustrate the prejudice with which Europeans then viewed Africans'.[17] A similar controversy on racism emerged over the Mexican character,

12 C Hitchens, introduction to Sacco (n 5).
13 *La Revue 21* <www.revue21.fr> accessed 15 April 2014.
14 O Balez and others, *Grand Reporters: 20 Histoires Varies* (Les Arènes XXI 2012).
15 See eg, the *Cartoon Picayune* <www.cartoonpicayune.com> accessed 15 April 2014, which has similar aims; the *Illustrated Press* <http://illuspress.com> accessed 15 April 2014; and *Comics Journalism* <www.comicsjournalism.com> accessed 15 April 2014.
16 See J Vrielink, 'Judging the Past: Discrimination Law, Hate Speech Legislation and the Colonial Imagination' (2012) 12 *International Journal of Discrimination and the Law* 99.
17 M Farr, *Tintin: The Complete Companion* (Egmont Press 2011).

Memin Pinguin, the subject of discussion in a legal journal.[18] The issue is also explored in the anthropomorphic detective series *Blacksad*, which portrays vicious inter-racial violence and segregation in the graphic novel *Arctic Nation*, pitting white-furred animal characters against black-furred animal characters and opening with a lynching.[19] These texts belong in the literary rather than the journalistic genre, and may be analysed *inter alia* from the established law and literature perspective and other interdisciplinary standpoints.[20] But they ought to be distinguished from the practice of graphic reporting.

Graphic reporting is clearly distinct from graphic novels even though the latter may raise questions of interest for human rights. Graphic reporting involves the overt and intentional depiction of human rights violations or conflict situations in graphic novel format. For example in India, the Dalits, at the bottom of the caste hierarchy, are developing graphic novels that examine questions of caste prejudice and atrocities. Thus *Bhimayana: Experiences of Untouchability*[21] is written and drawn in Gond art, and begins with a discussion around reservations, a legal affirmative action policy that was established in the Constitution of India in 1950 to address historic discrimination and uplift those at the bottom of the caste system. The legal elements are precise and draw on the historical struggle for equal treatment on the basis of caste through the personality of Ambedkar, a Dalit leader in the early twentieth century who drafted the Indian Constitution and infused it with legal protections against caste discrimination. This graphic novel is particularly concerned with the implementation of legal remedies, and the gaps between legal protection and everyday discrimination, violence and atrocities experienced by Dalits. A further publication, *A Gardener in the Wasteland*,[22] indicates a particular interest in Dalit graphic novels on the part of this publishing house. Similarly, as noted above, Sacco has explored the treatment of Dalits, portraying the subtleties and social mechanisms in an Indian village that keep

18 See TL Banks, 'Mestizaje and the Mexican Mestizo Self: No Hay Sangrenegra, so there is no Blackness' (2006) 15 *Southern California Interdisciplinary Law Journal* 199, 202.

19 JD Canales and J Guarnido, *Blacksad: Arctic Nation* (Dargaud 2003).

20 See eg, R Posner, *Law and Literature* (Harvard University Press 1998). The law and literature genre is well-established, although it has not engaged to any notable extent with graphic novels. See also Chapter 13 in this book, which reflects on the problems of global justice through two superhero works from DC comics.

21 D Vyam, S Vyam, S Natarajan and S Anand, *Bhimayana: Experiences of Untouchability* (Navayana 2011).

22 S Natarajan and A Ninan, *A Gardener in the Wasteland: Jotiba Phule's Fight for Liberty* (Navayana 2012).

Dalits subordinated despite constitutional bans on untouchability and other discriminatory practices.[23]

Graphic reporting is not the identification of human rights questions in literary works of graphic fiction, but rather purports to capture the reality of human rights violations as experienced. Thus Prajna Desai, in a commentary on *Bhimayana*, notes that beyond its graphic quality and pedigree, the book is 'unusually germane for being grounded in present-day journalism'.[24]

What is the 'added value'?

A specificity of this type of reporting is its graphic nature, which renders the report on human rights violations particularly vivid. The combination of text and illustration is known to offer a strong combination to mark the reader's mind. As highlighted by Jennifer George-Palilonis in her book on graphics reporting:

> the combination of words and visual within a story package have an extreme impact on catching a reader's attention, keeping it and even ensuring that he or she retains the information much longer than when a story is provided in the form of words alone. Information graphics generally stimulate more brainpower because they appeal to both the literal and visual regions of the brain. Information graphics can tell stories with a degree of detail that is often otherwise impossible.[25]

But the process is deeper than a straightforward combination of words and images. One commentator terms this the 'biocularity' of the graphic narrative, a complexity realised in Marjane Satrapi's *Persepolis* whereby:

> the author-artist's memory of a childhood in Iran, the creation of the child character-avatar, and the narrator-avatar's commentary collaborate to tell a complex verbal-pictorial story infused with memories and its emotions without detracting from the memoir's realism.[26]

23 See 'Kushinagar' in Sacco (n 2).

24 P Desai, 'Review of Bhimayana: Experiences of Untouchability' (*The Comics Journal*, 18 April 2012) <www.tcj.com/reviews/bhimayana-experiences-of-untouchability/> accessed 15 April 2014.

25 J George-Palilonis, *A Practical Guide to Graphics Reporting: Information Graphics for Print, Web and Broadcast* (Elsevier 2006) 4.

26 PJ Rader, 'Iconoclastic Readings and Self-reflexive Rebellions in Marjane Satrapi's *Persepolis* and *Persepolis 2*' in J Jakaitis and JF Wurtz (eds), *Crossing Boundaries in Graphic Narrative* (McFarland 2012) 127.

This 'narrative agility'[27] can have a major impact when it comes to reporting real life human rights violations. Not only does it provide more nuances, but these can stay in the reader's mind with more impact than traditional reporting. As captured in a review of Sacco's work, a reporter writes, 'The images Sacco draws are so powerful that they burn deep into your retina and reconfigure how you see the world'.[28] This statement highlights how graphic reporting can provide a very human and powerful description of some of the worst human rights violations. Evidently, graphic novels can report on human rights violations with a force that often eludes other media.[29]

Graphic reporting allows the reporter to integrate much more artistic and detailed elements when reporting on the suffering of trauma or violence. To give an illustration, much has been written on the genocide that took place in Rwanda in 1994. This has included newspaper reports, articles, films, documentaries and novels.[30] All this reporting vividly testifies to the extreme violence suffered by victims and survivors, and provides analyses on the relationship between the different communities involved. Recently, Jean-Philippe Stassens, a Belgian graphic author, has examined the Rwandan genocide from the angle of the graphic novel in his book *Déogratias*.[31] The work is based on months of investigative journalism in the country and region. In this graphic account of the genocide, one of the main characters transforms himself into a dog when violence erupts around him. This reporting on how violence can take hold of an individual provides the reader with a rich and traumatically graphic vision of extreme violence, as well as its triggers. Moreover, an important aspect of the use of graphic reporting relates to the way the author employs the narrative to allow the reader to move across timelines. Mass killings, and especially genocide, involve deep-rooted and embedded discrimination, which has brewed over time to unleash into a form of extreme violence. By its nature, graphic reporting allows the use of inter-temporal illustration to show how these historical and integrated forms of discrimination relate to the mass killing and its aftermath.

27 Ibid 136.
28 *National Post* (Toronto), as quoted in Sacco (n 2).
29 On this issue, see also R Versace, *This Book Contains Graphic Language: Comics as Literature* (Continuum 2007), which includes a chapter on war memoir and the unique ability of comics to capture its human/real-life details.
30 See eg, P Gourevitch, *We Wish to Inform You that Tomorrow We Will Be Killed with Our Families* (Picador 1999); J Hatzfeld, *Life Laid Bare: The Survivors in Rwanda Speak* (Other Press 2007); T George, K Pearson, D Cheadle and P Rusesabagina (eds), *Hotel Rwanda: Bringing the True Story of an African Hero to Film* (Newmarket Press 2005).
31 J Stassens, *Déogratias: A Tale of Rwanda* (Dupuis 2000).

In *Déogratias* this approach allows the author to address the issue of ethnic divisions and the way these have been consumed by the characters both in the past (before the genocide), during the genocide, and in its aftermath, all within the same movement of the pen (see Figure 14.1[32]). The text displays powerful juxtaposition of these three different time-frames, often within a same page, which allows the author to highlight how they need to be viewed together to capture the reality faced by individuals. A written account, or other forms of reporting including visual documentaries, could not include this trans-temporal element in a simultaneous manner. In the context of Rwanda it matters especially, as historical accounts and present day narratives on ethnicity play an immense role, often translated in written accounts as a dichotomy between the 'good Tutsi' (the victims) and the 'bad Hutus' (the perpetrators), a narrative that fails to integrate the complexity of the relationship and divisions in its historical span. *Déogratias* avoids this dichotomy by offering a trans-temporal account through the eyes of a character who is neither good nor bad, and whose ethnicity does not define the good or the bad. As summarised by Glover:

> The multimodality of the graphic novel exists in its combination of the literary and the visual, which enables the genre to visually represent multiple temporalities in sequences of drawn frames. The treatment of memory and trauma in these graphic novels is emboldened by the form's ability to visually layer, sequence, and juxtapose multiple temporalities.[33]

Arguably, this multi-layering of sequences and temporalities provides a vivid and rich account when it comes to the complexity of human rights violations, something not easily transcribed in official reports or other forms of written account of these atrocities. From this perspective, graphic reporting provides a valuable medium for reporting on atrocities or violations that need to be put into their temporal context.

A further element is the daily-life scenery that requires comprehension. Thus another 'added value' of graphic reporting relates to the fact that

32 Translation of dialogue:
Teacher: Who here is a Tutsi? The Tutsi are a Nilotic race who arrived much later from their faraway north. With their cows and their weapons, the Tutsi took advantage of the natural integrity of the poor Hutu peasants, and treacherously enslaved them. Lastly, there are the Twa. They are of Pygmy stock. They practice pottery and hunting.
Student: The teacher is a fool.

33 J Glover, *Narrating Crisis: Rwanda, Haiti and the Politics of Commemoration* (Doctoral Thesis, University of Florida 2011) 111.

Figure 14.1 From J Stassen, *Déogratias: A Tale of Rwanda* (Dupuis 2000). DEOGRATIAS © DUPUIS, 2010 – Stassen. All rights reserved.

graphic novels allow a much deeper and profound analysis of the hinterland than that afforded by textual reporting. The graphic novel provides a medium to allow the reporter to push the reader to integrate details in the background that are often not easy to transcribe in a text-only report. The attention placed on the details in graphic reporting provides useful and rich information to the reader that will allow a better comprehension of the overall situation. Hitchens, present as a journalist in Bosnia, noted this in his introduction to *Safe Area Gorazde*:

> Sacco's combined word-illustration makes me remember that distinctive Bosnian domestic architecture - the gable ends and windows - with a few deft strokes. You know where you are, in other words, and not in some generic hotspot. Then the additional details, such as the

> unforgettable 'bear's paw' scar that a mortar-shell makes on a pavement. And - more easily replicated but still impressive - the forlorn look of a wood-built house that's been reduced by fire to a silhouette and a brick chimney stack.[34]

There is evidently a wider potential appeal, with *Déogratias* and *Safe Area Gorazde* far more accessible to a broad audience than the decisions of the international criminal tribunals on Rwanda and the former Yugoslavia for example. This is not to indicate that these graphic works represent a popularisation of particular issues; it is just to emphasise that they act as a vehicle to bring serious human rights questions to the fore, in a manner that is idiosyncratic and innovative, and, although limited to their own means of expression, provides greater depth of analysis than text alone. They do not replace academic works of history or law; they provide colour and expression to the experience of human rights violations.

Is it 'serious'?

Comics and graphic novels are often seen as less serious than 'proper' media such as journalism. In the words of Doherty, comics are 'associated with the madcap, the childish, the trivial'.[35] This vision of comics and therefore graphic novels as childish means that for many people reporting serious human rights violations through the medium of the graphic novel is seen not only as inappropriate but as an insult to the 'seriousness' of the situation.[36] The extent to which it is recognised within media is difficult to ascertain, although Sacco claims, 'Comic journalism has also become respectable among many reporters . . . in that many co-journalists don't find it unusual or less worthy to pursue journalism in a comics form'.[37] Nevertheless, he also notes that a 'great disadvantage' relates to 'the sense of respectability from outside sources', whereby 'many people look at sequential mediums as an inferior medium'.[38] Hence in *Journalism* we see a defence of the comics journalist, including the necessary subjectivity inherent in all journalism, 'Ultimately, a drawing reflects the vision of the individual cartoonist. I do not think this exiles a drawn report from the realm of journalism'.[39]

34 C Hitchens, introduction to Sacco (n 5).
35 T Doherty, 'Art Spiegelman's Maus: Graphic Art and the Holocaust' (1996) 68 *American Literature: A Journal of Literary History, Criticism, and Bibliography* 69.
36 See eg, Versace (n 29) 8–9: Versace discusses *inter alia* the reception of the comic book adaptation of the commission report on the terror attacks of 9/11, in which the graphic account was seen as reductive and inappropriate.
37 Sacco, as quoted in Nalvic (n 3).
38 Sacco, as quoted in Nalvic (n 3).
39 Sacco (n 2).

As indicated, Sacco is perhaps the central figure in comics journalism and graphic reporting, providing the strongest arguments for its broader recognition, and it is appropriate to isolate his particular experience in explaining his medium to an individual firmly embedded in the architecture of international law and justice. In *Journalism*, he describes a meeting with Louise Arbour, then prosecutor at the International Criminal Tribunal for the former Yugoslavia (ICTY), and Gabrielle McDonald then president of the ICTY. Sacco seeks to portray them in his depiction of the Tribunal through interviews on the work of the institution as well as its aims. They responded with heavy scepticism, viewing comics as not being of sufficient seriousness to depict the workings of the ICTY. In this regard, they did not wish to support a medium that they believed might undermine the workings of international justice. Sacco expresses his exasperation, noting that the ending of his graphic snapshot of the Tribunal was somewhat spoiled by the absence of the viewpoints of the major actors within the Tribunal, which he had planned to include as his closing depictions. As a result, he notes, his final narrative appears somewhat truncated.[40]

In an analysis of the external perceptions of the sister International Criminal Tribunal for Rwanda (ICTR), Kingsley Chiedu Moghalu, Legal Adviser to the ICTR, demonstrates how the visibility of the Tribunal is relatively low, and outlines why the image and perception of the Tribunal both as a court and as an organisation is important.[41] He highlights the nature of international criminal justice as fundamentally different from that of national justice, involving crimes that strike at the heart of our common humanity such as genocide, war crimes and crimes against humanity, orchestrated by powerful political, military and other figures. Hence the impact of the tribunals goes beyond the forensic combat of the courtroom, and the perception of whether their trials and related activities can or will bring about results is just as important as what happens in their courtrooms.[42] He asks:

> But does the tribunal receive adequate coverage? The answer, nonetheless, is 'no'. Many stories on the tribunal, because they are filed by wire agencies, are 'spot news' reports that lack depth, content, and context that would truly enlighten readers. Thus, while the ICTR may be widely reported, it is not reported in an in-depth manner except on an occasional basis.[43]

40 Sacco (n 2).

41 KC Moghalu, 'Image and Reality of War Crimes Justice: External Perceptions of the International Criminal Tribunal for Rwanda' (2002) 26 *Fletcher Forum of World Affairs* 21. The analysis outlines how coverage of the ICTY is by comparison much more widespread and sympathetic.

42 Ibid 22.

43 Ibid 24. He notes that this under-reporting is despite the fact that the ICTR is the first international criminal tribunal to convict a head of government for genocide and to convict an individual for rape as a crime against humanity.

It would appear that graphic depiction of the workings of international criminal justice ought to be encouraged and supported, given its unique ability to provide 'depth, content and context'. Yet Sacco's meeting with Arbour captures the difficulties inherent in arguing for the importance of graphic reporting. There is a *prima facie* belief that graphic novels are not serious, in the sense that newspapers or other reporting mechanisms are. Furthermore, even if their seriousness is accepted, there is a lack of authority perceived in graphic novels, which cannot act in the same way as a report from a non-governmental organisation (NGO) or other monitoring group, and certainly cannot be considered 'objective'. In this sense, graphic novels are not afforded any human rights character or weight, and are considered merely as fiction. Sacco and others must combat this perception and are doing so through continued reporting from situations they consider require it.

This viewpoint that graphic reporting is not sufficiently serious is anachronistic. There is no evidence that graphic reporters are trying to undermine the institutions or incidents they wish to portray, any more than any other critical work may seek to do. Sacco's description of the demeanour of the judges in the ICTY in his short account is intriguing, as is his movement between the defendants and the events they are accused of, with very real attempts to ascribe their human attributes.[44] In this regard the work of graphic reporting humanises its subjects, removing atrocities from the realm of the abstract. It shows the existing accused - whether in a dock of an international tribunal or *in situ* while committing an act - as well as the existing victim - including their facial expressions, the scenes of the room or countryside or cityscape - and the reactions of those who are witnessing, or failing to intervene in, or passively observing,[45] or being affected by, the atrocity. This emotional impact forms part of a wider interest in how human rights atrocities are committed and why, and explores the conditions that foster an environment where widespread rights violations can occur.[46] It is a very serious enterprise.

It is unfortunate that the former prosecutor and president of the ICTY failed to recognise this. Increasingly, the international tribunals have become divorced from their wider context, and there are far too few insights into

44 See Sacco (n 2).

45 The 'bystander' has been the subject of analysis in international criminal law - see eg, LE Fletcher, 'From Indifference to Engagement: Bystanders and International Criminal Justice' (2005) 26 *Michigan Journal of International Law* 1013.

46 See eg, the creation of these conditions were elaborated in the so-called 'media trial' *Nahimana et al.* of the ICTR, where Ferdinand Nahimana and others were convicted for incitement to genocide through the broadcasts of their radio station and newspaper publications. See further, GS Gordon, 'A War of Media, Words, Newspapers and Television Stations: The ICTR Media Trial Verdict and a New Chapter in the International Law of Hate Speech' (2004) 45 *Virginia Journal of International Law* 139.

how they are working and their efficacy or otherwise in delivering international justice, as well as preventing further atrocities.[47] As Moghalu notes in relation to the ICTR:

> the Rwandan genocide, portrayed as 'tribal chaos and anarchy' in order to locate it within the prevailing stereotype of the African continent as one in perpetual crisis, was given wide global media coverage. The search for justice for the genocide by an international court sitting in Africa has not, however, attracted a fraction of that coverage.[48]

He concludes that 'the tribunal should pursue a much more proactive strategy to building external perceptions of its work',[49] which evidently prioritises targeting global television media outlets but also includes a media program bringing selected journalists to cover the tribunal. Such strategies should include graphic novelists. Commentators have noted the general ability of 'literature [to] do justice to the trauma in a way the law does not',[50] and graphic reporting can depict both the disconnected trauma of experience in the fictional figure of *Déogratias* and the faithful reportage of the international legal trials that follow, as attempted by Sacco. Thus graphic reporting may be particularly suited to the depiction of international crimes and their adjudication. Schabas observes that 'international criminal justice is different from "ordinary" prosecution at the domestic level',[51] due to the nature of the crimes pursued - genocide or crimes against humanity for example, rather than 'ordinary' crimes such as murder - the involvement of the State, and, crucially, the fact that those prosecuted are representative of the crimes committed. The goal of international criminal law is not to prosecute all perpetrators, but rather to prosecute only those most responsible. It has a symbolic as well as a narrow legal function. Hence the representation and dissemination of international criminal justice is integral to its workings.

47 Thus Fletcher (n 45) 1018 notes, 'tribunals should act outside the courtroom - through outreach programs and in conjunction with other institutions - to engage bystanders directly as a target audience. International tribunals currently are under-connected to other initiatives to promote social reconstruction'.

48 Moghalu (n 41) 35.

49 Moghalu (n 41) 40.

50 S Feldman, *The Juridical Unconscious: Trials and Traumas in the Twentieth Century* (Harvard University Press 2002) 8. The depiction of trauma in graphic novels is further discussed in L Dragulescu, 'Drawing the Trauma of Race: Choices and Crises of Representation in Art Spiegelman's *Maus*' in J Jakaitis and JF Wurtz (eds), *Crossing Boundaries in Graphic Narrative* (McFarland 2012) 138.

51 WA Schabas, *Unimaginable Atrocities: Justice, Politics and Rights at the War Crimes Tribunals* (Oxford University Press 2012) 22.

Irrespective of whether or not graphic reporting is accepted as legitimate by international actors, it is at the very least adding to the documentation of human rights atrocities and violations, and seeking deeper understandings of its causes and experiences, as well as moving into the realm of legal redress. It is perhaps inevitable that graphic novelists who have depicted the atrocities in Yugoslavia and Rwanda would seek out the international courtrooms which are holding those most responsible to account. The continuance and growth of graphic reporting points to a role that has not as yet been recognised, but is contributing to the array of human rights reportage and providing its own particular insights and testimonies.

The future of human rights reporting

Having examined some of the specificities of graphic reporting, it remains to be asked whether there is space for graphic human rights reporting under the current human rights agenda. It is apparent that this sub-genre of graphic novels perceives itself as analogous to journalism, but has not as yet considered fully its position within the human rights discourse. Human rights reporting is a central pillar of the UN supervisory competence in terms of compliance with international human rights law and has been mainstreamed within its operations. The extent to which graphic reporting can contribute to this has not been explored, but there is evidently much potential. Human rights reporting is at present varied, and human rights organisations use a range of tactics, as well as reflecting in themselves much diversity of constitution and outlook. It is apparent that integrating graphic reporting is very possible and can evolve beyond its present status.

There is evidence that some NGOs have started to use the medium of the graphic novel to support their campaigns and raise awareness. For example *Survival International*, a charity working to support the human rights of indigenous peoples globally, has produced a comic or graphic narrative called *There you Go!* This 'cartoon book' takes a satirical swipe at the 'development' of tribal peoples. Drawn by Oren Ginzburg, it tells the story of how tribal peoples are being destroyed in the name of 'development'.[52]

This represents a relatively rare attempt at using graphic material for campaigning and human rights awareness-raising, but it is possible that the so-called 'gatekeeper' human rights NGOs (*Amnesty International* and *Human Rights Watch*) could produce graphic accounts of human rights situations. They could employ graphic reporters to provide illustrations

52 O Ginzburg, *There you Go!* (Survival International 2006).

of the everyday reality of human rights violations in particular situations, and publish these as NGO reports. This would add character and situation to their aim of disseminating information on human rights violations. The suggestion is not to replace their existing legalistic approach, in which their reports combine accounts of rights violations by reference to international legal standards; rather, it would complement or supplement existing reportage. For example, *Human Rights Watch* has issued a series of reports and communications on the situation of migrant workers in Gulf States such as the United Arab Emirates and Qatar;[53] a graphic report on the horrific conditions and grind in labour camps in which many such migrant workers live would add to their impact. Evidently, smaller NGOs could also contemplate such innovative practices.

The UN is consistently seeking broader impact in terms of disseminating its message on situations of human rights, as well as providing legal remedies for violations. Graphic reporting is potentially a major tool in bringing the wider message of rights situations to an international audience. Although it may not be countenanced at present due to prevailing and outdated perceptions of the lack of gravity of graphic novels,[54] the UN mechanisms could integrate graphic reporting. The UN Special Rapporteurs, who hold mandates from the Human Rights Council to investigate particular situations or countries,[55] could invite graphic reporters to supplement their reports with depictions of the situations being described; this could begin with such established figures as Sacco. Indeed, the present authors believe Sacco would in fact make an excellent Special Rapporteur in his own right – one who could report to the UN Human Rights Council in graphic form on a variety of themes. Until such potential developments, the continued belief that graphic novels are not serious will hinder an effective form of dissemination and awareness on human rights issues.

The realm of graphic novels needs to take greater recognition of its potential in a human rights context. There are not many graphic reporters,

53 See eg, Human Rights Watch, 'Building Towers, Cheating Workers: Exploitation of Migrant Construction Workers in the United Arab Emirates' (Human Rights Watch Report, 12 November 2006) <www.hrw.org/sites/default/files/reports/uae1106webwcover.pdf> accessed 15 April 2014; Human Rights Watch, 'Building a Better World Cup: Protecting Migrant Workers in Qatar Ahead of FIFA 2022' (Human Rights Watch Report, 6 December 2012) <www.hrw.org/sites/default/files/reports/qatar0612webwcover_0.pdf> accessed 15 April 2014.

54 On why comics or graphic novels are yet to achieve legitimacy as a unique form of expression, see further A Nyberg, *Seal of Approval: History of the Comics Code* (University Press of Mississippi 1998).

55 A full list of the range of Special Rapporteurs is available at <www.ohchr.org/EN/HRBodies/SP/Pages/Welcomepage.aspx> accessed 15 April 2014.

with the majority of comics authors focusing on fiction. This can be contrasted with film, where documentary is probably the fastest growing genre in the industry and has gained in recent years major recognition beyond its previously niche status. Within documentary, we now see a variety of human rights film festivals, and many filmmakers are seeking to document lives and experiences in the context of rights violations rather than the more traditional story-telling aims.[56] By contrast, graphic novel festivals are dominated by superhero and other genres, and there is no representation for human rights in Comic-Con or in the Francophone equivalent at Angoulême.[57] These festivals of graphic writing need to find space for the small but important group of authors that are advancing human rights protection through innovative and effective reporting in graphic form. At the very least, a human rights or graphic reporting stall at these festivals would appear to be appropriate.

Graphic reporting is a means by which graphic novels can chart human rights violations and the mechanisms for their prevention. It deserves greater recognition from the graphic novels sphere as well as the human rights sphere. A number of interesting and important works have already emerged, signalling the development of a genre that does not overlap with existing reportage, but rather has its own distinct identity and function. The mechanisms for human rights protection are constantly evolving, and subsuming graphic reporting will bring important and heightened exposure to the reality of human rights abuses around the world.

Acknowledgements

The authors wish to thank the editor and reviewers for helpful comments and improvements to the chapter. They would also like to acknowledge the influence of Sacco, Stassens and other *bande dessinée* graphic reporters for inspiring the piece.

Bibliography

Balez O and others, *Grand Reporters: 20 Histoires Varies* (Les Arènes XXI 2012).

Banks TL, 'Mestizaje and the Mexican Mestizo Self: No Hay Sangrenegra, so there is no Blackness' (2006) 15 *Southern California Interdisciplinary Law Journal* 199.

56 For example, Human Rights Watch runs its own 'Human Rights Watch Film Festival'; see further <https://ff.hrw.org/about> accessed 15 April 2014. See also the One World International Human Rights Documentary Film Festival <www.oneworld.cz/2014/> accessed 15 April 2014.

57 Although some smaller alternative festivals, such as the Toronto Comic Arts Festival, afford particular space to graphic reporting.

Canales JD and Guarnido J, *Blacksad: Arctic Nation* (Dargaud 2003).
Crumm D, 'Sacco Nails down Comic Credentials in Journalism' (*Read the Spirit*) <www.readthespirit.com/explore/joe-sacco-nails-down-comic-credentials-in-journalism/> accessed 15 April 2014.
Delisle G, *Shenzhen* (Drawn and Quarterly 2000).
Delisle G, *Pyongyang* (Drawn and Quarterly 2003).
Delisle G, *Burma Chronicles* (Drawn and Quarterly 2007).
Delisle G, *Jerusalem* (Drawn and Quarterly 2011).
Desai P, 'Review of Bhimayana: Experiences of Untouchability' (*The Comics Journal*, 18 April 2012) <www.tcj.com/reviews/bhimayana-experiences-of-untouchability/> accessed 15 April 2014.
Doherty T, 'Art Spiegelman's Maus: Graphic Art and the Holocaust' (1996) 68 *American Literature: A Journal of Literary History, Criticism, and Bibliography* 69.
Dragulescu L, 'Drawing the Trauma of Race: Choices and Crises of Representation in Art Spiegelman's *Maus*' in J Jakaitis and JF Wurtz (eds), *Crossing Boundaries in Graphic Narrative* (McFarland 2012).
Farr M, *Tintin: The Complete Companion* (Egmont Press 2011).
Feldman S, *The Juridical Unconscious: Trials and Traumas in the Twentieth Century* (Harvard University Press 2002).
Fletcher LE, 'From Indifference to Engagement: Bystanders and International Criminal Justice' (2005) 26 *Michigan Journal of International Law* 1013.
George T, Pearson K, Cheadle D and Rusesabagina P (eds), *Hotel Rwanda: Bringing the True Story of an African Hero to Film* (Newmarket Press 2005).
George-Palilonis J, *A Practical Guide to Graphics Reporting: Information Graphics for Print, Web and Broadcast* (Elsevier 2006).
Ginzburg O, *There you Go!* (Survival International 2006).
Glover J, 'Narrating Crisis: Rwanda, Haiti and the Politics of Commemoration' (Doctoral Thesis, University of Florida 2011).
Gordon GS, 'A War of Media, Words, Newspapers and Television Stations: The ICTR Media Trial Verdict and a New Chapter in the International Law of Hate Speech' (2004) 45 *Virginia Journal of International Law* 139.
Gourevitch P, *We Wish to Inform You that Tomorrow We Will Be Killed with Our Families* (Picador 1999).
Groth G, 'Joe Sacco on *Footnotes in Gaza*' (2011) 301 *The Comics Journal* <www.tcj.com/tcj-301-joe-sacco-on-footnotes-in-gaza/> accessed 15 April 2014.
Hedges C, 'What War Looks Like' (*New York Times*, 24 May 2009) <www.nytimes.com/2009/05/24/books/review/Hedges-t.html?_r=2&> accessed 15 April 2014.
Holpuch A, 'Joseph Kony Graphic Novel Illustrates Personal Stories of Violent Campaign' (*The Guardian*, 15 March 2013) <www.theguardian.com/books/2013/mar/15/joseph-kony-graphic-novel-violent> accessed 15 April 2014.
Human Rights Watch, 'Building Towers, Cheating Workers: Exploitation of Migrant Construction Workers in the United Arab Emirates' (Human Rights Watch Report, 12 November 2006) <www.hrw.org/sites/default/files/reports/uae1106webwcover.pdf> accessed 15 April 2014.
Human Rights Watch, 'Building a Better World Cup: Protecting Migrant Workers in Qatar Ahead of FIFA 2022' (Human Rights Watch Report,

6 December 2012) <www.hrw.org/sites/default/files/reports/qatar0612webw-cover_0.pdf> accessed 15 April 2014.

Moghalu KC, 'Image and Reality of War Crimes Justice: External Perceptions of the International Criminal Tribunal for Rwanda' (2002) 26 *Fletcher Forum of World Affairs* 21.

Nalvic, 'A Quick Guide to Comics Journalism' (*Nalvic's Reviews*, 12 June 2012) <http://nalvicreviews.wordpress.com/2012/06/12/a-quick-guide-to-comic-journalism/> accessed 15 April 2014.

Natarajan S and Ninan A, *A Gardener in the Wasteland: Jotiba Phule's Fight for Liberty* (Navayana 2012).

Nyberg A, *Seal of Approval: History of the Comics Code* (University Press of Mississippi 1998).

Posner R, *Law and Literature* (Harvard University Press 1998).

Rader PJ, 'Iconoclastic Readings and Self-reflexive Rebellions in Marjane Satrapi's *Persepolis* and *Persepolis 2*' in Jakaitis J and Wurtz JF (eds), *Crossing Boundaries in Graphic Narrative* (McFarland 2012).

Sacco J, 'Kushinagar: A Comics Journalist Chronicles the Struggles of UP Dalits' (*The Caravan*, 1 January 2012) <www.caravanmagazine.in/reporting-and-essays/kushinagar> accessed 15 April 2014.

Sacco J, *Palestine* (Jonathan Cape 2003).

Sacco J, *Safe Area Gorazde* (Jonathan Cape 2007).

Sacco J, *Journalism* (Metropolitan Books 2012).

Schabas WA, *Unimaginable Atrocities: Justice, Politics and Rights at the War Crimes Tribunals* (Oxford University Press 2012).

Stassens J, *Déogratias: A Tale of Rwanda* (Dupuis 2000).

Versace R, *This Book Contains Graphic Language: Comics as Literature* (Continuum 2007).

Vrielink J, 'Judging the Past: Discrimination Law, Hate Speech Legislation and the Colonial Imagination' (2012) 12 *International Journal of Discrimination and the Law* 99.

Vyam D, Vyam S, Natarajan S and Anand S, *Bhimayana: Experiences of Untouchability* (Navayana 2011).

Index

For Product Safety Concerns and Information please contact our EU representative GPSR@taylorandfrancis.com
Taylor & Francis Verlag GmbH, Kaufingerstraße 24, 80331 München, Germany

www.ingramcontent.com/pod-product-compliance
Ingram Content Group UK Ltd.
Pitfield, Milton Keynes, MK11 3LW, UK
UKHW010958180926
475701UK00004B/440

9781138241664